routledge direct editions

CENTRALITY AND CITIES

JAMES BIRD BA, PhD, FCIT
Professor of Geography
University of Southampton

ROUTLEDGE DIRECT EDITIONS

ROUTLEDGE & KEGAN PAUL
London, Henley and Boston

First published in 1977
by Routledge & Kegan Paul Ltd
39 Store Street,
London WC1E 7DD,
Broadway House,
Newtown Road,
Henley-on Thames,
Oxon RG9 1EN and
9 Park Street,
Boston, Mass. 02108, USA
Manuscript typed by Vera M. Taggart
Printed and bound in Great Britain
by Unwin Brothers Limited
The Gresham Press, Old Woking, Surrey
A member of the Staples Printing Group

ISBN 0 7100 8445 5

'This magnificent butterfly finds a little heap of dirt and sits
still on it; but man will never on his heap of mud sit still. He
wants to be so, and again he wants to be so....' He moved his
hand up, then down....

Joseph Conrad

(The above is uttered by Stein, merchant and butterfly collector,
in conversation with Marlow, the narrator, when discussing the
problem of man's existence in general and the character of Tuan
Jim in particular, the protagonist and eponymous hero of Conrad's
novel, Chapter 20.)

CONTENTS

TABLES

MAPS AND DIAGRAMS

The photograph on the inside cover shows the City
Hall, Toronto (designer Viljo Revell, 1910-64),
where two office towers frame and emphasize the low
council chamber; with a pedestrian plaza, foreground,
which becomes a rink in winter (a truly *diagonal*
place, see pp. 10 ff). By courtesy of Toronto Fire
Department.

PREFACE

Centrality and cities, not cities and centrality. The choice of
the deductive order is deliberate in the hope of disarming those
who might complain of a lack of empirical underpinning. This
could not be presented in all its detail, though I have included
every reference used, and found useful which is not quite the same
thing. Pursuit of these references will quickly lead to field
work detail. It proved impossible to include separate sections to
correct the obvious concentration on the western city. Instead,
all that space permitted were interpolated indications of some
obvious discrepancies when the ideas are transplanted and tropical-
ized from western Europe and North America.

   In comparing, comparing, comparing, I have searched for simi-
larities over space and time. Very few references are paraded
merely to be rejected. Rather I have tried to erect an agenda
based on a link between a concept and a phenomenon where many
varied elements in an array of scholarship can each make its
logical contribution. The list of references, long as it is for
a book of this size, is but a sample from those loaded shelves of
any first-class library that are devoted to some aspect of the city.
Add in the hundreds of papers published each year in the journals
of such subjects as architecture, economics, engineering, geography, history, planning, political economy, and sociology, and it
may be that not enough has been read and quoted. I am very conscious, therefore, that the basic theme outruns the evidence.
Further work will show whether this theme is useful, and will
cause the associated ideas to be strengthened and developed, or
discarded and ignored. In the latter case their only merit was to
have entwined themselves into a lifeline for me to grasp amid a
tossing ocean of other ideas; and back from that line derives any
residual use that the book may retain.

   My thanks are due to my secretary, Mrs R. Flint, who courage-
ously took on the first draft over and above her other duties; and,
as usual Mr A.S. Burn, BSc., MCIT, Principal Experimental
Officer and Chief Draughtsman, and other members of the Cartographic
Unit, University of Southampton, have performed wonders in trans-
forming pen and pencil drafts. I am indebted to Mr A.W. Keir, MSc.
for permission to make use of a reading orientation erected by him

in an MSc, dissertation, 1973, for the University of London, on the rural-urban fringe. The Editor of 'Geography' kindly gave permission for inclusion of material which first appeared in vol. 58 (pp. 105-18) of the journal, and which here forms the basis of Chapter 6. I also benefited from reading the thesis on spatial axes which gained Mr J. Tuppen his Ph.D (Southampton) degree; and my colleague Dr I.B. Thompson also gave me advice on this topic.

I should like to thank Mr Peter Hopkins and Ms C.E. Gardiner, of Routledge and Kegan Paul who together with the patient typing of Mrs Vera Taggart have successfully translated the text into this Direct Edition.

Much of the book was written on study leave, kindly granted by my home university, and with my academic responsibilities covered by my colleagues. I was the fortunate recipient of a British Academy Fellowship, a Leverhulme Trust Research Grant, and a British Council travel grant, on attachment as Visiting Professor at the Department of Geography, Carleton University, Ottawa. My thanks are due to Professor P.E. Uren for the initial link and to Professor D.M. Anderson, chairman, and his colleagues; no climatic 'chill factor' could affect the warmth of their welcome to my wife and myself. And so, although the dateline is Southampton, England, it was in an apartment with a bird's eye view of a capital CBD that most of the book was written, perhaps an appropriate task for a resident of Ottawa in a district known as Centretown.

                                                        J.H.B.

ACKNOWLEDGMENTS

In respect of maps and diagrams the following are respectively
thanked: Fig. 1, editor of 'Geography'; 2a, 2b, Hutchinson
Publishing Group Ltd; 3, Holt, Rinehart and Winston; 4, J. Wiley &
Sons Inc.; 6, Professor B.W. Hodder; 7, Royal Town Planning
Institute and G. Albers; 11, Hutchinson Publishing Group Ltd.;
13, editor of 'Geography'; 17, M.I.T. Press Inc.; 18, 19, 20,
editor of 'Geography'; 22, E.J. Brill; 25, American Institute of
Planners; 26, Weidenfeld & Nicholson Ltd.

SPATIAL ASPECTS OF CENTRALITY

Endogenous Centrality

Note: in each diagram the city is represented by stipple. This may be the continuous built-up area, the city and closely associated suburbs, or the area bounded by 'city limits', however defined.

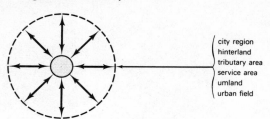

city region
hinterland
tributary area
service area
umland
urban field

Internal Centrality

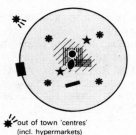

● peak land value intersection

⬬ religious and/or admin. precinct

≡ inner city, originally bounded by walls where appropriate

▦ central business district (CBD) or hard core area

out of town 'centres' (incl. hypermarkets)

⧄ urban core (includes hard core area and core fringe, or inner core area and frame)

★ transport nodes

▬ employment nodes (outside CBD) and including peripheral industrial estates

✳ commercial centres of a lower order (compared with CBD)

Exogenous Centrality

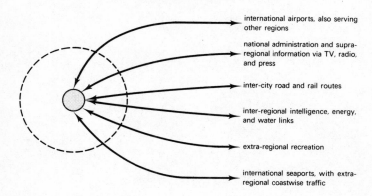

international airports, also serving other regions

national administration and supra-regional information via TV, radio, and press

inter-city road and rail routes

inter-regional intelligence, energy, and water links

extra-regional recreation

international seaports, with extra-regional coastwise traffic

FRONTISPIECE   Spatial aspects of centrality: diagrammatic representation
See also Table 23, p. 133, noting the equations:
total centrality = endogenous centrality plus internal centrality
               plus exogenous centrality
and
total centrality minus imagined total centrality = cognitive
                                   dissonance

INTRODUCTION
CONJECTURES ON CENTRALITY

This is a study about the concept of centrality, and cities are the
most obtrusive by-products of that concept on the surface of the
earth. The idea of centrality came before cities and has taken on
different forms within the modern metropolis. 'Centrality' is more
basic than urbanism, urbanization, or whatever word is used to cover
city formation and development - more basic and perhaps even more
complicated. The complications are entwined within a progression
from the straightforward idea of transport efficiencies to complex
symbolism in psychology. Because 'centrality' is a broader concept
than even that embraced by 'city', the agenda of this book would be
vast indeed unless the discussion were tied to something concrete
on the surface of the earth. And so in the foreground is kept the
aim of throwing some light on city centre origins and development,
in order to prevent the argument from drifting away above the real
world altogether - a hideous irrelevancy for a geographer.* That
expression 'the real world' is bound to give some trouble, but the
difficulty need not be encountered head-on at the outset.

DEDUCTIVE CONJECTURES

The following rather simple conjectures are placed below without
comment to erect some of the topics for later elaboration. They
should be regarded as mere headlines or preludes to the arguments
developed in this book. Deliberate is their very starkness. In
this way they might catch the eye of a browsing reader, thumbing
through the first pages and lure him on and in. As will be seen
later, the implication of a labyrinth is not inappropriate.
1 The idea of a centre involves the idea of a non-centre, or
    tributary area with distance decay to a periphery - a
    'worldwide habit' (Y.-F. Tuan, 1973, 416).
2 The idea of a centre involves a comparison between places

*The sub-title of this book might have been 'a study in proxemics
at the macro-scale'. 'Proxemics is the term I have coined for
interrelated observations and theories of man's use of a space as a
specialised elaboration of culture.' (E.T. Hall, 1966, 1)

  (and this produces spatial variety and spatial ordering).
3   Cognitive processes are comparison processes.
4   Comparison functions are basic* in human psychology.
5   There is a psychological human need to erect centres.
6   Centres in the real world reflect a need for centres in the
     inner world.
7   Regional economics requires centralized outputs to inter-
     regional and international trade when regions are regarded
     as open systems.
8   Urban centres are systems of organized complexity and can
     be analysed by general systems theory, or converted into
     synthetic models by statistical dynamics if treated as
     systems of disorganized complexity.
9   Because a centre 'here' can be contrasted with a non-
     centre 'there', a technique which makes use of polar
     opposites may throw partial insights into the problem of
     centrality.
The scale of this study is confined to those centres and peripheries that cannot be seen at once because they are so extensive
(a scale delimitation suggestion of R.M. Downs and D. Stea, 1973,
14). The pattern must then be apprehended via some form of cognitive representation, and apparently only vertebrates can so
experience space without actually traversing it (A.H. Esser, 1971,
3, citing F.S. Rothschild). However, the emphasis here is on the
concept of centrality rather than specific cognitive representations
of centres and peripheries.

TOWARDS CENTRALITY - A PERSONAL JOURNEY

Three separate avenues have led to the writing of this book, and
the first derives from work on seaports. For me this subject has
several attractions: the undoubted importance of seaports in the
modern world economy; and the multi-faceted nature of their function, at a place where land and sea meet, and where many different
professions come together to effect transport exchange, and often
to process what is exchanged. The curious paucity of academic work
on seaports twenty-five years ago gave a pioneering aura to any
subsequent attempt to remedy the situation. The seaport presents
an intriguing locational paradox, palpably a centre for so many
activities, yet palpably eccentric to the hinterland served.

*'basic' explanatory note. In H.S. Sullivan's three modal stages of
experience (1959, 25-30): prototaxic (infant), parataxic (maturing
infant-child), syntaxic (most mature level), even at the parataxic
level, there is differentiated perception, interpretation of stimuli
and realization of their relationship to others (idem, 83-4). However, the effective projection of centres into the real world, i.e.
'generating cognitive representations', would occur at the syntaxic
level where also would be received a series of 'generated cognitive
representations' of centres from an environment so ordered. For the
generating/generated dichotomy see R.M. Downs and D. Stea (1973, 82-
4). Sullivan's general theory is not unlike those of H. Werner and
J. Piaget, conveniently summarized in R.A. Hart and G.T. Moore
(1973).

Today, seaports are better represented in academic literature, and this has been an inter-disciplinary effort with geographers playing their part alongside workers in other disciplines and the studies emanating from official sources. But it is still not easy to fit seaports into the mainstream of theoretical development of work in urban geography and location theory. For over forty years workers in human geography have been bedazzled by central place theory. W. Christaller's (1933) famous formulation has been hailed as the counterpart in geography to the perfect competition model in economics and 'geography's finest intellectual product' (W. Bunge, 1966, 133). Apart from its own intrinsic value, the theory has stimulated a vast body of research (see B.J.L. Berry and A. Pred, 1961), and central place theory has been given an unassailable paradigmatic position in human geography. Most seaports are places located eccentrically in their hinterlands. Therefore seaports are cases exceptional to the prevailing paradigm in human geography. This is not only a crude syllogism but also very dispiriting for the student of ports.

In many texts on locational theory ports appear as exceptions or distortions. There are some fine general studies in human geography, and even many specific studies of settlement and urban geography that do not mention ports at all. Such unconscious omission of discordant data is a common side-effect of belief in a powerful paradigm (T.S. Kuhn, 1970, 24). Cumulative frustration led me to write two papers (1970 and 1973a) in an attempt to combat the imbalance by bringing back seaports into the general fold of locational theory in geography. 'Seaports are not aberrant cases' was my cry, and encouraged and helped by parallel work on gateways in Canada by A.F. Burghardt (1971), an attempt was made to weld seaports into a theory framework compatible both with central place theory and agglomeration and scale economies (see Chapter 6 below). Meanwhile, from different directions, others were reaching or had reached the conclusion that central place theory was but a partial theory framework, notably J.E. Vance with his mercantile model of settlement derived from a study of wholesaling (1970, Chapter 7).

A second avenue also arose from port studies, and this was the theme of development downstream which I had first studied on Lower Thameside in 1952. At that time I attempted to demonstrate how ports developed towards the sea, and especially was this true of ports founded near tidal limits at the heads of drowned estuaries in north-west Europe. This was a reference to dock and industrial development as the total port grew in size along the estuarine axis, rather than a study of those discrete annexes of the port established on the threshold of the sea, and at that time called outports in a classic study by N.J.G. Pounds (1947). By 1957 I had become aware that not only do ports develop downstream, but they also indulge in a flight from the centre, rather like the concept of a hollow frontier in migration studies. Indeed, this downstream migration and concomitant abandonment of a central area by the port of London can be demonstrated at an early date (cf. nos 24-30 with 1-23 on Fig. 1, noting no. 8).

From this it follows that, as a devoted port student, I was driven from the centre, following the migrating port function, which very often had been the reason for the site of the downtown

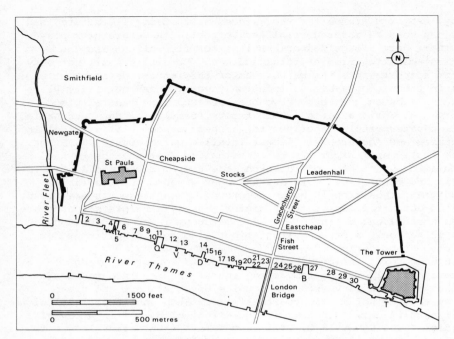

Upstream of the Bridge

1	*Puddle Wharf*	13	Tenements
2	A Brewhouse	V	*Vintry*
3	Baynard's Castle	14	A Brewhouse
		D	*Dowgate*
4	A Messuage	15	A Dyehouse
5	*Pauls Wharf*	16	Former depot of
6	Earl of Huntingdon's		Cologne merchants
	property	17	*Hay Wharf*
7	City of London	18	Tenements
	property	19	Dyers Hall
8	Broken Wharf (a ruin)	20	Brewhouses
9	*Brookes Wharf*	21	Fishmongers Hall
10	*Timber Wharf*	22	*Fish Wharf*
Q	*Queenhithe*	23	*Drinkwater Wharf*
11	*Salt Wharf*		
12	Black Swan Brewery		

Downstream of the Bridge

24	*Buttolphes Wharf*
25	*Lion Key*
26	*Sommers Key*
B	*Billingsgate*
27	*Smarts Key*
28	*Porters Key*
29	*Wool Wharf and Custom House*
30	*Galley Key*
T	Tower of London

FIGURE 1 Functional differentiation within London, 1603
The military strongpoint at the vulnerable point where the walls
meet the river downstream, has the religious centre as counterpoise;
the markets (named) have become specialized; and although the port
is still confined to the city waterfront within the walls, the port
function (properties listed in italics) is markedly more important
downstream at the 'Legal Quays'. (For complete list of these in
1746, see J. Bird, 1964, Fig. 40, 205.)
Sources: (for riverside functions) J. Stow (1603): (for markets)
K.L. Buzzacott (1972).
Reproduced from 'Geography', 1973, vol. 58, 109, by permission of
the editor.

centre in the first place. No wonder that an interest was maintained in such centres, which often expand over former port areas.
Temptation was too great in one instance, and port study was tem-
porarily deserted to investigate the development and modern functions of Billingsgate (1958), which has become the interesting
phenomenon of a central wholesale fish market which receives no
fish by water. This feature of port-abandoned central areas was
seen repeated in studies of other ports in Britain (1963), in the
EEC (1967), and in Australia (1968).

Here were two avenues leading me to consider the problem of central places on the one hand and central areas of cities on the
other. The one problem that both subjects have in common is that of
centrality, and it gradually became clear to me that 'centrality' is
an idea, and that the appearance of a centre on the surface of the
earth is basically the manifestation of an abstract idea.

problem

A third main avenue towards centrality derived in the first instance from two books which were subsequently heavily criticized in
a third. The first of these thought-provokers was P. Teilhard de
Chardin's 'The Phenomenon of Man' (1959), a book which caused a
great stir when it was published. The title was attractive, but
interest tended to wither away as one tried to decipher its convolu-
ted and often vague deductions. However, in 1963 I drew attention
to one idea that might be useful to geographers - that of the noosphere. Here is the passage where this concept first appears in the
1959 volume:

> Geologists have for long agreed in admitting the zonal composi-
> tion of our planet. [Père Teilhard was at one time Professor of
> Geology and a distinguished palaeontologist.] We have already
> spoken of the barysphere, central and metallic, surrounded by the
> rocky lithosphere that in turn is surrounded by the fluid layers
> of the hydrosphere and the atmosphere. Since Suess, science has
> rightly become accustomed to add another to these four concentric
> layers, the living membrane composed of the fauna and flora of
> the globe, the biosphere, ...an envelope as definitely universal
> as the other 'spheres' and even more definitely individualised
> than them. For, instead of representing a more or less vague
> grouping, it forms a single piece, the very tissue of the genetic
> relations which delineate the tree of life.
>
> The recognition of a new era in evolution, the era of noogene-
> sis, obliges us to distinguish correlatively a support propor-
> tionate to the operation - that is to say, yet another membrane
> in the majestic assembly of telluric layers....Much more coherent
> and just as extensive as any preceding layer, it is really a new
> layer, the 'thinking layer', which, since its germination at the
> end of the Tertiary period has spread over and above the world of
> plants and animals. In other words, outside and above the bio-
> sphere there is the noosphere. (pp. 181-2)

In the above passage the vital deductive step is made when Père
Teilhard writes that the genesis of an intellect gives rise to
another in the series of spheres - a sphere in which thought spreads
and has inter-relations with component intellects.

The concept of the noosphere has interesting implications for the
student of centrality. For example, there are obvious drawbacks to
crude environmental determinism, but some argue that if determinism

is thrown away altogether, it will be much harder to achieve laws in human geography and more difficult to show effects flowing from causes. E. Jones (1956) studied this attitude and provided the following illustration:

a spring-line at the base of a scarp does not determine the distribution of population and the pattern of settlement in the sense that people are forced to live along that line. If a generalisation could be deduced at all from a pattern of villages along the foot of the scarp, then it must be deduced from the *collective behaviour* of the human beings concerned. Motivation in individual cases in this example would vary enormously, but taken as a mass the human reasons may be generalised and stated as a sociological law. Again there is nothing in a mere hilltop compelling men to use it as a defensive site; any compulsion to make such a specific use of a hilltop arises inside the *society* from a *state of tension* or of actual *warfare*. Physically it is a site; sociologically it becomes a defensive site. (p. 374) [italics added]

Now it might be possible to replace the words in italics in the above quotation with the word *noosphere*, an omnibus word which embraces 'society', 'collective behaviour', 'states of tension', 'motivation', 'warfare', even 'planning', all of which are close to values or attitudes of mind (see Table 6). The noosphere will change as man's thinking changes, and if we wish to understand the 'centres' erected upon the earth's surface, it is necessary to understand the relevant stage of the noosphere when the sequence of causal events was conceived. A bald statement here suggests itself. Man's actions are not determined by the environment, physical and social, but by what he thinks the environment determines him to do, given the knowledge that he has at any one particular time. And Père Teilhard considers the noosphere to be a vital part of the total environment.

In practical description it may be necessary to isolate parts of the environment, but in seeking explanations of the geographical pattern of phenomena, it is unwise to neglect any part of the environment, including the noosphere. If the tools of the noosphere, that is to say the store of information about techniques and machines, raise a man to a technological level beyond what was possible previously, then he will view the landscape with a different eye (J.C. Malin, 1950, 296). R. Hartshorne (1960, 172) once defined geography as the 'study that seeks to provide scientific description of the earth as the world of man'. Parallel with this, and germane to the present topic, an editor of a book on the internal structure of the city perceived a theme that permeated definitions of the city - it was the city as the 'home of man' (L.S. Bourne, 1971, 13). The home and the world of man include not only the visible environment and man himself but also the mental climate and stored learning with which we come into contact during every day of our lives. P.B. Medawar (1961) has dealt with this point at length. He distinguishes between:

endosomatic or internal heredity for the ordinary or genetical heredity we have in common with other animals; and *exosomatic* or external heredity for the non-genetic heredity that is peculiarly our own - the heredity that is mediated through tradition,

by which I mean the transfer of information through non-genetic
channels from one generation to the next. (p.96)

This is comparable with K.R. Popper's (1972b, 74) thesis of the
three Worlds: World 1 (physical world, objective); World 2 (subjective world of conscious experiences); and World 3 (objective
knowledge, as in the *logical contents* of books and libraries and
computer *memories*). [Note: books, libraries, computers are World
1 objects.] The links between these worlds are summed up in:
What may be called the second world - the world of the mind -
becomes on the human level, more and more the link between the
first and the third world: all our actions are influenced by
our second-world grasp of the third world. (ibid., 148-9)

Worlds 2 and 3, exosomatic heredity, and noosphere seem to be
concepts that are compatible. If the noosphere (combining Worlds
2 and 3) is accepted as part of the total environment where explanations of current geographical patterns may legitimately be
sought, the dichotomy of Man and Environment is obliterated (see
also W.H. Ittelson, 1973, 18). In addition, the concept of Nature,
with a capital N, by its very nature, leaves out an indispensable
feature of our evolving world - Man's past and current thoughts
which react upon us all and upon everything around us, and our view
of both (Medawar, 1961, 100 et seq. for expansion of the 'Nature
does not know best' thesis; see also R.L. Heathcote, 1960; and Y.-F.
Tuan, 1971).

The second seminal volume was Arthur Koestler's 'The Act of
Creation', published in 1964. This was literally two books in one,
and the first part was certainly the most stimulating and enter-
taining, with an endeavour to understand the act of creation via
the idea of *bisociation,* and incidentally beginning with about the
best explanation of humour that I have come across. (Curiously
enough, E.H. Gombrich (1961, 3,5; also 395) begins his study of art
and illusion with a pictorial joke and a pictorial pun.) 'I have
coined the term 'bisociation' in order to make a distinction between
the routine skills of thinking on a single 'plane', as it were, and
the creative act on more than one plane' (A. Koestler, 1964, 35-6).
Fig. 2a shows Koestler demonstrating the perceiving of a situation
in two self-consistent but habitually incompatible frames of reference or 'matrices of thought', M1 and M2 (cf. E.H. Gombrich, 1961:
'mental set', p. 60). Consider two 'self-consistent frames of
thought': offenders are punished by being locked up; cheats are
dealt with by being kicked out. These can be *bisociated,* and the
resulting tension of the incongruity, the essence of the joke, is
relieved by the explosion of a laugh, or at least the wince of a
smile: 'A convict was playing cards with his gaolers. On discover-
ing that he cheated they kicked him out of gaol' (ibid., 36).

The pun is the simplest form of bisociation, a double frame of
thought in one word. The triple structure of many jokes is
explained by the Koestler scheme: establish a matrix of thought;
reinforce it; and then suddenly introduce a different matrix of
thought. This explains the traditional form of 'The Englishman,
Irishman, and Scotsman' jokes in British humour; and the final
enforced bisociation has become known vividly as the punch line in
American humour. In literature bisociation can be traced in chias-
mus, oxymoron, syllepsis, syllogism, synecdoche, zeugma; above all

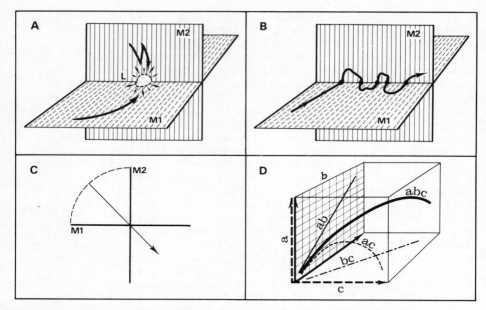

FIGURE 2   Bisociation, multisociation, and diagonalism
A   Koestler's idea of the act of creation when two different mat-
    rices of thought are 'bisociated' (op.cit., 196, Fig. 2).
B   Illustration of the comic or tragic results of combining a real
    world (say M1) with a fantasy world, M2, as in 'Don Quixote'
    (idem, Fig. 3).
C   Koestler's two matrices in elevation to show that diagonalism may
    take any combinatorial path through the quarter-sphere contained
    within the planes of M1 and M2 and the quarter-sphere circumfer-
    ence, schematically represented by the pecked arc.
D   An example of combination of variables in three dimensions. A
    notional tri-variate curvilinear regression line abc is inside
    a cube.

Similar diagrams to A and B have been produced by C.D. Broad (1923)
and V.E. Frankl (1969), see J.R. Smythies (1969, 241, 245; and 255
in subsequent discussion). Perhaps the most important forerunner of
Koestler is A.A. Moles (1957), where diagonalism is implicit in many
of the methods of scientific creation discussed and is rather explicitly illustrated in Figs I-1, I-2, VII-3, and VIII-1.

in metaphor and simile; and in rhyme, a bisociation of sound and
sense. Perhaps bisociation is a simple idea to demonstrate, but
the most convincing illustration seems to be Koestler's deft exposition of the basic gimmick in 'Don Quixote'. Fig. 2b shows what
happens when the Don oscillates between his own romantic fantasy
world (say M1) and the harsh 'reality' of the other characters.
The resultant collisions have their comedy and pathos. Cervante's
conception was so original as to give us a new word - quixotic -
to describe the tragico-comic double-think. But how far this idea
of bisociation can be extended into the general field of creativity
is doubtful.

    Curiously enough, the two books referred to, one by Teilhard, the

other by Koestler, came in for trenchant criticism by P.B. Medawar
(1967) in his 'The Art of the Soluble', and he was particularly
devastating in the case of the former. Perhaps this could be understood as a nice demonstration of the Popperian view of the scientific method, to which Medawar adheres, in which progress towards
knowledge is made by error elimination or reduction, as in the following sequence: (1) initial problem, (2) proposed theory, (3) deduction of testable propositions, (4) testing, i.e. attempted refuta-
tion, (5) preference established among competing theories, and further problems emerging (K.R. Popper, 1961, 131-4; 1968, 32-3; 1972a,
406-7; see also B. Magee, 1973, 56; and J. Bird, 1975). Medawar's
criticisms of bisociation are based on five instances which he puts
forward to test it; and he prints Koestler's reply to his criticisms
and then his final reply (1967, 85-96). Leaving the details of this
debate where it is for the interested reader to follow up, it can be
noted here that Medawar would substitute the hypothetico-deductive
system for bisociation. He says that this system would meet two of
the points he makes against bisociation, and that the other three do
not arise.

The hypothetico-deductive system, outlined in the five-stage process above, is in fact a dialogue between the possible and the
actual, and Medawar has given the argument a very clear exposition.

Like other exploratory processes, ... [scientific method] can be
resolved into a dialogue between fact and fancy, the actual and
the possible; between what could be true and what is in fact the
case. The purpose of scientific enquiry is not to compile an
inventory of factual information, nor to build up a totalitarian
world picture of natural Laws in which every event that is not
compulsory is forbidden. We should think of it rather as a logi-
cally articulated structure of justifiable beliefs about nature.
It begins as a story about a Possible World - a story which we
invent and criticize as we go along, so that it ends by being, as
near as we can make it, a story about real life. (1969, 59)*

At this point we have three concepts in this third avenue towards
centrality: noosphere, bisociation, and the hypothetico-deductive
system. At first sight they appear to have little in common, and
yet each involves the justaposition or two or more ideas in a
cerebral comparison: the noosphere against the other spheres;
bisociation explicitly requires an explosive juxtaposition; and the
hypothetico-deductive system involves a continuous comparison between 'what could be true and what is in fact the case'. Koestler
probably stopped at the two-dimensional bisociation, because it was
the easiest combination to demonstrate (see C. Tunnard and B. Pushkarev, 1963, 362); though a combination in three dimensions can be
illustrated (Fig. 2d). The computer takes over in the many dimen-
sioned world of multi-variate analysis. J. Taylor (in correspondence, 10 August 1973) would prefer the term multi-sociation to
describe brain processes; and this is also the view of F. Hayek
(1969, 323), though he is searching for a 'really appropriate
name'. Regression is a possible candidate for the general idea of

*This hypothetico-deductive system, based on Karl Popper's philo-
 sophy of the scientific method, is advanced by B. Harris (1966) in
 the theoretical investigation of urban systems.

mental comparisons, but the word would have an odd ring in usage outside quantitative methodology. The word derives from the idea of offspring reverting to the size of stature of their parents, a statistical concept developed by Francis Galton in 1877 (see K. Pearson, 1930, vol. IIIa, 6 ff). 'Correlation' also coined by Galton, which is even closer to the idea in question, now has too close a statistical connotation.

DIAGONALISM

'Bisociation' and 'comparison' describe the process of spatial perception only at its simplest manifestation, or only partially, because many variables are usually involved in a mental process affected by interplay between the conscious and the unconscious at different hierarchical levels. Faced with trying to express a similar idea of the process in question, in connection with perceiving urban environments, A. Rapoport and R.E. Kantor (1967, 210) decided to use the word 'ambiguity', in the following sense: 'Arising from language admitting of more than one interpretation...duplexity of meaning' (Webster's Dictionary). This is one of the meanings of ambiguity, and if it could stand alone, it is sharper than the definition adopted by the verbal analyst, W. Empson (1953, 1), whom Rapoport and Kantor cite as a scholarly authority for their deductions: 'any verbal nuance, however slight, which gives room for alternative reactions to the same piece of language (see also the discussion in A.W. Steiss, 1974, 228 ff). E.H. Gombrich (1961) also makes important use of the word ambiguity in his study of art and illusion (index entries and 395-6), 'the theme song of this book' (ibid, 313). Y.-F. Tuan (1973) believes that 'ambiguity' in attitudes towards environment are due to (1) the complexity of environments (or stimuli); (2) the discrepancy between the search for spatial symmetry and the asymmetry of the human sense of time and the goal-directed processes of human life; and (3) the tendency for feelings and ideas to polarize. But Rapoport and Kantor expressly disown another meaning of ambiguity given by Webster: 'doubtfulness, or hesitation, uncertainty'. Because use of 'ambiguity' in this context involves a deliberate discard of one of its normally accepted meanings, it seems advisable to turn elsewhere and is the excuse for a neologism. The mental process of *diagonalism** is a simultaneous comparison on two or more levels leading to superimposition, overlap, or combination between 'the expected and the experienced'

*I am aware that concepts may manifest themselves in a number of
  different ways (H.H. Price, 1969, 353) and that there are several
  orders of control systems in the brain - W.T. Powers (1973) suggests as many as nine or ten. 'Diagonalism' is offered merely as
  an umbrella term embracing many forms of concept combination, comparison, and overlap which can be analysed into many hierarchical
  levels. For example, A.A. Moles (1957) offers no less than twenty-
  one heuristic methods of scientific creation and eight 'infralogi-
  cal' methods, many of which depend on some form of comparison or
  combination. The practice of diagonalism avoids the criticisms
  directed by H. Marcuse (1964) against one-dimensional thought.

(E.H. Gombrich, 1961, 60), or between ideas (Fig. 2c). One may
travel along a line through a corner where any number of axes meet.
The verb *diagonalize* is always transitive with two or more objects.
Strangely enough, the antithesis of diagonalism has already been
defined as cognitive dissonance, the non-fitting relationships
among cognitions (L. Festinger, 1957, 3). It was some time after
coining this word, that I noticed the importance of the diagonals in
the diagrams of Patrick Geddes (1915, republished in 1949, 194, 201,
and 204); and these gave rise to the following sentence: 'Related-
ness is the parent of reality; objects by themselves have no meaning, they only become real when understood in *relation*' (J.W. Turner
and W.P. Keating Clay in Geddes, op.cit., 203).

M. Peckham (1965) has argued along similar lines, leading to what
might be called 'Peckham's paradox'. This argument runs that to
every situation a human being brings an orientation (called a dispo-
sition by F. Hayek, 1969, 314; and a generic perception by S.
Kaplan, 1973, 70). He then diagonalizes the orientation and a particular situation which has been generalized by suppressing those
elements of it which the orientation, successful in previous similar
situations, tells him are not relevant. Every successful diagonal
employment of an orientation and successive situations reinforces
the tendency to 'order' the situations in this way. Compare this
with T.S. Kuhn's (1970, 113) 'What a man sees depends both upon what
he looks at and also what his previous visual-conceptual
experience has taught him to see.' But, following Peckham further,
this 'drive to order' has a built-in danger of a too-stereotyped
response to every related situation, even when these change significantly such that the orientation ought to be restructured (positive
feedback being required). Peckham believes that it is the business
of the arts to seek out what appear in current orientations to be
irrelevancies and reveal that they ought to be incorporated in newly
adjusted orientations: 'Art is the rehearsal for the orientation
that makes innovation possible' (op.cit., 314). The idea of a comparable orientation can itself be compared with J. Monod's (1972,
140) idea of imagination as the representation and simulation of
external events and programmes of action.

The name of D.O. Hebb (1949, 1951, 1958) is perhaps the one most
associated with brain activity as the establishment of connections
between neurons, and he appears to follow the Popperian view of
thought processes as the setting up and testing of hypotheses
(notably, 1951, 49; for discussion of neural circuits see 1958, 80),
as in comparing an orientation with successive situations. This
idea of 'comparison' was cogently expressed by J. Taylor (1971):

I am suggesting then, that mental sensations have their non-
physical character in that they are composed of relationships
with other ongoing sensations as well as past sensations. It is
this process of comparison which gives content to the mind.
(p. 735)

The idea of diagonalism is contained within the following description of a creative mind by a cyberneticist, particularly in the
twice repeated idea of 'bringing back' [for comparative purposes]:

A machine that incorporates randomness, deviation-amplification
and deviation counteracting may be both efficient and flexible.
It can search for all possibilities. It can try to amplify

certain ideas in various directions. It can stay at a relevant
idea (which may change from time to time during the invention)
and bring back to it other ideas for synthesis. In fact, open-
ness to strange hunches, ability to elaborate on them and bring
them back to a synthesis are what is found in the process of
human creative minds. (M. Maruyama, 1963, 179)
Compare this with E. Cassirer (1944): 'It is not enough to pick up
isolated data of our past experience; we must really re-collect
them, we must organize and synthesize them, and assemble them into
a focus of thought' (p. 51). Man's mental concepts are held
together by a functional bond (vinculum functionale, ibid., 68),
and diagonalism is used in this study to indicate the process by
which this bond is discovered and activated.

Diagonalism has been my guide through a very varied literature,
and, as I hope to show, throws an illuminating light upon the concept of centrality in relation to cities. D. Harvey (1970, reprinted 1975, 302 ff) can be seen working his way to something like this
process at what he calls the interface between geographical and
sociological approaches to city problems: 'simple problems can be
treated in both dimensions simultaneously' (ibid., 303-4); for more
complex problems we are often forced to use an interative sequence,
successively keeping constant spatial form and social process (see
also D. Harvey, 1973, 46-9). But notice that this assumes that we
can diagonalize the two dimensions, because even if one dimension
is held constant, it must be translated into the language of the
other at each step of the iterative process.

C. Lévi-Strauss (1969, 84) is also bold enough to believe that
there are 'fundamental structures of the human mind' and for him
one of these is the notion of reciprocity, regarded as the most
immediate form of integrating the opposition between (diagonalizing)
the self and others (cf. A.W. Gouldner, 1960). He asks that whether
or not these structures account for the phenomena in question can be
answered only by consideration of the whole study. I should like to
follow that lead, comforted by the sure belief that at the very
least this book will provide plenty of scope for the Popperian process of error-elimination. One more quotation will bring this section firmly back to cities. No one will deny the powerful influence
on urban planning exerted by the ideas of Ebenezer Howard (1902).
Perhaps the secret of their power lies in the diagonalism explicit
in the very expression 'garden city', made even more explicit in
these words: 'But neither the Town magnet nor the Country magnet
represents the full plan and purpose of nature. Human society and
the beauty of nature are meant to be joined together. The two
magnets must be made one' (p. 48). (For diagrams showing how this
idea grew out of an Edenic diagonalism between city and wilderness,
see Y.-F. Tuan, 1971, 36-7.)

The idea of polar types is continued in Fig. 3 and Table 4. The
reader will have guessed by now that the thesis here will be that
the idea of a city can be approached only by diagonalizing at least
two approaches, and then at many levels. The classification is not
irrelevant because even the extreme types have engendered different
approaches to urban design which have actually become manifest on
the ground. A demonstration of these polar attitudes when applied
to city lay-outs is given by the juxtaposition of the following two
quotations, each attacking the opposite view (continues on p. 17).

TABLE 1 Summary of related terms, from centrality to the
hypothetico-deductive system

1	Idea in question:	*centrality*
2	Realm of ideas, incl. those about space:	*noosphere,* combining *Worlds 2 and 3*, via *endosomatic* and *exosomatic heredity*
3	Simplest idea of centrality:	*bi-polar*, referring to a distinction between a centre and a non-centre
4	Simplest idea of idea creation:	*bisociation*
5	Creative process (including both 3 and 4):	*diagonalism*, or *multi-sociation*, or *ambiguity* (restricted to 'duplexity of meaning') or *orientation compared with situation*
6	*Manifestation of 5*:	*vinculum functionale*, such as axiom, belief, equation, diagonal, hypothesis, model, myth, orientation, postulate, regression line, theory, all when compared with perceived reality
7	Opposite of 5:	*cognitive dissonance*
8	Reduction of 7, and search for and refinement of 6:	via *hypothetico-deductive system*

NOTE: The text summed up in the above table, dealing as it does
with the concept of regularity expectation, with supporting references, is open to the objection that I as author with a conjectural
orientation of diagonalism will find supporting references because
of the predisposition. This is unavoidable, and ought to be dis-
counted by the reader. However, demonstration of the following
interesting sequence was irresistible:
1 Koestler's idea of bisociation criticised by Medawar (1967, 85-
   96);
2 Medawar acknowledges debt to Popper (1969, 45);
3 Popper dedicates book to Hayek, with favourable references to
   him (1972a, passim and vice versa 1969, 317);
4 Hayek proposes 'much the same process' as bisociation (1969,
   323).

TABLE 2   Polarities and syntheses in nine systems

System	Polarity	Synthesis
Actualism	function/structure	consciousness-energy
Alchemy (1)	sulphur/salt	mercury
Astrology (1)	cardinal/fixed	mutable
Einstein	radiation (c)/matter (m)	energy (E)
Electricity	positive (proton)/ negative (electron)	neutral (neutron)
Gurdjieff (2)	affirming force/denying force	reconciling force
Mathematics	+ / -	=
Tantra	Siv/Sakti	Brahman
Taoism	creative $(yang)$/ receptive (yin)	Tao

1   'I do not hesitate to take the synchronistic phenomena that
    underlie astrology seriously. Just as there is an eminently
    psychological reason for the existence of alchemy, so too in the
    case of astrology. Nowadays it is no longer interesting to know
    how far these two fields are aberrations; we should rather
    investigate the psychological foundations on which they rest'
    C.G. Jung (1959, 344, footnote).
2   G.I. Gurdjieff (1950) 'All and Everything'. New York: Dutton.
Source of table: R. Metzner (1971) who believes that the list could
be extended indefinitely because the principle has appeared in every
civilization, culture, and philosophical or scientific endeavour.
The psychologist G.A. Kelly (1955, I, 109) also ascribes a dichotomous quality to all human thinking. For example (using the same
headings as in Metzner's table) in K.R. Popper's system (1972b, 74):
polarity, World 1 (physical world, objective)/World 3 (objective
knowledge) as in the *logical contents* of books and libraries, and
computer memories): synthesis, World 2 (subjective world of conscious experiences).

TABLE 3   Some polarities associated with centrality and cities

Type	Polarity	Possible result of bisociation
Spatial-formal	centre/umland (1)	central place theory (2)
	centre/hinterland centre/foreland	port (gateway) (3)
	central place/agglomeration	regional centre with manufacturing (4)

Type	Polarity	Possible result of bisociation
Spatial-formal	gateway/agglomeration	major industrial port (4)
	hearth (5) / domain hearth/hollow frontier (6)	diffusion (5)
	centrality/excentricity	centre-periphery model (7)
	quadrate cross (8) / walls (9) grid (10) / boundary	urban morphology
	individual buildings (11)/ built-up area (11)	urban renewal
Spatial-locat-tional	site/situation	settlement location
	Von Thünen (12)/Weber (12)	optimum locations
Spatial-func-tional	inputs (13) or imports/ outputs (13) or exports	manufacturing and trading centres
	zone of conflux (14)/ zone of dispersion (14) centripetal forces (15)/ centrifugal forces (15)	spatial tensions in city regions
	node (16)/ edge (16)	graph theory network analysis
	urban system in tree (17) form/ same components of urban sub-system in different tree	urban semi-lattice (17)
	tree networks/circuit networks	urban structures (18)
	buildings (19)/ inhabitants (19)	social area analysis (20)
	Öffentlichkeit (21)/ Privatheit (21)	intensity of urban core sociability
Methodo-logical	models/reality	urban problems
	genetic/end- or goal-directed (22)	city region structure planning
	individual/collective	urban culture
	native/nonnative	level of collective need for spatial variety (23)

Type	Polarity	Possible result of bisociation
Dynamic (i.e. with a particularly important time element	adaptive (24)/adoptive (24) causality (25)/indetermism (26)	real world survivors as cities

NOTE: Using the terms of the psychologist, G. Kelly (1955, I, 109), the above table is a construct system about centrality and cities evolved via (1) an experience [of the literature] corollary; (2) an organization corollary; and, most obviously (3) a dichotomy corollary. An example of empirical work on the thinking about cities via bipolar personal constructs is given in P. Sarre (1972, 35-40). Personal constructs are scales between opposites for the person concerned, though not necessarily for anyone else.

1   First proposed by A. Allix (1914), as the trade or tributary area of a town with a fair, see A. Allix (1922, 553).
2   W. Christaller (1933), translated by C.W. Baskin (1966).
3   A.F. Burghardt (1971).
4   See Fig. 18.
5   T. Hagerstrand (1952).
6   W. Zelinsky (1967).
7   J. Friedmann (1966). Considered as an elaboration of the heartland-hinterland model by B.J.L. Berry et al. (1976, 257).
8   R.E. Murphy and J.E. Vance (1954).
9   S. Chang (1970).
10 R. Pillsbury (1970).
11 L. Holzner (1970).
12 J.H. von Thünen (1826, see P.G. Hall, 1966); A. Weber (1909). That von Thünen and Weber form a polarity is summed up in the essence of their respective models: the optimum activity for a given location; the optimum location for a given activity.
13 W.W. Leontief (1966).
14 J.E. Vance (1960).
15 C.C. Colby (1933), C.B. Wurster (1963).
16 K.J. Kansky (1963).
17 C. Alexander (1965). Tree and semi-lattice are discussed on pp. 138-9, below; see also A.A. Moles and E. Rohmer (1972, 65, Fig. 18).
18 E.S. Dunn (1970).
19 L. Holzner (1970).
20 E. Shevky and W. Bell (1955); D. Timms (1971, 123-210), gives an extended review.
21 H.P. Bahrdt (1961). These terms are difficult to translate into English. W.F. Heinemeyer (1967, 91) interprets the first as 'urban core sociability', and the second refers to the private familial sphere of the individual (based mainly on the home).

'Öffentlichkeit' has also been translated as the community of
publicly oriented private persons (ibid.).
22 A. Mori (1964). See also G.W.S. Robinson (1967).
23 J. Sonnenfeld (1966).
24 A. Alchian (1950), C.M. Tiebout (1957), and G. Krumme (1969).
25 E. Jones (1956).
26 L. Curry (1966).

[The] ... rectangular system of dividing land, when applied to
cities, was perhaps satisfactory for the cities of America,
Australia, and other new countries. The inhabitants of these
cities were primarily concerned with survival. They lived only
for gainful production, and produced only to live. It mattered
little to them that they were packed up in barracks like herrings
in casks. (C. Sitte, 1889, 1945 edn, 84-5)

The Pack-Donkey's way [the line of least resistance] has been
made into a religion.
    The movement arose in Germany as a result of a book by Camille
(sic.) Sitte on town-planning, a most wilful piece of work; a
glorification of the curved line and a specious demonstration of
its unrivalled beauties....
    The structure of cities reveals two possibilities: a progres-
sive growth, subject to chance....
    Or on the other hand, the construction of a city as the
expression of a preconceived and predetermined plan....
    We struggle against chance, against disorder...; we strive for
order, which can be achieved only by appealing to what is the
fundamental basis on which our minds can work: geometry. (Le
Corbusier [C.E. Jeanneret-Gris], 1929 edn, 8, 91-3)
Note: Le Corbusier and Sitte partially exemplify respectively the
flat principle and the *principle of static, modelled form* (see
Fig. 15).

THESIS, ANTITHESIS, AND DIAGONALISM WITHIN A GENERAL MODEL

It is possible to combine the first seven of the 'deductive conjectures' presented at the opening of this introduction: *the development of spatial centralities derives from, among other things, a
psychological need for varied external phenomena on which to exercise the comparative processes of a conscious brain, and the resultant spatial variety and ordering satisfies fundamental, if often
unconscious, human needs based on the stage of technology reached
in regions regarded as open systems.* First reaction to this is
likely to be conditioned by one's personal position in the native/
nonnative polar typology of J. Sonnenfeld (1966, see Table 5; cf.
the conclusion of J. Abu-Loghod, 1968), which may change with age.
But accept the statement for the moment as a model presented in
advance of the supporting evidence. The question has to be asked
as to whether this is a normative process model or a predictive
model (the polarity is that of M.J. Webber, 1971).
    It is obviously very vague on processes. Though cities have been
the most obvious expression of spatial centrality, the statement

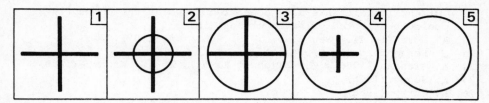

FIGURE 3   Code numbers and notation for stages on a continuum from
romantic (1) to classical (5)
See Table 4
Source: P. Thiel (1970, 607).
Note. The middle stage (3) of this continuum is identical to what
R.S. Lopez (1963, 7) has cited as the earliest ideogram denoting
a city. The title of his reference is 'The crossroads within the
wall'; see also T.C. Stewart (1970, intro.).

implies not only that centres precede cities, but also that they
will outlast the idea of a uni-centred city as the scale of spatial
thinking changes with changing technology. The model is therefore
predictive, and its predictions can be tested. By basing the statement on a deductive conjecture about brain processes, as yet unpro-
ven, and by applying it to the 'real world' of cities, I hope on two
counts to avoid K. Popper's class of irrefutable (and therefore non-
scientific) theories (1972b, 199). This is because the statement
will be tested by future work in the field of perception strategies
and also because it fits into a suggested model solution to some of
the problems involved in city study. Hence the expression 'among
other things' in the italicized statement is not as weak as it
looks because parts of this model can be tested.
     I am referring to the general model, and the general model with
extensions, proposed by F.S. Chapin (1974, and illustrated here as
Fig. 4). Chapin agrees with the sequence: motivation ➔ choice
➔ action ➔ pattern (op.cit., 32-3). Diagonalism helps to
explain the box in the top-left corner of the general model. In the
extended model Chapin has inserted two feedback loops. The satis-
faction-dissatisfaction levels involved in the top loop are very
much conditioned by the opportunities for diagonalism in the activity
pattern. I have inserted a third feedback loop because in a similar
fashion to the determination of levels of satisfaction-dissatisfac-
tion, the measurement of 'congeniality' of surroundings is conditioned by the levels of opportunity for diagonalism in their appraisal (a point referred to below in Chapter 7, esp. pp. 147-8; see
also Fig. 25).
     In this connection spatial *variety* is important. If this is so,
the antithesis of the italicized statement should also be true, in
the spirit of diagonalism. Let the statement, in its antithetical
form, start: *the development of spatial peripheries*....The following ideas will immediately come to mind: 'the wish to get away
from it all','the dream of a wildscape','the cry of back to
nature'; and the urban dweller who has ever felt the need of a
change via a rural, seaside, or foreign travel holiday might feel
that there is some truth in the antithesis of the thesis. In the
opposite direction rural dwellers go 'up to town' for their spatial

TABLE 4   Polar attitudes and attributes

Code Number (1) (as in Fig. 3)	1	2	3	4	5
Polar type	Romantic (2)			Classical (2)	
Examples:	Dionysian (2)			Apollonian (2)	
	Heraclitean (3)			Parmenidean (3)	
	tree-like			*egg*-like	
	open-ended			*closure*	
	movement			*rest*	
	incompleteness			*completeness*	
	dissolution			*cohesion*	
	imbalance			*balance*	
	asymmetry (4)			*symmetry (4)*	
	cities of heterogenetic change (5)			cities of orthogenetic change (5)	
	clouds (6)			clocks (6)	
	system of values dominant in the limbic brain (7)			system of values dominant in the neocortex (7)	

1   P. Thiel (1970, 607), with his examples italicized in the table.
2   'Two basic morphological archetypes' of G. Kepes (1956, 286-7).
3   H. Tuzet (1965, 18-19), see also pp. 40-1 below.
4   E. Johns (1969).
5   R. Redfield and M.B. Singer (1954), see also pp. 41 below.
6   K.R. Popper (1966, reprinted in idem,1972b, 206-55), where clouds represent physical systems which are irregular, disorderly, and unpredictable; and clocks represent systems with opposite characteristics (p. 207). The ensuing discussion shows that the statement 'all clouds are clocks' represents physical determinism, and 'all clocks are clouds' represents physical indeterminism.
7   P.F. Smith (1974, 212-13).

variety or dream about it, just as those characters in Russian drama dream of Moscow, particularly after more than a month in the country (see J.F. Wohlwill, 1966, 34; cf. the antithetical view of social life [public life versus privacy], in A.A. Moles and E. Rohmer, 1972, 148).

Chapin further proposes a four-stage programme for studying human activity patterns in the city: description, explanation (embodied in the models), simulation, and evaluation. As in this

TABLE 5   The native/nonnative typology

	Characteristics
native:	to a city, or region, or country; or to a rural, urban, or suburban environment.
nonnative:	migrant, transient, 'native to somewhere else', moving from rural to urban, from city to suburbia, from 'south' to 'north', etc., from mid-latitude to tropics: includes two extremes as sub-groups: the adventurous and hyperactive; the rootless or dis-possessed.
	Values
native:	have values that adjust to changes in the home landscape given time.
nonnative:	values freedom, opportunity, discovery: may turn into 'native' if adjusts to new environment; or may retain values requiring environmental trans-formations as in 'a city of rapid change', or as in further migration, permanent or temporary.
	Adaptation level
native:	datum is home environment as previously experienced.
nonnative:	datum may be that of previous environment, and there-fore may demand more variety than present environment offers.

Source: Based on J. Sonnenfeld (1966) for typology, characteris-tics, and values. In turn Sonnenfeld based his typology on ideas derived from adaptation level theory,H. Helson (1964, 335-7), see p. 29 below). Nonnatives may be further subdivided into 'cosmopo-litans' who have social and functional contacts wider than their local region and 'centralists' who are those cosmopolitans that actually live close to a city centre (C. Hamnett, 1973).
Additional note. A thesis in this book on centrality and cities is that everyone needs spatial variety, the nonnative explicitly, the native subconsciously, and this latter state may be consciously revealed when vacation time comes around, unless poverty binds him to his region.

study, Chapin does not reach the last two stages of his R & D pro-gramme, but he does cite the beginnings of work going forward to simulate human activity patterns (p. 216).
   In similar fashion to the argument so far in this chapter, Chapin believes it necessary to move from the individual actor upwards to the group.
   ...to understand behavior patterns of such segments of a metro-
   politan community, it is necessary to conceive of these patterns
   in terms of the behavior of individuals. Since individuals

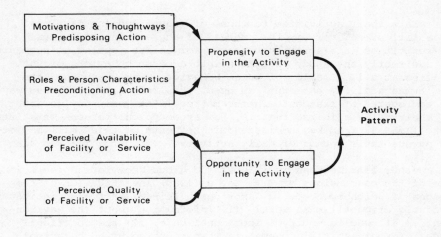

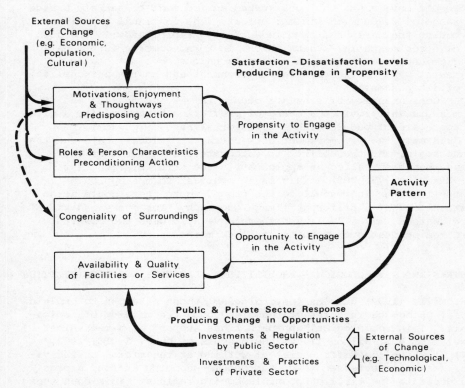

FIGURE 4   Chapin's general model for explaining human activity patterns
Top: The general model. Bottom: The general model with extensions. The feedback loop indicated by the pecked line with arrow has been added.
Source: F.S. Chapin (1974, 33 and 212), reproduced by permission of J. Wiley & Sons Inc.

relate their activities to those of groups and institutional
entities, however, in the process of aggregating individual
activities into activity patterns for entire population segments,
indirectly the study is taking into account behaviors of entities at all... scales of human behavior. Thus when the term
'human activity patterns' is used, this refers to patterned ways
aggregates of residents in the metropolitan community go about
their daily affairs, that is, how archetypical persons (statistical means) from key socioeconomic segments of this small society
pursue their rounds of daily activity. (op.cit., 11; see also
21).

Another link between individual and group behaviour appears in
one of the conclusions of T.R. Lee's (1968) investigation of the
images of neighbourhoods in Cambridge. This extract also indicates
a double diagonalism at work: (1) information about the environment is allowed to modify a locational code; (2) the locational
code, or socio-spatial schema, is then compared with the actual
locality to 'govern' movement within it.

People move about the local urban environment to satisfy a wide
range of needs with minimum effort. The continual locational
coding that arises from this activity precipitates in the form
of a socio-spatial schema which, in turn, governs future navigation and movement. Each schema is unique, but is related in
lawful ways to the physical environment and to the personality
of its possessor.

   Consentaneity of schemata occurs in varying degrees and its
measurement provides a means of predicting behaviour for a given
aggregate of people with a territorial base. (p. 263)

Such easy two-way movement between the individual scale and the
group scale, and the ability to integrate one in terms of the
other, has been called an approach via the structural context
(D. Massey, 1975, 203). This is in contrast to the approach
always from the individual to the group, where there could arise
difficulties of a different 'image geography' for every individual
(J.W. Watson, 1975, 272); and there have also been two powerful
warnings against such a building-block methodology.

CENTRES AND PSYCHOLOGISM - PROHIBITIONS, DANGERS, AND POSSIBILITIES

C.W. Mills (1959) dubs as 'psychologism' those attempts to explain
social phenomena in terms of theories about the make-up of individuals. This sociological approach finds support at a mechanical
level from A.G. Wilson (1970, see discussion by P. Gould, 1972,
694) in which the difficulties of working at the micro- or individual scale are stressed; e.g. ten people shopping at four stores
can generate one trillion possible configurations. This does seem
rather daunting.

At the moment it appears respectable for geographers and sociologists to reduce down as far as somewhere in 3 in Table 6, provided that they remain at the group or institutional level. (For
examples of this attitude in the French school of geography see
P. Claval, 1974, 180.)

W.D. McTaggart (1965) marshalled references to those who have

TABLE 6   Five stages of psychological reduction

---

5 spatial pattern, function; social pattern, structure
    4 behaviour
            3a values and/or attitudes*
            3b motivation to comply with norms*
            3c normative beliefs*
                2 psychological drives
                1 brain processes

---

*For a discussion of these as 'three kinds of variables that func-
tion as basic determinants of behavior' and for readings in attitude theory see M. Fishbein (1967). It is useful to follow
J. Meddin (1975) and regard an attitude as directed towards concrete objects in the environment as opposed to value which has a
more abstract connotation.

taken an opposite view:
    there are those who contend that social phenomena must be
    explained in terms of the perspectives and fields of action of
    individual persons; overall trends are therefore to be inter-
    preted as the sum total of individuals' actions which are com-
    prehensible as such. (p. 222)
In the theoretical study of the perception of environment, B. Sadler
(1970-1) has observed that 'the concepts involved [in the processes
of individual perception and response] can be extended to groups of
individuals' (p. 53). L. Svart (1974, 302) and R. Hudson (1976)
also discuss the problem, moving upwards in Table 6, the 'links between individual choice and group behaviour patterns' (1976, 171).
C. Renfrew (1972) faced the difficulty of psychologism when putting
forward his multiplier effect theory for the emergence of civilization.
    Changes or innovations occurring in one field of human activity
    (in one system of a culture) sometimes act so as to favour
    changes in other fields (in other subsystems). The multiplier
    effect is said to operate when these induced changes in one or
    more subsystems themselves act so as to enhance the original
    changes in the first subsystem. (p. 37)
Renfrew admits that his theory depends very much on individual
behaviour, and after discussing the problem (p. 495), he concludes
that the individual component in a theory is not a weakness. While
grouping of units enables them to be described statistically as far
as their behaviour is concerned, this cannot be so easily explained
if reference to individual units is omitted (p. 496) (for Popper's
three-world concept 'reduced' to the level of an individual see the
diagram and associated discussion by brain physiologist,
J.C. Eccles, 1970, p. 167, Fig. 36).
    Focussing the discussion on cities, J. Jacobs (1961) in her
interesting if idiosyncratic book 'The Death and Life of American
Cities' (p. 429 ff) confronted the methodological problem. She
relied on W. Weaver (1967, earlier version 1958) who listed three
stages in the development of scientific thought:
1 ability to deal with problems of simplicity containing two factors which are directly related to each other;
2 ability to deal with problems of disorganized complexity by

means of statistical mechanics (randomness of patterns suggests randomness of forces);

3 ability to deal with problems of organized complexity where the variables are interrelated (any randomness of pattern masks complex interaction of forces, see D.A. Pinder and M.E. Witherick, 1972, 282).

Many of the problems concerning cities are treated as though they were of type 2, and though much progress is achieved thereby, cities obviously present problems of organized complexity. J.W. Forrester (1969, 9-10) comes to a similar conclusion. He notes that complex systems present apparent causes that are often coincident systems, such that symptoms are often erroneously labelled causes from analogy with simple systems. When M.M. Webber realized this he seemed in despair because he felt that the locational planning task was so complex a job that it defied efforts to comprehend what it meant, much less to discuss it effectively (a letter quoted in H. Fagin, 1965, 239). Faced with this problem, A. Rogers (1967) advocated a probalistic approach as one way forward, generalizing the combined effect of a very great number of interdependent factors.

The system approach has been advocated as an analytical tool in solving problems of organized complexity (for example by C. Renfrew, 1972, 17-26; and by H.M. Proshansky, W.H. Ittelson, and L.G. Rivlin, 1970, 278). W. Michelson (1970, 24) calls for an intersystem congruence model which would study the interdependence of the physical environment and the social structure. He criticized the school of human ecology because the assumptions and point of view of its adherents were not adapted to the treatment of attitudes, sentiments, and motivations, i.e. level 3 and below in Table 6 (Michelson 21, quoting A. Hawley, 1950, 180). General systems theory has undoubted analytical value in studying a system of organized complexity like a city, but it does not of itself provide clues to the leading part in the process of centralization, to use the very terminology of systems theory. This point is worth expanding, and the quotation below is from a survey of definitions in general systems theory by O.R. Young (1964).

1.9   CENTRALIZATION AND DECENTRALIZATION
1.91   CENTRALIZED SYSTEM - 'one element [the leading part] plays a major or dominant role in the operation of the system' (A.D. Hall and R.E. Fagen, 1956, 22).
1.92   LEADING PART - 1) a component, knowledge of which permits a high degree of prediction about outputs from the system (supplied by ORY) 2) the leading part causes and does not simply indicate these outputs (supplied by ORY).
1.93   PROGRESSIVE CENTRALIZATION - 'one part of the system emerges as a central and controlling agency' (Hall and Fagen, 22).
1.94   DECENTRALIZATION - 1) control over the system is spread widely among its elements - there is no leading part (supplied by ORY) 2) knowledge of any given component does *not* permit a high degree of prediction about the system's outputs (supplied by ORY).

Here 'decentralization' is used as defining a state of the system. But it is also a process operating at different scales, notably within or between cities ('proper decentralization'), and at

regional or state level ('general decentralization' - the terms are
from C. Woodbury, 1953, 207-11).

Ethologists try to identify the leading parts of human behaviour
by analogy from the animal world. This has led to some excesses in
popular literature and severe criticism from psychologists. (H.M.
Proshansky et al., 1970, 178). One must agree that man's social
structure, broader experience, and symbolic reasoning (A.M. Rose,
1962, 6), transmitted from one generation to another make such
analogies very dangerous. Y.-F. Tuan (1975, 206) distinguishes between 'liberals' who seek to deny differences between animals and
people and conservatives, like this author, who believe that man's
symbolic reasoning places him apart. In a review of the historical
evolution of territoriality in man, E.W. Soja (1971, 28 ff) builds
upon the idea of change from a social definition of territory to a
territorial definition of society (ibid., 13). Territoriality of
whatever type, as both F.F. Darling (1952) and R. Ardrey (1966) discovered, inevitably involves a consideration of both centre and
periphery, to which Ardrey adds a third element - identity. His
'castle and border' interpretation of territory* combines the
security of a centre and the stimulation of danger at the border,
with the combination being the foundation of identity.

> I find it useful to define the three terms in terms of their
> opposites: to think of security as the opposite of anxiety, of
> stimulation as the opposite of boredom, of identity as the
> opposite of anonymity. (p. 170)

This chimes in with D.O. Hebb's (1949) belief that many of our
activities give clear evidence of the need to raise the level of
excitement (1958, 252-4). The physical environment needs to offer
the maximum freedom of choice (S. Carr, 1967, 529): sometimes to
be where the action is; sometimes to be away from it all. J.F.
Wohlwill believes that *novelty, complexity, variation, surprising-
ness,* and *incongruity* are all involved (1966, 32 ff.).

Most human beings have a 'home' which they regard as a 'centre'
for varying proportions of time. Yet an individual knows that this
is not the centre for his community. So a continuous double-think
is a requirement of living in a community and particularly in a
community geared to an urban centre. A.A. Moles and E. Rohmer
(1972) consider these two philosophical systems so important that
they open their study of the psychology of space with a discussion
of the polarity: me, here, now a personal philosophy of centrality;
and a philosophy of objective Cartesian space within which there are
impartially observed discontinuities, like centres and peripheries
(7-10). For these two authors this is 'a fundamental irreducible
contradiction between two concepts of space' (145; see also Y.-F.
Tuan, 1973, 416). There are also the concepts of territory and
orbit (A.E. Parr, 1965). The first is an area which an individual
or a close-knit group claims as its own; whereas an orbit is an area
through which there is habitual or occasional movement and may contain two or more territories (home and office for example, see Fig.
22, below).

The debate about psychologism could continue for some time, and

*cf. the prospect and refuge concept at the heart of the experience
 of landscape in J.H. Appleton (1975).

more workers from contrasting disciplines could be marshalled to
speak for both sides. The matter might be brought nearer to an
issue if diagonalism does operate at the individual level, for then
we could infer that it would also operate at group and institutional
levels, giving an explanatory tool for spatial ordering. Some would
say that because work on psychology and brain processes does not
give sufficient support to the hypothesis of diagonalism, we must
recognize it as a conjecture running ahead of the evidence, for the
time being one hopes (cf. A. Koestler, 1949, 44). Others are
bolder. For example, P.F. Smith (1974), an architect, bases an
approach to a theory of aesthetics on the 'bipolarity of human men-
tation' (p. 19):

> Emphasis on the autonomy of the two cortical systems [limbic
> brain and neocortex] should not obscure the fact that there
> is interaction between them. Maybe it is approaching an
> explanation of the aesthetic response to suggest that it
> derives from their simultaneous and harmonious involvement.
> (idem, p. 213)

The proving of a physiological basis for the way we think crea-
tively, recreatively, and aesthetically about space may be difficult. Fortunately, R.L. Gregory (1973, 55-6) in distinguishing
between the brain's physiological and strategic functions has shown
that cognitive strategies can be investigated without the associated physiological processes being completely understood.

Search for a psychological explanation can easily lead into the
problem of an infinite regress. K.R. Popper (1972b, 47) faced this
difficulty in his system for scientific discovery, where a hypothesis, or frame of reference, or 'expectation' must precede observation. Popper is even driven to the idea of inborn expectations
(for an example, see J.S. Bruner, in A. Koestler and J.R. Smythies,
1969, 324). One of the most important of these is the expectation
of finding a regularity. Here we have arrived close to inborn diagonalism between an internal orientation and an external situation.
This is how the idea of a centre could be projected on to an apparently featureless plain, and we have begun our story about the
emergence of centres in a possible world.

Chapter 1

CENTRE GENESIS

Beneath such a bold title, a text must run some risks, and so it
will be. The centres in question are those that flourished and
grew into great urban places. So here is that basic subject 'the
origin of cities' which has been the concern of many eminent students; and it would be agreeable to report some degree of consensus, but at first sight this hardly seems to be the case. Fortunately, the difference between some suggested explanations are more
apparent than real, more relative than absolute. Instead of being
daunted by the confusion, it is better to rejoice in the fact that
many thinkers of very varied backgrounds have pondered the problem.
There are perhaps two very great attractions in the subject. Much
of the human world, now and throughout history, has been mediated
via a hierarchy of cities - an idea neatly encapsulated in the one
word 'civilization'. A study of city origins throws a great
searchlight on the march forward of human society. Second, there is
a fundamental attraction in genetic explanation of any phenomenon
under study. Space navigation is a pure form of genetic deduction:
'We know where we are because we know how we got here.' M. Eliade
(1961, 83-91) goes further and believes that to know the origin of
something (that is to say its raison d'être in the religious sense)
is to gain power from it, and power emanates from a centre (see also
idem, 1964, 27-38). This pithy view, with its 'centre' allusion,
neatly anticipates some of the detailed subject-matter that follows.
Discussion of how cities can originate (and the manner in which
their centres arose, and these must have come first), and how growth
occurs, gives a useful hindsight through which to see problems of
present-day city centres. This chapter will certainly survey causes
of city formation over a long span of time, but emphasis will be
given to those studies dealing with the earliest city origins.
These were the first attempts to build notable focal centres of some
permanence on the surface of the earth, and this was how the plane
of thought first significantly intersected the plane of the earth's
surface, which was of course thought to be a plane in the first
instance (cf. Y.-F. Tuan, 1971, 18 ff).

Several difficulties arise at once. The first cities antedate
the written record; there were several nuclear areas of primary city
development; there are culture variables; and some would hold that

there is a fundamental distinction between a city 'then' and a city 'later', a particular instance being the contrast between the pre-industrial city and the industrial city which has diffused outward from western Europe. A further practical difficulty is that each primary nuclear area demands a specialist skill in a particular culture manifested through material remains and early languages, perhaps in the form of ideographs. The author-experts on these primary sources have not unnaturally tried to isolate a dominant variable, and the facts are seen through the prism of its contri-butory logic. In face of these intricacies, one might wonder whether a return into the distant past of cities was really worth while, apart from the attraction of a puzzle for its own sake. But allow for the moment some stark propositions, which will receive some underpinning in due course: (1) the city must be studied ulti-mately in terms of its function not in terms of its form, which nevertheless may give useful evidence; (2) statements about origin and development ought to be explanatory and not delineatory; (3) the function of cities is a dependent variable and human motivation an independent variable; (4) in a further equation, human behaviour is dependent on the way the world is seen. This appears to have led us straight into one of the basic difficulties. Surely, people in various cultures have seen the world differently.

> in the field of anthropological comparison I was very dubious about the validity of comparing some of the very disparate soci-eties, disparate in time and space and in structure, that were instanced....Here I find myself unconvinced by the underlying assumption that there are unchanging or relatively unchanging patterns built into the behaviour of the hominids which express themselves in any conditions of time and space. (S. Piggott, 1972, 948).

This would put the student of centre genesis at a disadvantage com-pared with, for example, the geologist and geomorphologist who can adopt the principle of uniformitarianism. 'The same physical pro-cesses and laws that operate today, operated throughout geologic time, although not necessarily always with the same intensity as now' (W.D. Thornbury, 1954, 16). The benefits of this concept can be obtained by adopting a little more generality, and asserting that the human method of confronting reality has always been the same in that the brain is basically a comparing machine which pro-vides spatial orientation; E.T. Hall (1966, 99) goes as far as to say that 'to be disoriented in space is to be psychotic'. Man pro-jects his desired world, with its centres and non-centres, on to the perceived world and then organizes the latter in an effort to gain the former, which itself is governed by the positive feedback of experience. The elements of this association (genotype) may be very differently arranged in different cultures (phenotype), or operated with different intensity, but the basic comparative method always operates, giving a cross-cultural regularity.* Here is a basic assertion of this book, the text of which is designed as supporting evidence. A bold illustration would be that even though the earth was a large billiard ball and man could have survived and

*For brief discussion of 'genotype', 'phenotype', and 'cross-cultural regularity' see p. 149 below.

evolved upon it, he would have designated some points as central, and this would have implied a distance-decay to intervening peripheries.

If all this offends by over-abstraction, at least there are for study those tangible central points that remain as the archaeologists' excavated town site or even the proto-centre of a still living city. The very first centres were certainly not cities, and 'centre' in this sense not only pre-dates cities, but as can be seen in our own generation, post-dates the uni-centred city which dominates so much of human history. Beginning at the stage of effective village agriculture, the time which R.J. Braidwood and G.R. Willey (1962, 348) called 'probably the point in all human history at which man commences to manipulate seriously and to control the environment', then already there is a 'here' (where we are sheltered) and a 'there' (where we till or farm). But this is a geometric differentiation rather than a hierarchy. Farming prospers, man prospers, the population increases, and, again according to G.R. Willey (ibid., 94), there is a change from village to villages-and-centre. A splitting-off from the original settlement becomes necessary for the increasing population. As a result some centres are older than others, and the past of the community is enshrined in their present. In Mesoamerica this stage is believed to have been reached as early as 1000 BC. Once there are central villages and non-central villages simply on a basis of age, many other factors come into play including H. Helson's adaptation level theory (1967, 284 ff) in the psychological study of perception. This states that where significant characteristics of an object vary from members of a class, a particular object is perceived not as it really is, but as its characteristics compare to a subjective average of all similar characteristics experienced in the past as a frame of reference (the adaptation level). Thus once a location acquires some centrality because it embodies conscious or subconscious memories of a group, it is at once perceived or held to be more central than it is by people who do not live in that central place.

S.L. Thrupp (1963) came close to this comparative effect when she postulated that the first centres were a cultural requirement for social continuity which was obtained by inventing the idea of order.

Initially this took form in the mind's eye as a spatially constructed cosmos with different levels in it for gods and men, connected by a hollow central shaft. (122) [And later] There is a symbiosis between the city and the country. (255)

For her, the first centres and the cities that succeeded them in a state's graded hierarchy were 'ideas', and there was 'much sympathy' for this viewpoint among a conference of specialist historians of the city in 1961 (O. Handlin and J. Burchard, 1963, 255).

If predilections are reinforced by expediency, they become powerful indeed. A colleague, C. Renfrew (1975) has indicated an economic reason for the emergence of the first central places.

If we imagine village A making water jars and fine pottery, village O producing fibers and poultry products, and village Z salt, flowers, and maize we can imagine each exchanging its products for those produced by the other. If the number of production points is N, each producer will need to visit or be visited by $(N-1)$ village representatives from other villages to

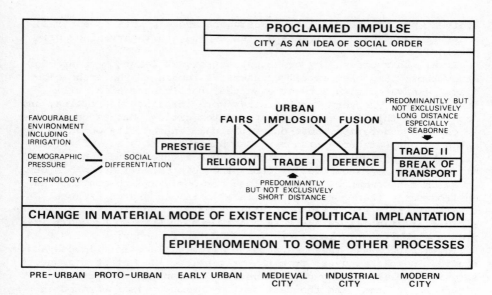

FIGURE 5   General relationship between some suggested causes of city genesis and time

The number of exceptions to the designedly vague time-scale is vast and could have been reduced by further combination of causes, but this would have over-complicated the diagram and given an unlooked for air of precision. Cf. Table 7.

The horizontal axis of this diagram might be compared with the axial schema of H. Lefebvre (1970, 26) with the following stages on the way from nil urbanisation to a totally urbanised society: political city, commercial city, industrial city, critical zone (in which industrialization plays an important role alongside other factors, like a rural exodus, and a subordination of a basic agricultural economy to an urban way of life).

effect full distribution, with the consequential $N.N-1$ journeys.

If, on the other hand, a system of redistribution $\frac{}{2}$ operates, and one village functions as a central place as well as a small production location, inhabitants of the surrounding villages will have to travel only to the central one, and its inhabitants will not need to travel at all, so that the total of journeys will be $N-1$. (loc.cit., 9)

When the subject 'origin of cities' deals not just with the earliest forms but with city-formation throughout history, the number of possible 'explanations' begins to proliferate, most of which are put forward as the leader among several independent variables. Table 7 attempts to summarize suggestions that have been put forward, and Fig. 5 is a rough sequence of them in a time continuum. In face of such variety, common sense would tell us that in most cases a conjuncture of many variables would be necessary to produce a city on the ground. In this case, common sense would leave us in a state of idiographic-type confusion in that each city would have its own unique combination of causes, if indeed these

TABLE 7 Some possible prime or validating agencies for the origin of cities

		Representative proponent(s) and/or examples where appropriate
1	Trade	C. Renfrew (1975)
2	Favourable environment	Physical environmental determinists
3	Demographic pressure	G.R. Willey (1962), E. Boserup (1965)
4	Technological development	V.G. Childe (1950)
5	Religion (or myth)	N.D. Fustel de Coulanges (1864); E. Isaac (1959-60, 1961-2) Third World examples, esp. in Africa; R.M. Adams (1960, 1966), Mesopotamian cities; P. Wheatley (1969, 1971), early Chinese cities
*6	Markets	H. Pirenne (1925), medieval European cities; S. Tsuru (1963)
7	Irrigation	K. A. Wittfogel (1957)
8	Defence and attack	H. Blumenfield (1949); E.E. Bergel (1955)
9	Periodic fairs at religious festivals	A. Allix (1922); E.G. Eriksen (1954)
*10	Urban implosion of palace and temple	L. Mumford (1961), R.E. Dickinson (1951, 1962), L. Mumford (1962)
*11	Fusion of fortress and market	M. Weber (1921), A. Boskoff (1962)
12	Idea of social order	S.L. Thrupp (1963)
13	Proclaimed impulse	J. Bird (1965), Australian seaport capitals
14	Epiphenomenon to some other causal chain	R.L. Meier (1962), M. Maruyama (1963)
15	Change in the material mode of existence	D. Harvey (1972, citing Engels and Marx; 1973), H. Lefebvre (1972)
16	Prestige in a pre-market ordered universe	H.W. Pearson (1957)
*17	Agent of trade	J.E. Vance (1970)
*18a	Break of transport (coastal gateway)	J. Bird (1970)
**18b	Break of transport (inland gateway)	A.F. Weber (1899), R.D. McKenzie (1933), R.E. Murphy and J.E. Vance (1954), and A.F. Burghardt (1971); U.S. and Canadian cities

	Representative proponent(s) and/or examples where appropriate
**19 Political implantation	Secondary urbanization, bastides, medieval burgs and bourgs, colonial cities, new capitals, new towns; S.B. Jones (1954)

NOTES

1   The order in this table is the order of treatment in the text.
2* Signifies an agency best not regarded as applying to the earliest cities in nuclear areas of urban growth.
 ** More in evidence after the establishment of the universal oekumene (i.e. post-industrial revolution and post-Western expansion) (see R. Redfield and M.B. Singer, 1953, 56-7).
3   Nos 5, 12, 13, and 16 are perhaps better considered as validating agencies; this is the view of P. Wheatley in regard to religion.
4   C. Renfrew (1975) discusses the interaction of other processes in an endogenous (Nos 5, 4, 2) and exogenous (19, 18a, 16) classification.

could ever be distinguished. Yet if the idea of 'human motivation' is retained from the earlier stark propositions, the various listed suggestions begin to look different from one another. The idea of defence as a first cause falls down because there must be something to defend a priori, and trade can be invoked only if the trade is at a time or place agreed a priori on other grounds, because trade does not need a permanent settlement for its prosecution.
    Religion, on the other hand, involves a belief in powers unseen, alongside the seen reality of this world. This double view does appear to lead to a selective conferring of the quality of centrality on relatively few parts of the oekumene, and it makes use of the very idea of comparison that man employs when he uses his brain. In paraphrasing the thesis of those who believe that cities evolved out of primitive religious centres, alternative hypotheses will be given their place, especially in connection with cities of more recent historic time.

THE RELIGIOUS IMPULSE

The clearest expression of the religious impulse towards a centre is to be found in M. Eliade (1959, Chapter 1) where he points out that space cannot be homogeneous for men who oppose sacred space to the profane space that surrounds it - the revelation of an absolute reality at a chosen spot amidst the non-reality of the immense surrounding world. If man is to orient himself in the world, he must somewhere erect a fixed point - a centre; and this centre becomes the centre of man's religious world, an irruption of the sacred into the profane with the literal threshold between them a counterpart to the threshold ('seuil' in French philosophy, see p. 137) between man's imagined and perceived worlds. In this argument no radical difference is erected between myth and religion (E. Cassirer, 1944, 87). P. Wheatley makes important use of the work of M. Eliade (1971, 418) and frequently acknowledges a debt to R.M. Adams (1966 etc.). In attempting to summarize their views very heavily, the empirical underpinning is omitted, and the order of the arguments altered. Bear in mind that even the selection has its own built-in subjectivity.

Referring to table 7, agencies 2-4 are seen not as prime movers, but rather as

> components in a series of processual changes between...levels of socio-cultural complexity... Social organization, in fact, is the dependent variable which constitutes the nub of the problem of urban origins, and the next step towards an understanding of this evolutionary process is an examination of the forces working to produce social differentiation. (P. Wheatley, 1971, 281)

Adams (1966, Chapter 2, esp. 48 ff) has pointed out that in the primary nuclear urban areas of Mesopotamia and Mexico there was no one ecologically undifferentiated region favourable to the growth of city concentrations. Instead there were a number of distinctively specialized zones so that agriculturalists needed to have a centralizing authority to make regional interrelationships fruitful. Large population increases generally followed rather than preceded urbanization (ibid. 44) and the appearance of merchants (trade) and craftsmen (technological development) 'Occurred too late to be regarded as precipitating factors behind the growth of cities, class stratification, and the emergence of dynastic authority' (R.M. Adams, 1960b, 32-2). Wheatley is uncompromising in his view that for the seven regions of primary urban generation the beginnings of urban form are dominated by a ceremonial complex (op.cit., 225), and that religion provided a primary focus for the earliest urban dwellers. He provides evidence from his research into early Chinese cities, but acknowledges a distant forerunner (idem, 302) in N.D. Fustel de Coulanges (1864, 1916 in translation), who seems to have been endowed with intuitive insight:

> In the beginning the family lived isolated, and man knew only the domestic gods....Above the family was formed the phratry with its gods....Then came the tribe, and the god of the tribe....Finally came the city, and men conceived a god whose providence embraced the entire city...; a hierarchy of creeds and a hierarchy of association. The religious idea was among the ancients, the inspiring breath and organizer of society....
>
> Social laws were the work of the gods; but these gods so powerful and beneficent were nothing else than the beliefs of men....
>
> If the first cities were formed of a confederation of little societies previously established, this is not saying that all the cities known to us were formed in the same manner....When a chief, quitting a city already organized, went to found another, he ... never failed to organize the new state after the model of the one he had just quitted. (translation, op.cit., 175-6)

In this remarkable passage there is the idea of a settlement hierarchy, a demonstration that secondary urban foundation is a different matter from the first evolutionary origins, and the fundamental point that religion is basically what man feels constrained to believe. Later (idem, 177), Fustel de Coulanges boldly states that the first cities arose overnight by tribal unification and agreement after the hierarchical substructure had developed sufficiently (cf. E.W. Soja, 1971, 13). If, however, 'city' is taken to be a canonized form of centre at the apex of a hierarchy, then the evolutionary idea of ever more important centres can be retained, within a religious symbolization of space (E. Isaac, 1959, 15).

The archaeologist seeks his answers through deductive theory based on the study of man's material remains. Hence the following summary of Adams's views culled from a short paper (1960a), antedating his longer comparative work on early Mesopotamia and pre-Hispanic Mexico (1966), has, even in these brief extracts, those inserted tie-backs to material evidence that modern archaeological scientists demand of themselves.

the first clear-cut trend to appear in the archaeological record is the rise of temples. Conceivably new patterns of thought and social organization crystallizing within the temples served as the primary force in bringing people together and setting the process in motion.

Whatever the initial stimulus to growth and reorganization, the process itself involved the interaction of many different factors. Certainly the institutions of the city evolved in different directions and at different rates, rather than as a smoothly emerging totality....

the Early Dynastic period ... saw the full flowering of independent city-states between about 3000 and 2,500 B.C.

Of all the currents that run through the whole interval, we know most about the religious institutions. ...we see a complex of workshops and storehouses surrounding a greatly enlarged but rigidly traditional arrangement of cult chambers....

At some point specialized priests appeared, probably the first persons released from direct subsistence labor. Their ritual activities are depicted in Protoliterate seals and stone carvings. If not immediately, then quite early, the priests also assumed the role of economic administrators, as attested by ration or wage lists found in temple premises among the earliest known examples of writing. The priestly hierarchies continued to supervise a multitude of economic as well as ritual activities into (and beyond) the Early Dynastic period, although by then more explicitly political forms of organization had perhaps become dominant. For a long time, however, temples seem to have been the largest and most complex institutions that existed in the communities growing up around them....

There is not one origin of cities, but as many as there are independent cultural traditions with an urban way of life. Southern Mesopotamia merely provides the earliest examples of a process that, with refinements introduced by the industrial revolution and the rise of national states, is still going on today. (loc.cit., 8-10)

Adams and Wheatley show how other factors become welded on to the religious impulse, and both acknowledge that cities founded at later periods may be surfacing on other prime agencies. But their work has the particular interest of dealing with the earliest centres that can be called cities.

FURTHER AGENCIES OF CITY ORIGIN

Turning to other theories or concepts of city origins, one must
beware of seizing on a particular idea, valid for one set of cities
at a particular time and of over-extending the generalization.   In
particular, there is the danger of over-projecting it backwards in
time, perhaps even as the ultimate explanation of first genesis.
This applies to the idea of a city founded as a market.   P. Wheatley
(1971, 282) observed that markets in the ancient world were not
autonomous price-fixing markets but subject to pressures in the
sphere of society's moral values, outside economics.   The self-
regulating market where demand, price, and cost are the determinants
of what shall be produced and to whom it shall be distributed (W.C.
Neale, 1967, 370), relying on values other than culture, can cause
social differentiation and is therefore more likely to aid city
generation.   This seems to fit in with B.W. Hodder's sequence (1968,
203-5) whereby periodic markets evolve into daily markets provided
that there is a political control of a kind to guarantee the market
place, and a sufficient density of population (Fig. 6).   If the density of population is insufficient, then as E.L. Ullman (1974, 128-
9) has pointed out, the periodic market is one way of substituting
time for space, and enabling a population to support a higher-order
central place than its absolute numbers would support as a permanent
feature.   H. Pirenne (1925) rather overdid the market and trade
factor when he refused the title of city to an urban community that
did not foster long-distance trade and have a large mercantile
middle class (pp. 56, 65; 75-6).   This was to incur the wrath of
L. Mumford (1961, 253 and 616), a proponent of another type of
explanation (see below).   Irrigation as a prime agent of urban
origin has a rather fragile basis, because it would require evidence
that it was a vital part of the ecological and societal patterns in
every nuclear area of city genesis.   Adams (1966, 68-76) shows this
not to have been the case in Mesopotamia and Mexico, and Wheatley
reviews the anti-irrigation evidence in other areas (op.cit., 289
ff).   And we follow Wheatley again in considering another suggested
prime agency for founding cities - institutionalized warfare.

> Like large-scale irrigation, it presupposes rather than generates
> superordinate authority. ... There is some reason to think that
> warfare may have played a relatively more important part in stim-
> ulating social differentiation and inducing institutional dev-
> elopment in regions of secondary urban generation, but in the
> realms of primary urban generation it appears, in the light of
> present knowledge, to have arisen only when emergent foci of
> power began to manipulate technological innovation to create
> gross inequalities in productivity.   (op.cit., 301-2)

Here is A. Allix (1922, 534) on the coincidence of religion and
trade:

> To minimize inconvenience movement of caravans at an early date
> became regular, that is periodic....Naturally the return of cara-
> vans at fixed times to their accustomed 'ports' was followed by
> gatherings for trade.   As the great religious festivals also
> drew great concourses of people, it was mutually advantageous to
> have them coincident: the caravans found it to their interest to
> arrive at the times of festivals; the sovereign power that

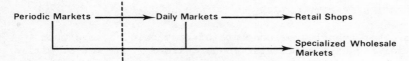

FIGURE 6   From periodic markets to modern shopping
Markets are normally on fixed locations to the right of the vertical
pecked line, here inserted.
Sources: B.W. Hodder (1968) and K.L. Buzzacott (1972).

established the fairs - as was the case in historic times for
the most part - fixed them on the great feast days. The word
'fair' (the etymology is no longer in doubt) is from feriae,
feast. [sic: Lewis and Short give 'days of rest, holidays,
festivals'.] (See E.G. Eriksen, 1954, 29.)

Some other ideas are also combinatorial. Mumford's 'urban implo-
sion' of palace and temple, a state of dynamic tension and interaction within the strict enclosure of a city wall (1961, 34 ff); and
M. Weber's fusion of fortress and market (1960, in translation, 77)
are in this compound mould. Later, while still advocating a twofold
origin, L. Mumford (1962) appears to be willing to place more emphasis on religion. S.L. Thrupp's view of the city as an 'idea of
social order' is in fact very close to the Adams-Wheatley thesis as
far as first city genesis is concerned. She even makes use (op.cit.,
122) of M. Eliade's phrase (1957), which Wheatley employs with appro-
val - the 'cosmicizing of an area' once chosen as a centre (op.cit.,
index, 566).

My own idea of the 'proclaimed impulse' (1965, 297-9), is in a
somewhat different category in that it was an attempt to answer a
'how' rather than a 'why' question. If a city is basically an
agreed centre, that agreement has to be proclaimed back to the par-
ties concerned and to any others who come within functional distance
of it. 'Proclaim' appears to be the right word because it means
that a decision is made openly, solemnly, and publicly, and has
taken many forms throughout history. The centre can be proclaimed
visually by means of height, massive scale, or richness in decora-
tion. A market must have its proclaimed rules of time and place
(see the quotation from A. Allix above), and a port must have its
legal customs basis proclaimed for ships. In British and American
law the word is used only of notices by an administrative or execu-
tive officer, and it is right that every city in the world should
cherish a charter of some type or other. A superficial view would
take this as mere symbol-worship, but such a document is the legal
basis of the city's continuous proclamation of its own centrality,
its raison d'être, and a reference to its very beginnings (see also
the symbolic importance of archives in D. Lowenthal, 1975, 11). A
survey is effectively a proclamation writ upon the ground, and the
date of the foundation of a town is often usefully taken as the date
of the first official survey, if that can be known. Whether or not
such a settlement grid ever becomes a city depends on the consensus
of opinion, forced or otherwise, continuously to proclaim it so.
The idea of the proclaimed impulse appears to correspond with the
decision stage, provided it is validated, of S.B. Jones's (1954)
unified field theory with its thesis of a political idea eventually

projected on to an area.

The proclaimed impulse seems compatible with Wheatley's idea of
the 'validation' of the centre (op.cit., 267, 315, 319). Indeed,
he ascribes an important position to this term in this extract
from his conclusion:

validating the augmented autonomy resulting from each institutional adaptation, providing the expanded ethical framework
capable of encompassing the transformation from ascriptive, kin-
oriented groups to stratified, territorially based societies, and
from reciprocative to superordinately redistributive economic
integration, was a religious symbolization.... The material
expression of this symbolization ... was the ceremonial centre,
which afforded a ritual paradigm of the ordering of social interaction at the same time as it disseminated the values and incul-
cated the attitudes necessary to sustain it. (idem, 477-8)

The origins of cities is a non-problem to those who consider
cities as epiphenomenal by-products of some other process. One
might observe that it seems strange that the same type of by-product
should evolve from the different prime agencies demonstrated over
historic time in Fig. 5. But let a quotation from R.L. Meier (1962)
give the flavour of such an argument.

A teleological explanation for the construction and organization
of cities would imply that they were determined by some basic
collective goal. Thus a new nation may have to create a proper
capital, and a new city might thereby come into being. Normally,
however, the creation of cities cannot be considered an *end* or
goal of societies, but only as a means to a variety of ends
sought by some important sub-populations. (20-1)

Perhaps this view is only apparently at variance with other explanations. Let a religious satisfaction be the sole objective of founding a city; the religious satisfaction is the ultimate goal, and the
city is the means. Achieving the means is in itself an objective,
and a goal or objective in the future can be a cause of action in
the present.

	Future	Present
religious satisfaction	ultimate goal	cause
city building	goal-enabling objective	means

(cf. L. von Bertalanffy, 1968, type of finality, 2 (iv), 79)

So instead of the city being an epiphenomenon of various processes,
it is rather the same solution for different purposes or for different combination of purposes, except that according to the
Wheatley-Adams thesis the first cities were founded with the goal of
some form of religious symbolization.

For Meier an intensification of communications, knowledge, and
controls seems to be highly correlated with the growth of cities (p.
41). The basic argument seems to be that

bond-formation between humans is encouraged by the acquisition
and retention of knowledge, and that the product of this knowledge tends to accelerate the exchanges of artifacts and messages
which inform humans about each other, and thereby causes an elaboration of the variety of bonds as well as strengthening those
that are most used....(p. 31)

This looks like a process of cumulative causation based on an initial proximity and the growth of transactions, which are the basic units and always involve some communication of information. Such deduction shows that communications theory has obviously much to contribute to the understanding of cities as urban systems, but does not seem able to help in understanding the differential selection of some sites over others for initial city foundation. Meier writes 'that some sites were enabled to grow into towns' (p. 21) and 'A few of the favourably situated towns evolved into city-states...' (idem). But why 'some' sites were chosen and not others is not discussed; and if by 'favourable' situation is meant 'favourable for city growth', the statement is clearly circular.

City-genesis as epiphenomenal to some other causal chain appears in M. Maruyama's (1963) version of cumulative causation as the second cybernetics.

  1st cybernetics: deviation-counteracting feedback networks -
                         morphostasis
  2nd cybernetics: deviation-amplifying feedback networks -
                         morphogenesis

This idea is made particularly relevant to the present discussion in Maruyama's example of the genesis of a city on a homogeneous plain (166-7).

1 Initial homogeneous plain.
2 First farm location by pioneer ambitious farmer by chance. *Initial kick.*
3 Several farmers follow first example.
4 First shop opened.
5 Village develops.
6 Village makes a more favourable location for farms nearby.
7 Increased agricultural activity leads to industrial activity.
8 City arises.
9 City increases 'inhomogeneity' of plain and inhibits growth of other cities nearby.

Given the initial kick, a deviation-amplifying mutual causal process has produced a city in one place and not in another, even although the plain was postulated as homogeneous at the outset. Cumulative causation of this type must certainly be involved in the growth and success of great cities, but there is doubt as to whether it is satisfactory as a complete explanation ab initio. First, no plain is homogeneous; and, second, any 'inhomogeneity' must be that as perceived by the first settlers or city founders. Moreoever, 'several farmers follow first example' implies that there is some other repeating mechanism which causes them to see the inhomogeneity of the plain as the first farmer did. Third, any local consensus to establish a centre must be upheld by the relevant political power, local or distant, to give the proclaimed impulse which validates the initial kick. In short, the deviation-amplifying interactional process is most useful once a centre exists; but the process, by definition, does not deal with the origin of the deviation. As A.W. Gouldner (1960) observes, 'starting mechanisms' are outside the usual perspective of functional theory which deals with already established systems. In the case of centre genesis, to say that this is caused by random processes is to confess ignorance of a generalisation applicable to all cases. Here it is argued that because the origin of some centres is known, the origin of others may be inferred, if it is believed that at a sufficient level of generality, some common processes of centre genesis are in operation.

There is one attempted explanation of first city genesis, by D. Harvey (1972 and 1973), that does clearly run counter to the Adams-Wheatley thesis and even inverts it. Harvey uses an economic change in the material mode of existence as a prime agency. The easiest way to demonstrate the antithesis is to put the two sequences side by side in tabular form (Table 8), if care is taken to observe the concomitant elements in each scheme (marked by 1, 1a, etc.).

TABLE 8   Thesis and antithesis in the founding of the first cities (S = stage; P = process)

Adams-Wheatley sequence			Harvey Sequence*		
Pre-1	(S)	Egalitarian society	Pre-1	(S)	Egalitarian society
1	(P)	Religious movement	1	(P)	Material mode of existence transformed economically
1a	(P)	Secular forces assist			
2	(S)	Redistributive and rank society based on effective space (umland) giving surplus	2	(P)	Transformation in consciousness due to 1.
2a	(P)	Surplus maintained by stable peasantry attached to religious image projected from a centre	2a	(P)	Change in ideology
			3	(S)	Redistributive economy and rank society
			3a	(P)	Surplus produced by a peasantry with low migration potential

*D. Harvey (1972; and 1973, 220-31); see also H. Lefebvre (1972, esp. 99-103).

Both Wheatley and Harvey avoid the deterministic belief that cities arise where there is a surplus, and evidence for counteracting this idea is to be found in a paper by H.W. Pearson (1957). He makes a careful distinction between an absolute surplus over subsistence needs biologically determined and a relative surplus over needs socially defined. Pearson argues that data for establishing an absolute surplus cannot be derived unless it is argued that any time not spent in pursuit of subsistence satisfaction proves the existence of a surplus. He dismisses this line of reasoning as a 'crude kind of economic determinism' and goes on to say that an economy, at all levels, is a *social* process of interaction between man and his environment. Although there may be a complex interplay of variables, the effect of the surplus is given by the way it is institutionalized. This seems to add weight to the Wheatley-Adams thesis, and indeed Wheatley makes use of Pearson's paper as supporting evidence. But the paper does go on to discuss the means of establishing surpluses in pre-redistributive forms of economy - the actual institutionalising process. For these early cases Pearson finds an agency in 'prestige', including the desire to accumulate prestige wealth, which can be intrinsic or, more frequently,

symbolic. The concept of prestige thrives inside a hierarchical
Apollonian-type framework (see below). Prestige symbols will then
be regarded as central to the society: adornment symbols giving a
personal hierarchy; and, more significant to the present purpose,
static symbols giving a hierarchy of spatial relations outwards from
the symbol's central location with a distance-decay effect over the
area where it wields psychic sway. Differential spatial prestige
leads back to a basic premise - the idea that centres arise following actions involving spatial comparisons, and these ideas seem to
be compatible with the Adams-Wheatley thesis.

Prestige may well be associated both with symbols and that early
form of trade - exchange of gifts which appears within the following
evolutionary three-stage system of M. Mauss (1954, 45): (1) total
prestation ('anything or series of things given freely or obliga-
torily as a gift or in exchange; and includes services, entertain-
ments, etc., as well as material things' idem, translator's note,
xi); (2) gift-exchange; (3) pure individual contract, the money
market, sale proper, fixed price, and weighed and coined money.
A.W. Gouldner (1960, 176-7) also discusses reciprocity as a possible
starting mechanism of relationships between people or groups.

J.E. Vance's (1970) exogenous mercantile model has some affini-
ties with long-distance trade as a chief factor in city origin and
others with the break of transport idea (see below). His prime
mover is the 'agent of trade' (later the merchant-wholesaler) who is
sent forth to organize and conduct trade from 'points of initiation'
(p. 4) to 'points of attachment' in new lands (p. 151). The model
grew out of a need for a main frame of analysis for wholesale trade
in the United States (p. 9), and to counteract the dominantly endogenetic nature of Christaller's central place theory (p. 5). Other
applications of the mercantile model are possible in Canada and
Australia, and indeed in any land where there has been an organized
trading push from outside. The model has more to say about the
results of that push than its origin in the first place, and here
the 'first place' means not only in preceding time' but also
literally in the first *place*. Thus the application of this model
seems of greater utility in later human movement than in times of
earliest city development (i.e. more within Trade II than Trade I in
Fig. 5, but cf. the movement of caravans in A. Allix, 1922, cited
above).

'Break of transport' is frequently invoked as an origin of cities,
and certainly all settlements founded as ports on rivers or sea
coasts would come under this heading. The idea implies a break of
movement at some physical barrier between a distant origin, possibly
a parent core area, and a desired destination, possibly an area ripe
for development. The phrase has a relatively modern ring about it,
but it does distinguish city genesis where the umland served is an
open system vitally linked on to another system. The other polar
type of city genesis is where the centre crystallizes out as the
apex of a locally-constructed city hierarchy.

A good example of this contrast is given by Winchester and Southampton, only 18 km. apart in Hampshire, England. In the later
seventh to ninth centuries

Winchester would be the traditional in many senses the ceremonial,
centre, while Southampton would take the part of an emerging

urban community with a relatively dense population of lower
social status, engaged in manufacture and long-distance trade.
(M. Biddle, 1973, 246-7)

The contrast has persisted. Southampton (pop. 215, 118) is a
regional centre and a major port of Britain; but Winchester (pop.
31,107) has retained its administrative pre-eminence in Hampshire.
Wheatley (op.cit., 392) follows the typology of R. Redfield and
M.B. Singer (1954) where these two types - gateway city and city
which has emerged as a leading central place in a relatively local
hierarchy - are called respectively cities of heterogenetic and
orthogenetic transformation (p. 59). At the spatial organization
level the fundamental contrast has recently received emphasis as
the hinterland/heartland contrast (B.J.L. Berry et al., 1976,
236-67).

H. Tuzet (1965, 18-19) delineates a comparable polarity in
philosophy between Heracliteans and Parmenideans. Because Hera-
clitus and Parmenides were founders of actual schools of philosophy
with ramifications wider than this polar delineation, the names
Dionysian and Apollonian are respectively substituted (see Table 4).
Dionysians prefer diversity, 'progress', change, continuous rather
than discrete order, not 'being' but 'becoming' - a romantic aesthetic. Apollonians hate change, yearn for perfectionist patterns;
but since the world cannot be totally perfect, they incline to her-
archical structure - a classical aesthetic. These ideas find
expression in modern geographical thought when the exogenous gateway concept is considered alongside the endogenous central place
theory (see pp. 117-29 and esp. Fig. 21). There are even such alternative approaches within central place theory itself. W. Christaller (1933) favoured a fixed k hierarchy* and might therefore be
termed classical, as opposed to the variable k hierarchies of A.
Losch (1943), who thus appears as Dionysian and 'romantic'. (W.
Bunge, 1966, 152, demonstrates the k contrast; see also G. Rowley,
1974, 271a.)

'Political implantation' can cover a vast number of cases, and is
nearly always an effective umbrella covering twentieth-century city
foundation now that the world is effectively divided up into organized territorially-based state units. The already-mentioned unified
field theory of S.B. Jones (1954) provides useful theoretical underpinning here. 'Agglomeration and scale economies' (see p. 121-2)
have been omitted from the table of prime agencies because they
appear to be secondary factors fostering the growth of settlements
once established. A possible case which might slip through the
elaborate net is the city founded on a highly localized resource.
Yet a mining settlement must export to survive, and therefore it
could be classed as an inland gateway which might soon develop
industries and a momentum of its own through agglomeration and scale
economies and the two-way haul of raw materials. Neither break of
transport nor political implantation can be projected backwards in
time as a first cause of the first centres, although political
implantation covers a number of earlier cases if it is allowed to
subsume defence.

*A hierarchy of settlements in which each order contains some fixed
number, k, for each settlement of the order above.

In concluding this section it is necessary to distinguish centre-genesis from city-genesis. Some cities were planned to be the most important places in their region ab initio, and the space around was deliberately adapted to focus upon them. Other cities may have begun as agricultural villages, at havens for ships, near a mine shaft, or at a minor node on a transport net. Subsequently, the development of the area threw up an urban hierarchy requiring a high-order centre, and such sites found themselves selectively adopted.

Throughout most of written history, cities have been the most spectacular embodiment of selective centrality on the surface of the earth; yet, despite modern urban physical obtrusiveness, the city is the expression of a function rather than a morphological phenomenon. This is certainly Wheatley's view: 'We have argued ... that no specific morphological feature, or even assemblage of features, is an adequate indication of urban status, which can be defined only in terms of function' (op.cit., 394). Compare this with the present author's consistent view on that particular class of cities called seaports. 'any attempt to define ports by an inherent characteristic of form is impossible. It is much more convenient to define a port in terms of its function rather than in terms of its form' (J. Bird, 1957, 13). 'A seaport is best defined in terms of its function...' (J. Bird, 1971, 13). This does not imply that the 'trace on the ground' is neglected, because a centre is not only the expression of a function, an 'organizing and regionalizing principle' in Wheatley's words (op.cit., 477), but also a place where the centralising function is proclaimed in vivid three-dimensional form.

MORPHOLOGY OF FIRST CENTRES

At the beginning of cities, or at the beginning of any individual city, morphological features ought to be easy to interpret. Sometimes this is indeed the case; at other times decidedly not. The Apollonian/Dionysian dichotomy provides useful clues, often manifested by evidence from cities with grid lay-outs compared with cities of so-called organic growth. Such a superficial contrast may reflect a basic difference between deductive centrality and inductive centrality. The former refers to the consciously planned conference of centrality on to a chosen location such that within the plan there is from the outset a centre and a periphery. Inductive centrality is where the idea of the centre is projected on to a city after it has grown from its first beginnings. Instead of an a priori centre, there is an original area and a later area. The differences between deductive and inductive centrality come mainly from differences in the combination of space and time.

This section is concerned with deductive centrality because according to M. Eliade (1949) and to Wheatley who follows him, the first centres were projected images of cosmic order on to the plane of human existence. Such multiple imagery, called *diagonalism* in this study, is more likely to arise within religions holding that human order was brought into being with the creation of the world, so that the city lay-out relates to the idea of cosmic order

(E. Isaac, 1961-2, 12; and B. Bogdanović, 1975, 142).   Cosmic order
in its turn could be conceived only where man had learned to have
a theoretical concept of space to place alongside observational
space (E. Cassirer, 1944, 45); and observed space can be combined
diagonally with objective space to form ego space (R. Beck, 1967,
21) in which centres will appear.   Harvey (1972, 511) has countered
this idea of cosmic order as a precursor to first city origins by
pointing out that projected images exist in non-urbanized societies;
and he cites Stonehenge.   This seems merely to make the point that
while such centres may grow into cities, this is not necessarily
always the case.   T.C. Stewart (1970, intro) expressed the
sequence vividly by declaring that the psychic condition exists
first, and then a site is sought on which to realise the inner mental pattern.   In Stewart's anthology, the majority of the morphological patterns appear as based on the square, the circle, or some
form of axis, particularly one in the form of a cross.   The resultant detailed pattern depends upon which of the three elements is
dominant (see also the suggested notation of P. Thiel, 1970, quoted
in Fig. 4 above).

Examples suggestive of cosmic order are the Pole Star, around
which it was believed the heavens revolved, the pattern of four
seasons; and, in a Chinese context, the *yang* (masculine, dominant,
precipitous, sunny, south-facing) and the *ying* (with opposite
characteristics).   S. Chang (1970, 66) argues that a preference for
the north (sunny) bank designated *yang* is testified by the great
preponderance of that character in Chinese place-names.   Eighty
cities have this character and all are sited on the north bank of
a river, while the total number of cities with the character *ying*,
sited on the south bank, adds up to less than ten.   At this point
quotation of a poetic *trouvaille* unearthed by Wheatley (p. 428) in
the *Chou Ritual*, is irresistible.   This refers to the choice of a ·
centre in China, probably in the third century, or earlier.'   'the
place where earth and sky meet, where the four seasons merge, where
wind and rain are gathered in, and where ying and yang are in harmony.'

The square and the circle are of course shapes in which the idea
of a centre is subtended at a geometric point within them.   Inter-
secting axes certainly give a much more explicit centre, and evoke
the mandala theme (see P.F. Smith, 1975, 161).   Indeed, R.S. Lopez
(1963, 27) draws attention to the ideogram for a city in the earliest writing that can be read; it consists of a cross within a
circle.   A vertical axis projected down from the Pole Star, provides an 'axis mundi', 'the place where earth and sky meet'.   From
this projected axis the idea of centrality emanated and was diffused over the tributary area by means of roads, perhaps aligned to
the four cardinal points, often accentuated by four great gates.

In China, the ancient Hsien capitals were usually square or rectangular in exterior shape, oriented to the cardinal points (Y.-F.
Tuan, 1974, 414).   Chang (p. 70) observes that the earth was regarded as square in ancient Chinese thought; and the number four (four
sides) had a particular and popular significance.   These are further examples of an alternative world of thought and belief being
projected on to the real plane of the earth's surface.   In the
Chinese city the axis between the north and south gates was the main

basis of the ground plan, but the full vista was interrupted and
the panoramic promenade consisted in a progressive unrolling for
the pedestrian, rather as in viewing a Chinese scroll painting, as
Wheatley suggests (p. 425). One of the causes of this successive
enclosure effect derived from the detailed arrangement of the axes
of the two main roads. The north and south limbs of the main axis
were often offset at the centre, and sometimes the east-west axis
had a similar displacement. This pattern has obvious defensive
advantages, but Chang reports (n. 23) that the Chinese believed
that evil spirits or demons travelled in straight lines, and the T-
junctions formed by the offset axes would prevent them from winging
their way into the heart of the city.

There seems to have been little competition in the ancient
Chinese city for location at the geometric centre. The square
enclosed by the early-built walls was often too large for continuous occupation at an initial stage. Plenty of sites were available, and those facing south had a premium. No one building dominated. The Confucian temple, the city temple, the seat of the
magistrate might each have become the nucleus of their own functional precincts, producing a mosaic pattern that eventuates in the
western city only after centro-symmetric ordering has taken place
(see below p. 68 ff). In addition, the zone above 100 Chinese
feet was believed to be the cruising height of evil spirits so that
temples and towers seldom exceeded ninety-five feet in height - an
indication that non-persons could dictate the morphology of the
city in another dimension. This idea could be expanded to a statement which says that city morphology has to conform to both an outer
and an inner reality, the latter of course being real possibly only
to those who founded the city and to those who continue to use it
without adaptation. Such is the only relevant inner reality in
early city morphological explanation.

The Chinese case is easy to demonstrate in that the enclosing
wall is there in its massive reality, but in many modern cities the
urban boundary is often firmer on maps than it is on the ground.
This inner presence of an invisible boundary was often found in some
other early cities, 'to keep the citizens together, sheltered *from*
the cold, wide world, *conscious of belonging to* a unique team, proud
of being *different from* the open country and *germane to* one another'
(R.S. Lopez, 1963, 27) [The added italics indicate a contrast
stated twice over - implicit diagonalism].

When at later periods a centre was based on mainly militaristic
principles, it would certainly form part of a power hierarchy, as
under the Tokugawa regime in late seventeenth-century Japan. Urban
morphology was dominated by a castle as the source from which the
functionally binding power emanated first over the city and then
over the tributary domain beyond. The word strongpoint is literally
apt here. In the Japanese castle town of the eighteenth century,
the hierarchical nature of the power emanation is reflected in the
town morphology: the caste was central, with the upper military
caste close by, the lower caste warriors on the periphery, and arti-
sans and merchants in separate districts (T. Yazaki, 1963, see
illustrations preceding the text).

City plans based on the overt projection of spatial patterns are
forms of the 'ideal city'. As we have seen, reflections of the

cosmic order were probably the first class of such projections, but as H. Rosenau (1974, 30) remarks:

> during the Greek evolution the ideal plan was isolated from its cosmological background; in a similar way the magical connotations, although still felt receded into the background during Roman developments; Judaism contributed the projection into the hereafter and thus stressed the symbolic aspects of the Messianic hope, as realized in the Heavenly Jerusalem. The Greek, Roman and Jewish heritages influenced the Middle Ages in the representation of ideal cities, either from a formal point of view, or in a symbolic manner.

ESTABLISHING A CENTRE

Finally, here are a few highly generalized summary thoughts about how founders of centres, which might or might not grow into cities, could be discovered going about their job.

1 The selected location must conform to an inner desired symbol or pattern, or be capable of being made to conform.
2 The natural morphology of the site, or the interpenetration of land and water, must be of such a pattern that this can be interpreted as a framework which untouched or retouched gives an impression of a within and a without.
3 The area so framed must be large enough for the required settlement, but not so large as to give an impression of an undifferentiated area. The sprawling modern city often has to adapt itself by means of outgrowths from the original site beyond which there is terrain difficult for urban construction. In this respect, those modern cities are fortunate if the original focus was where a small stream, now easily buried, met a larger river with wide flat river terraces, or where the city was founded on a small as opposed to a large indentation of a coast or lakeshore. Difficulties arise if the amounts of flat land immediately adjacent to the original site are extremely limited.
4 If a location is between two or more varied surfaces, this may be an attractive feature for founders. Varied environmental resources are a hedge against uncertainty and may promote exchanges.   They may also cause an unavoidable halt in movement.
5 The sphere of locational choice is often constrained by the direction from which the original founders arrived. Or, put another way, the choice might be influenced by the easiest transport routes to a national or folk core area. Success of such a choice would depend on the ability to maintain such links.
6 The growth of a centre is often assisted by the possession of some symbol of centrality, even if this is merely the intangible reflected symbolism of a name, perhaps after a saint or a monarch, or even after another city. It must be remembered than even an apparently meaningless name can acquire significance very quickly if the centre is validated and subsequently successful. This can be summed up by saying that no one knows what 'London' means, yet everyone knows what London means. If that sounds enigmatic, consider that New Orleans is no longer just a New World souvenir of Orléans; and it even takes an effort to remember that there was

ever the nominal connection.

7   All centres which generate cities have names from an early date.
    Perhaps it is strange that no league of cities has developed in
    which each is identified by a number, even if such a system has
    to be invented for the use of modern communication industries.
    Changes of city name can be highly significant because they may
    be indications of an increase in psychologically felt central-
    ity.

8   In post-literate societies, the legal seal on city centrality,
    the proclaimed impulse, will be enshrined in a document, always
    a highly cherished possession.

These observations presuppose the concomitance of power, often
manifest as military or political power, or social consensus, or,
even more simply the common beliefs of a human group. Sometimes
these beliefs were subconsciously disguised as the works or com-
mands of gods. But, to repeat the words of Fustel de Coulanges,
those gods, however powerful, however awful, were really 'nothing
else than the beliefs of men'.

Chapter 2

EVOLUTION OF CENTRAL AREAS

The central area of any city has an important time dimension sometimes jealously preserved and often symbolically flaunted before the
visitor. An account containing 'evolution' in the title is bound to
pay careful attention to progression through time, and this will
allow the next chapter more freedom to roam around the modern city
centre. The Ariadne thread in the last chapter was a concentration
on the origin of the first centres, and this permitted only the most
general forward survey. It was shown that throughout history many
different reasons could be invoked for centre or city genesis as
soon as there is a dive below the general level of the centre as an
a priori idea. To realize how complicated the problem can become
one has merely to turn to a brief volume of readings dealing with
one country at one period. J.F. Benton (1968) attempted a review
and paraded eight major theories of town origins which had been put
forward for medieval England. He concluded that it would be a ster-
ile exercise to decide which one was 'right'. Instead each theory
ought to be continually subjected to the evidence in an attempt to
obtain an acceptable compromise between generality over a large
number of cases and congruence with large numbers of individual segments of evidence. This proves to be useful advice if the study of
centrality and the city is to be brought closer to the present day.
To retain generality over a large number of cases, the focus will be
held on the evolution of the central area of a city; otherwise, the
great number of variables contributed by different cultures will
overwhelm the discussion.

As the total city increases in size, the centre evolves. There
is an important distinction between growth and development on the
one hand and evolution on the other. Biologists have encountered
this difficulty, and J. Huxley (1959, 27) remarked that evolution
was an anti-entropic process running counter to the Second Law of
Thermodynamics where there is a tendency towards decreasing order
(P.B. Medawar, 1967, discusses the problem, 43 ff). In the case of
a city centre, there is often an initial randomness of functional
location which becomes more ordered as the centre grows. The modern
metropolitan system as a whole may tend towards an entropy state of
functional location, as suggested by A.G. Wilson (1970), with the
relaxation time towards this end prolonged by a number of

constraints, many of which are classed under the general heading of
inertia (P. Gould, 1972, 700). A suggestion offered here is that
while urban systems as a whole obey the Second Law of Thermodynamics,
their centres and later their plurality of centres, diffused outward in innovation leaps from the original centre, manifest an evolution towards organization and negentropy. There results a great
mix-up of ordered centres and functionally diverse tributary areas
in the biggest city regions, as the citizens become more mobile.
Three pathways have been noted for the transmission of innovations
through an economic system: nationally outward from the manufacturing belts, down the urban hierarchy, and outwards from urban
centres into their surrounding urban field (B.J.L. Berry and
E. Niels, 1969, 295). City centres are important loci of transmission for at least two of these channels. A similar three-scale
basis has been identified in explaining the distribution of income
disparities in Canada, making up a composite centre-periphery model
(D.M. Ray and T.N. Brewis, 1976; and see below pp. 112-14).
    A 'centre' is of itself an open system, dependent not only upon
transport links with its tributary area but also having extra-
territorial links to other organizing centres. L. von Bertalanffy
(1968, 144-5) has shown that while closed systems obey the Second
Law of Thermodynamics and proceed towards increasing entropy, open
'organismic' systems can import negentropy via their extra-system
links, and this causes them to tend towards an increasing inner
order.

CITY IN PLAN AND CENTRE PLAN

To encounter a city in plan makes matters simpler at the outset.
There is an obvious prime contrast between cities developed on a
radial plan compared with those that are rectilineally designed.
A city based on a radial plan has a ready-made centrality imposed on
whatever is placed at the centre - cathedral, palace, government
building, or symbol. In such a city one can easily discern the
direction in which the centre lies merely by observing the angles
at which radial roads, sub-radial, and ring roads meet. One diff-
culty with the radial pattern is that the growth of the total system
by means of ribbon development along the spokes merely throws more
centrality upon the original centre whence it may be difficult to
expand over already built-up areas. Open-ended solutions are difficult to find in such designs, as L'Enfant realized when he came to
plan the lay-out of Washington in 1789.:
    although the means now within the power of the Country are not
    such as to pursue the design to any great extent, it will be
    obvious that the plan should be drawn on such a scale as to
    leave room for that aggrandizement and embellishment which the
    increase of the wealth of the nation will permit it to pursue at
    any period however remote. ... (Letter to George Washington,
    11 September 1789 see E.S. Kite, 1929)
Washington is often considered as a radially planned city that
stands out from the run of grid-based American cities, but the
L'Enfant 1791 plan is in fact a radial-grid combination, details of
which were dictated by careful attention to the site morphology.

The radial plan is not the only city plan to throw progressive
strain on the centre (see Fig. 7), but it must be remembered that
not all citizens are obliged to visit the centre at one time.
Given sufficient stimulus, tremendous efforts are made to expand
the centre in plan or in profile, up or down. A radial city can
equip itself with an intra-urban hierarchy of centres, or expand by
means of satellites when it will turn into another of the types
classified in Fig. 7. The city centre is not the sole focus for
citizens: place of work, local services, and access to open space
must all be catered for. These are achieved with varying success
by the different basic lay-outs. With any single plan it is difficult to reconcile the necessity for open-endedness, to allow for
growth, with a desire for economy in the use of existing centres.
The plan which allows the easiest additions is the linear, but it
is also the plan in which any increment throws the original centre
furthest off the geometric centre. If accessibility to open space,
the reverse of access to the centre, is a prime requirement, the
linear lay-out is also the most efficient; but almost as much could
be achieved by linear city components arranged as radials with green
wedges protected between them.

The rectilinear pattern is the best-known format in the United
States and has often formed the basis of those towns that began as
colonial bridgeheads. The design is extremely easy to survey and
is suitable for lot-selling in an open-ended situation over a period
of time. In 'Town Planning in Frontier America' by J.W. Reps
(1969), map after map shows the grid pattern imposed on a tremendous
range of morphological sites. Two cases may be quoted where the
introduction of radial streets led to local difficulties. In
Washington the combination of radials, between dominant urban functions, and an underlying grid gave dozens of awkward intersections
and strangely shaped building sites - not a very sound economic
proposition in an infant capital city. A paradoxical benefit
resulting from long periods of disuse of such plots is the opportunity for laying out small parks and sites for monuments which would
certainly not have been available in a totally regular grid. A more
vivid illustration of the inappropriateness of fancy planning in a
frontier setting is given by Reps's example of Circleville, Ohio
(1969, 299-303). When it came to a choice of site for the administrative centre of Pickaway County, Ohio, a location was fixed on
where there was a relic of Indian culture, a mound running in a
large irregular circle, about a thousand feet in diameter. The
original design made use of this for the alignment of the principal
street, with four diagonals, north-east to south-west and north-west
to south-east. The odd-shaped lots that resulted were considered
to waste valuable urban land, and over a period of years the town
was re-planned on a regular grid by a private redevelopment company
called, of course, the Circleville Squaring Company. H. Carter
(1972, 152) comments that it was an inappropriate symbolic preserva-
tion in the town form of Indian rites and usages. The settlers had
the grid pattern firmly in their psyche as the 'normal' lay-out for
a town. A telling detail provided another reason for abandonment of
the original plan which included a spacious 'circular square' around
the central courthouse. It had become a foraging haunt for local
swine. No other comment could further remove frontier America from

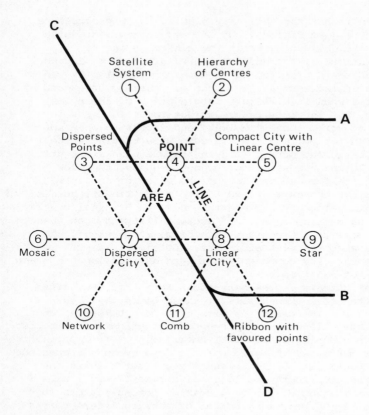

FIGURE 7   A classification of city plans in relation to point, line, and area

Around 4, is organized the concentric city. Line AB encloses those lay-outs which are likely to possess an inherently legible city centre (AB types). Line CD separates off types to the right where there is a city centre at the apex of a hierarchy of centres. (Note. AB types may easily develop into AC types.) Lay-outs to the left of CD have no explicit centre but will develop them in functional practice, if indeed the dispersed types ever come into being in the first place.

Source (for underlying framework): G. Albers (1968).

the sophisticated aesthetics of the Italian Renaissance piazza, and no wonder that such ideas could rarely be bodily transplanted to the pioneer fringe and hope to survive.

R. Pillsbury (1970, 437-9) puts ease of survey and lot selling as a subsidiary reason for the diffusion of the grid form in the United States, alongside the role of the central government in promoting middle-sized boroughs, concentrating the market function in a few select locations. He ascribes the chief innovative reason for rectilinear regularity to the classical revival in Europe and the United States; and D. Stanilawski (1966, 108) also stresses the importance of anterior models. The Greeks had shown great skill in adapting the grid pattern to sites of differing morphology.

TABLE 9   References or examples for classification of city plans (Fig. 7)

---

1   E. Howard (1902)*, Greater London and post Second World War 'out-county' estates.

2   British new towns, Mark I.

3   Nonplace community in M.M. Webber (1964, 108-14), theory.

4   E.W. Burgess (1925), theory.

5   Hook*, a planned satellite town of London never built, see 'The Planning of a New Town', etc., 1965.

6   Chandigarh*, designed by Le Corbusier, see N. Evenson (1966) and R. Khosla, 1971.

7   Broadacre City, F. Lloyd Wright (1935), never built.

8   A. Sonia y Mata (1882)*, theory, see L. Keeble (1964, 95-6).

9   The Nation's Capital - a Policies Plan for the Year 2000' [Washington] (1961)*.

10   L. Hilberseimer (1944)*, Milton Keynes.

11   MARS plan*, see E. Maxwell Fry (1944), theory.

12   Brasilia*, see C. Alexander (1966, 50) and N. Evenson (1973). The architect of Brasilia considered the basic form of his design to be 'two axes crossing each other at right-angles', see Envoi, below.)

---

*For references or examples marked *, and many illustrated plans see L. Keeble (1964, 95-7); and designer of underlying framework for Fig. 7, see G. Albers (1968, 17).

Hippodamus of Miletus is often credited with inventing this type of lay-out, but the hard evidence for this appears not to be at hand (see P. Zucker, 1959, 33 ff). Classical influences in America extended only to the plan, and not to three-dimensional details of the urban scene. Although the sheltered boardwalk might be a cheap timber copy of the colonnade, the peristyle was rarely found. A subconscious attraction of the grid lay-out may have been its appeal of geometric equality in a nascent democracy; and yet secure political control is necessary for a uniform cell-by-cell addition. A difficulty with this plan rigidly adhered to, is that the centre of the city is merely the peak land value intersection, or the busiest crossroads. Centrality can flourish even under these adverse conditions, as Piccadilly Circus bears witness, but the concept of centrality is certainly enhanced if one or two blocks are missed out of the grid lay-out to provide some sort of container setting.
   One solution to the problem of a centre in a grid is found in many an American county seat - the courthouse square. As in the case of the totality of the rectilinear pattern, there is an exotic origin for the innovation; in this case it is Londonderry, in Ulster, transferred at first to south-east Pennsylvania, and then

diffusing with the migrating Pennsylvanians (E.T. Price, 1968, 41).
The courthouse square suffers from the problem inherent in all
central areas of expanding towns. Price notes that the 'edifice of
government in a cavity surrounded by business' rarely survives in
the centre of a town which grows above 25,000 in population. The
original squares had an interesting mixture of form and function,
but this, it is suggested, does not fit in with the American psyche
which is held to prefer one thing at a time rather than mixing
several activities (polychronism or diagonalism). The strung-out
Main Street is supposed to reflect not only the American structuring
of time but also the lack of involvement with others (E.T. Hall,
1966, 163), leading to an emphasis on the *flat principle* in architecture (see p. 96 below, and Fig. 15). One might add that there
is also a lack of involvement with the total three-dimensional
effect of the city centre. So the courthouse square may find few
defenders if it interferes with traffic and trade as the town grows.

On the other hand, European medieval street patterns can be surprisingly long-lived (J. Majewski, 1971). Main arteries may be
progressively modified to take more traffic, and the originally
residential outskirts of the core, over which central functions
have expanded, can often absorb the traffic increases of the last
two centuries. Fixed site boundaries, the inertia projected upwards
from the network of subterranean services, and insufficient municipal resources for full-scale redevelopment have often postponed the
impact of twentieth-century demands perhaps sufficiently long enough
for the modern 'environment lobby' to argue powerfully for preserva-
tion. The centrality of Amsterdam within Dutch life has been much
influenced by the inner complexity of its 'ancient rustique inner
city', its entertainment centre, so 'exclusive and varied', and what
has been called the monumentality of the inner city with its
seventeenth-century houses and street canal lay-out (W.F. Heinemeyer
and R. van Engelsdorp Gastelaars, 1971, 209-10).

THE CENTRE IN A FRAME

Price's study of the courthouse square provides an instance of the
nature of effective centrality, and his phrase 'the edifice... in
a cavity surrounded by ...' may be broadened to the centre as 'a
functioning symbol within a contrasted frame focussing upon it'.
Any central symbol gains in power by being set among other city
functions which are separated from it, yet look towards it. The
symbol gains additional sway, if when approached, it can actually
be entered, so that the feeling of centrality recedes further into
the interior. Central symbols placed on high are effective at a
distance, but when approached become less meaningful, when the real
centre of action is obviously beneath the cathedral spire or the
civic tower. These ideas find expression in the detailed lay-out of
one of the most powerful central symbols on earth, the very name of
which is synonymous with the idea of a place as a centre - the
Prophet's Mosque at Mecca.

The very centre of Mecca is within the Mosque, the Kaabah, the
cube, believed to have been originally conceived as a literal reflec-
reflection on earth of the throne of God (E. Esin, 1963, 16), a

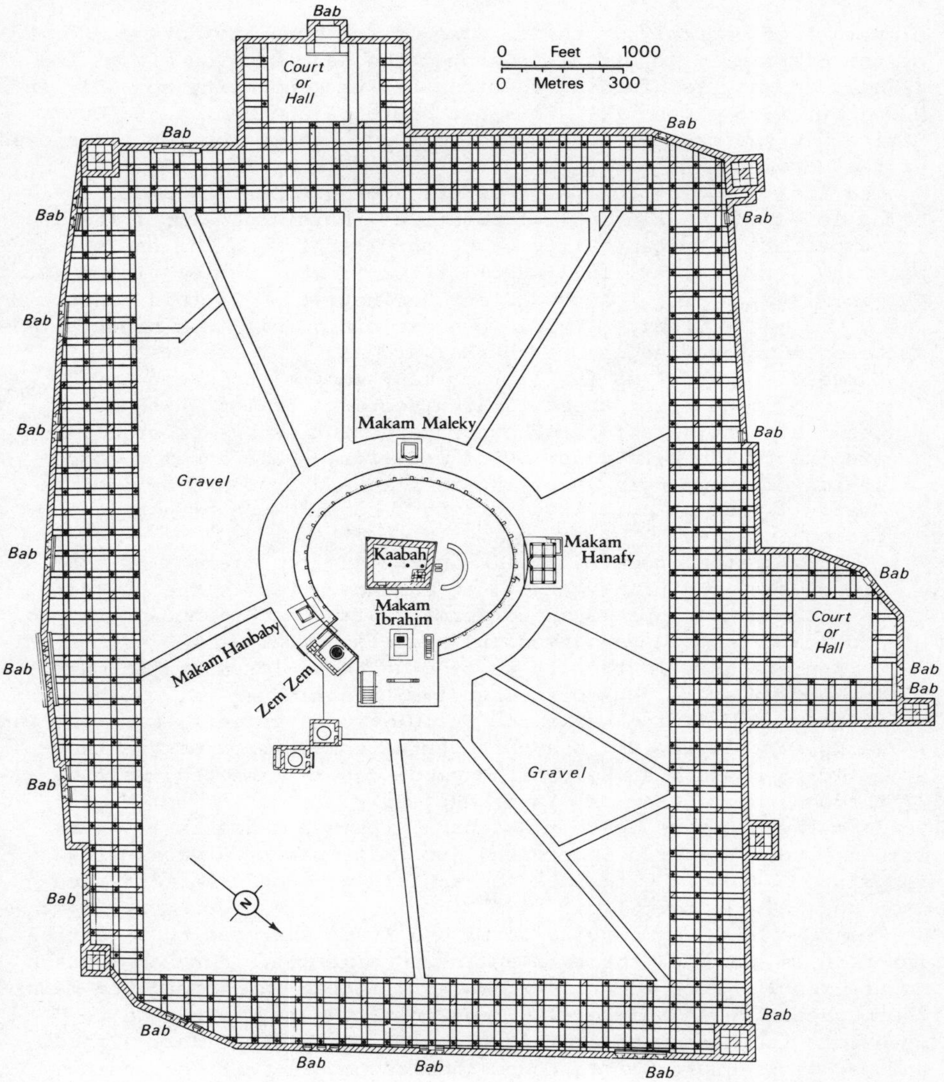

FIGURE 8   The Prophet's Mosque, Mecca
makam, stations for prayer; *zem zem*, holy well; *bab*, gate to the
mosque through the surrounding cloisters. Based on and highly simplified from a plan of the Prophet's Mosque at Mecca by Ali Bey
(1814), quoted in R. Burton (1855, vol. II, 294-5); see also a
sketch of the interior of the Kaabah by Burton (idem, 208).

veritable axis mundi of a Apollonian-type of religion (see Fig. 8).
Reconstructed many times, the cube itself contains sacred stones
built into the wall, and it is possible to go inside (see plan,
R. Burton, 1855, 208). The cube is covered with embroidered silk
(the *Kiswa*), renewed annually, and the discarded covering is cut
into strips and sold to pilgrims - almost a literal dismembering and

dispersal of centrality itself. One of the symbolic acts performed
by the pilgrim is to circulate around the Kaabah seven times (the
tawaf), thereby reinforcing the idea of its centrality not only in
Mecca but also in the religious structure of the believer. But
notice how the cube is set in the rectangle formed by the cloisters
of the Mosque.

The idea of going towards a centre, coming upon it, and then
being lured on towards and, if possible, inside the symbol itself,
is compatible with centrality being unrolled like a Chinese scroll
painting (P. Wheatley, 1971, 425) or the idea of serial vision (G.
Cullen, 1961, 17-20). An excellent demonstration of this concept
was given by W. Gropius (1950) when explaining his idea about a
succession of quadrangles to the Harvard Alumni Society:

> Harvard's 'Yard,' so familiar to many sons of this country,
> shows a sound basic theme of architectural design which has
> been reverently kept throughout the centuries by almost all the
> architects who have contributed individual buildings; a compo-
> sition of quadrangles, varying in size and confined by indivi-
> dually different buildings, offers a sequence of arresting sur-
> prises in space.
>
> This spatial theme fulfills an ancient requirement of the
> art of architecture - namely, to balance artfully the building
> masses and open spaces in conformity with the human capacity to
> experience and sense harmonious space and scale....
>
> Architecture is the art to provide the fulcrums which make
> space finite and thus comprehensive to human senses. Spaces
> in between defining walls and buildings, as streets, squares, and
> yards, are essential in architectural composition as are the
> building masses themselves. Anybody can realize that walking
> through the old Harvard Yard.   (p. 69)

Perhaps the ultimate form of a centre within a frame is a centre
within a centre - or a labyrinth, but this must be a reassuring
labyrinth and not one that causes anxiety through disorientation
(see pp. 146-7, below).

The idea of a town square forming a frame surrounding a central
function is apt when there is an included market. Many an English
square results from the rise of markets, often in a broadened main
thoroughfare, with a lateral extension if the market begins to
interfere too much with traffic circulation. Settlements already
endowed with squares often found them encumbered with periodic
markets such as upon the parvis before a cathedral. Alternatively,
markets arose on enclosures such as a village green or *Anger*, originally a common space resulting from the pattern of houses facing
inward to obtain some psychological togetherness if not actual
defensive shelter in a marchland region (H. Thorpe, 1949). These
organically evolved squares are to be contrasted with the planned
square, such as those originating in a survey which leaves open the
required number of blocks in the Hippodamic system post 470 BC.
P. Zucker (1959) is at pains to stress that the square is the result
of societal and psychological attitudes to the perception and use of
space. He points out that Spain did not foster the public life or
life in public that flourished in France and Italy and is therefore
less rich in town squares (pp. 2-4). Argument by antithesis is
followed by Zucker when he advances the theory that the lack of

effective town squares in the nineteenth century was due to the
fact that interest in three-dimensional aspects of space was then
dormant until re-awakened by Cezanne and the cubists (ibid., 6).
This emphasis on the three-dimensional quality of such urban foci
is important to counteract the too simplistic morphology of plans
alone.

Much of the modern thinking about city centre lay-outs in
regard to squares and vistas has been conditioned by a seminal book
first published in 1889, though not translated into English until
1945. This work by Camillo Sitte has already been noted in connection with his critique of rectilinearity (pp. 17 quotation). The
general effect of his philosophy of town planning led to what has
been called the informal revival (E. Saarinen, 1943, 114-28; see
also G.R. and C.C. Collins, 1965). He advocated what his contem-
poraries called a 'closed architectural effect'. The influence can
be seen in Zucker's classification (Table 10), where the subjective
category 'amorphous squares' indicates that the square is rendered
'shapeless' because the perimeter has been opened out by access roads
or by building profiles out of scale; and this is held to produce
an undesirable lack of closure. F. Schumacher considered that the
major contribution of Sitte was his emphasis on rhythmic spatial
relationships (see Collins and Collins, op.cit., note 77), such that
the eye beheld a varied succession of shapes rather than monotonous
vistas (cf. 'serial vision' etc. above; see also the contrast between the *flat principle* and the principle of *static, modelled form*,
Fig. 15 and p. 96 below). Two quotations will make these points
clearer.

The Place Saint-Michel at Nimes is an example of excessive
opening of a plaza enclosure by the entrance of oblique streets.
(1945 translation, 64)
What an impression is made by several grouped squares on the
person who goes from one to the other! The eye encounters a
new scene at every instant, and we feel an infinite variety of
impressions. This may be observed in photographs of St. Mark's
and of the Signoria of Florence. There are more than a dozen
popular views of each square, taken from various points. Each
one presents a different picture, so much so that it is difficult
to believe that they are all views of the same place. When we
examine a modern square of strict right angle design, we can get
only two or three views of different quality, for in general they
express no artistic feeling. They are only surfaces of so much
area. (ibid., 38)
As might be expected, Sitte objected to the placing of statues,
fountains, or obelisks in the centre of squares; indeed he lauded
the classical practice of placing statuary at the periphery of
plazas. As regards the grouping of buildings, he tended to favour
the principle of occult balance, exemplified by an adult closer to
the fulcrum of a see-saw in order to balance a child at the other
end. The opposite of occult balance is called 'unresolved duality'
by A.H.J. Brown, H.M. Sherrard, and J.H. Shaw (1969, 174, 178) –
perhaps equivalent to non-diagonalism. This occurs when two elements compete for attention, dividing the interest and dissipating
the possibility of any focal importation by the observer. Sitte was
very conscious of the three-dimensional essence of squares, offering

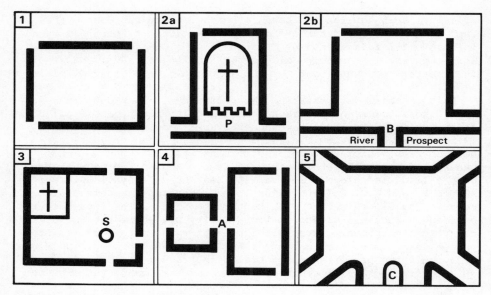

FIGURE 9   Simplified outlines of schematic town squares in the
classification of P. Zucker (op.cit)
1, closed; 2a, 2b, dominated; 3, nuclear; 4, grouped; 5, amorphous.
P. parvis; B, bridge; S, statue; A, arch; C, central reservation of
a boulevard (divided highway).   Cf. Table 10.

as a rule of thumb the idea that the breadth of a square ought to
equal the height of the principal building adjacent, and that the
length should not normally exceed twice that height (p. 28).   We
must remember that Sitte had no experience of skyscrapers, but no
doubt he would have suggested that they be balanced against horizontal surfaces of squares and buildings of a contrasted profile,
making sure that they were not located symmetrically with reference
to major traffic arteries.

If a centre gains by having some sort of container setting, the
effect of this is even greater if this is irregular.   Perhaps one
of the neatest points made by Sitte was his revelation that the
classical interpretation of symmetry stressed an aspect very different from its most usual modern meaning, and he quotes a gloss
supplied by Vitruvius: 'the appropriate harmony arising out of the
details of the work itself; the correspondence of each given detail
among the separate details to the form of the design as a whole'
(ibid., 33).   And perhaps one might add that in well-designed town
centres some portion of the necessary diagonalism between the symmetry of the parts and the symmetry of the whole is artfully left
for the observer to do for himself.

RELATIONAL DIMENSIONS OF THE CITY CENTRE

Because cities vary greatly in age, they must vary in the types of
technology prevalent at the time the centre first developed and
during any period of maximum growth.   This results in great

TABLE 10   Morphological classification of town squares serving
public life and traffic

---

1   Closed squares: e.g. post-Hippodamic *agora* in Greece; reappears
    in French bastides of thirteenth century and foundations of
    Teutonic knights in Germany.
    Type example: Place des Vosges, Paris

2   Dominated squares, with church, arch, fountain, or gate; or
    external axis (such as a square fronting a bridge); or external
    void (such as a lagoon, river, or distant landscape).
    Type examples: Notre Dame Cathedral, Paris and
    parvis; Praço do Comércio, Lisbon.
    Original apogeal period: late Middle Ages.

3   Nuclear squares, with a strong enough nuclear element to bind
    together the space around.
    Type example: Piazza di SS Giovanni e Paolo,
    Venice.
    Apogeal period: Renaissance

4   Grouped squares, with one square used as an antechamber to the
    next in axial alignment, or otherwîse, possibly via some visual
    linking symbol.
    Type example: (at right-angles) Piazza and
    Piazzetta, Venice.

5   Amorphous squares, which are squares in plan, but function mainly
    as crossroads, because unified impression does not result either
    because surrounding structures too heterogeneous, or width of
    roads leading off and height of surrounding buildings out of
    scale with dimensions of square.
    Type examples: Washington Square, New York;
    Trafalgar Square, London; Place de l'Opéra,
    Paris.
    Apogeal period: nineteenth century.

Source: Based on P. Zucker (1959, 8-17); cf. Fig. 9.

contrasts in the amount of adaptation necessary for the city fabric
to match the current technology, which itself varies across the world
array of cities at any one time. If technology is held constant,
differences due to age contrasts can easily be revealed in taking
data from one country. L.F. Schnore (1965, 127-30) classified the
cities of the United States according to whether the 'centre' was
gaining numbers relative to the 'ring'. These terms were defined
respectively as the largest city in each SMSA (Standard Metropolitan
Statistical Area) in which it is located, and the rest of the SMSA.
This is a rather coarse division in that the 'centre' is in fact the
built-up area rather than the central core, but the study provides
some interesting comparative pointers.
    Very few of the larger SMSAs exhibited patterns of centralization
(city gained, ring lost; or both gained, city faster). Schnore
notes that all of the thirty-two areas where the central city reached
50,000 before 1880 are decentralizing. If the data are adjusted to

include annexations by the central city, it is clear that the eight
cities that were centralizing up to 1960 were located in newer and
smaller SMSAs. Such comparisons can be upset if one includes the
areas which have been annexed by the city. These are often in
large units within the process of disjointed incrementalism whereby
it pays to develop real estates on the margin in as large a zoned
unit as possible (R. Montgomery, 1968, 194; and O. White, 1969, 7).
In an historical model of urban form, D. Harrison and J.F. Kain
(1970) came to the conclusion that the timing of development and
metropolitan area size explains over 70 per cent of the variance of
incremental density during a ninety-year period and across eighty-
three diverse United States metropolitan regions. Changes in
income, technology, and taste were identified as the principal
determinants of urban form, varying far more over time than among
cities at any one time. Extrapolating these findings from the
United States, it is made clear why cities in other continents of
even greater variation in age show even greater variations on a
theme of growth emanating from a centre (G.A. Wissink, 1962, 49-50,
284; see also F.L. Hauser, 1951; and for British cities, R. Drewett,
J. Goddard and N. Spence, 1976, 17 and 24).

Even when cities within different cultural value systems are
studied, G. Sjoberg (1960) maintained that technology, that is the
available energy, tools, and know-how, seemed to be the most satisfactory explanatory variable. He was thus able to produce a comparative study of what he called the pre-industrial city. In his
generalized morphology (ibid., 323-4), a certain amount of functional spatial segregation has occurred, but perhaps the greatest contrast with the modern city of the western world is the concentration
of higher-class residences close to the centre, with a decline down
the social strata to the periphery, a pattern also observable in the
Japanese castle town of the eighteenth century (T. Yazaki, 1963, see
illustrations preceding the text). Industry by definition is still
at the artisan stage in very small units, and the tertiary sector is
almost non-existent as a separate category. Ethnic quarters are
found. The centre is characterized by a religious focus, a government centre, and multi-purpose public buildings. Along the streets
are facades indicating many functions mixed together (business,
commercial, educational, religious, and residential).

From a city with an early type of technology, let the focus
shift to one without a free market in land values and rents. Until
the early 1960s housing was subsidized in Prague, and rents were not
differentiated according to location within the city. Instead there
was a strong correlation between age of occupants and age of housing, under a policy which allocated new housing mainly to families
with small children (J. Musil, 1968). The result was that distinct
social areas had largely been eliminated, yet the core remained,
still roughly coincident with the old walled town. The civic meeting place of Wenceslaus Square seems to have acquired great symbolic
force, because under the above policy constraints, the only urban
contrast for a citizen of Prague would be between residential areas
of uniform type and the core. To this must be added the fact that
Prague has been one of the few state capitals to have an almost
unchanged total population before and after the Second World War.
The result would be a tendency for the economic demand upon the core

to remain stable, undiluted by the competition from sub-centres arising within discrete social areas.

At this point the Harrison-Kain axiom bears repeating. Variations in cities over time are likely to be greater than variations among cities at any one time. This is not to mask the very considerable variations that exist between metropolises of advanced western nations, communist cities, and regional cities of the third world. For example, to tropicalize a Western metropolitan model by applying it to an inland city in a developing country of Africa is bound to set up a good deal of information noise. Various cultural sub-systems are certainly a constraint in the diffusion of a basic city lay-out throughout the world. Generalizations erected over a particular sub-system can be regarded as its 'real' models. But these are transmuted into 'ideal' models when compared with other sub-systems, a major utility then being derived from the resultant comparative insights (A.E. Smailes, 1971, 9).

Fortunately, these difficulties are not so severe if concentration is held upon the centre of the major city. Brushing aside the semantic objection that a centre is a dimensionless point, a clue is borrowed from the last section: there the centre was discovered as a place that one goes towards, enters, explores, and finally experiences as the centre for which one was searching. The centre should be large enough to promenade in, and even if composed only of downtown blocks, the area should be large enough for people to walk about, to utilize, to see and enjoy the variety of specialized components (B. Trigger in P.J. Ucko, etc., 1972, 578).

Let it be granted for the moment that it is possible to measure the dimensions of the city centre. Of course, this would entail agreement upon what kind of functions are distinct to the city centre and a method of measuring them in three dimensions. Next suppose there is a comparable method of measuring the total size of the cities in which the centres are set. Naturally, measurement problems would be eased if the centres and cities were in the same uniform data universe. Given these conditions, the law of allometric growth can be tested. This states that the rate of relative growth of an organ (the centre, if the biological analogy holds) is a constant fraction of the relative growth of the total organism. S. Nordbeck (1971, 54) has derived a refined mathematical formulation of this law. He also provides an alternative formulation which instead of referring to a growing organism at different times surveys an array of different sizes of the same family. Then the law of allometric growth states that it is possible to estimate the size of one variable from the measured values of the other variable.

R.W. Thomas (1972) tested this alternative formulation in the cases of twelve central areas in Britain, the cities in which they were set having a wide population range. The conclusion suggests that there is a proportional relationship between the size of the central area (total floor space), as a volume, related to total city size (total population): = volume: volume = 3:3, but there is no guide to the horizontal or vertical components of the volume. Thomas goes on to argue that the retailing function of the central area taken alone can be regarded predominantly as a ground-floor activity and that total retail floor space is a variable representing a two-dimensional form. In that case an allometric growth law

relationship of central retail floor space to city size was demonstrated: = area: volume = 2:3. But it would be expected that as a
city grows larger, some of the retail functions in the core would
decentralize, while the demand for office space might increase as
the city imposes itself more strongly in its tributary area and
develops its national and international relationships (W. Hartenstein and G. Staack (1967, 43). These results are a timely remin-
der that rules of thumb such as 'the centre of a city is likely to
be of an area of one acre (4047 sq.m.) for every thousand population' are likely to be unsound if projected upwards among the larger
cities. The allometric relationship is hardly to be expected if
there is a fundamental constraint on the growth of the city centre
and if growth at newer centres in and around the organism are substituted for growth at the original centre - a common North American experience.

If 'size of the CBD' is indicated by CBD retail sales volume, the
relationship with the total population might either be: (1) linear
(Model I); (2) a continually increasing function if sales related to
increases in population, in conformity with central place theory
(where increases in sales depend on the position in the hierarchy -
the higher the position the greater the increment in sales generated
by each unit increase in population) (Model II); or (3) following
the law of allometric growth (Model III). R. Briggs (1974) tested
these three models using retail sales data for the United States.
The order of goodness of fit of models based on the above propositions was I, III, and II, though only about 60 per cent of the variation in CBD sales was explained. Briggs was concerned that, of
these 'simple models' (his term), the one with the weakest theoretical base is the best predictor. He feels that technological
changes in transport ought to be included in more refined models,
where 'the rate of growth in office employment is proportional to
the level of office and employment' (i.e. similar to Model II in the
retail sales sector and demonstrated in P.W. Daniels, 1975b, 103).
This refinement would be a bow in the direction of agglomeration
economies via increased opportunity for linkages with a higher
number of offices. A tendency towards a linear relationship between
population size and CBD size may be due to opposing tendencies:
increase in size = increase in agglomeration economies = a unit
increase in population generates a greater unit increase in the CBD;
increase in size gives greater opportunities for sub-centres to
arise within the urban area, because distance and congestion costs in
travelling to the centre = a unit increase in population size generates a lesser unit increase in the 'central CBD'.

What has been called the 'grain size' of the city (K. Lynch and
L. Rodwin, 1958, 205-6; and R. Llewellyn-Davies, 1966, 170), that is
the dimensions between the main arteries, should not materially
affect the dimensions of the city centre. For example the grain
size may be very narrowly meshed in the pre-industrial city and as
large as a one-kilometre grid in a late twentieth-century new city
such as Milton Keynes, England. In the former case the centre will
have to expand across several converging radials or across several
grid blocks, giving rise to the confusion of through traffic and
central circulation; whereas in a very wide grid, the main arteries
serve automatically as by-passes of the central area.

Another dimension that gives a clue to the relation of the
centre to the rest of the city is the population density gradient
of the city, radially outwards from the centre. In western cities
this drops off towards the periphery, and there is a 'crater'
towards the centre because of the absence of a night-time population except in downtown hotels. The change in profile direction at
the lip of the crater is a good guide to the dimensions of the
centre. J.S. Adams (1970, 39-42) summarized some density gradient findings with reference to United States cities following the
pioneer work of C. Clark (1951). Older cities tend to have higher
densities, with 'central density' being an extrapolated value fil-
ling in the crater; older cities also tend to have steeper density
gradients compared with newer cities of the same size. There are
some complicated relationships because large and small cities co-
exist at any one time, but here are some comparative results, all
still referring to the United States. Both in 1900 and 1960 older
cities have steeper density gradients than younger cities. In
1900 the density gradients in both cases are steeper. In all
cases in both years, the gradient decreases in steepness with
increasing city size.

A.Z. Guttenberg (1960) believes that the flattening of the density gradient with growth at the periphery is accompanied by a decline in density at the centre. His model of urban form is dependent on the one factor of accessibility between people and facilities. If facilities provided and density of population could be
combined in a single index, the result would be that the profile
would not flatten as time went on but approach concavity near the
centre (e.g. curve A2T2 in Fig. 10).

A main implication of these findings for central areas is to
suggest that for a given city size, difficulties of core expansion
will be greatest for older cities, because they will encounter
higher population densities in their path compared with more evenly
developed newer cities. The extreme case of a very ancient city
which undergoes little expansion until some sudden twentieth-
century demand entails a massive urban development often poses so
great a problem that a double centre may appear, the new offset
from the old. (For compact accounts of work on population gradients see B.J.L. Berry, 1965, 97-103; B.E. Newling, 1969, 329-37,
page numbers referring to reprints in L.S. Bourne (ed.), 1971; see
also D. Thomas, 1972, 81-3; for adaptation of density gradient to
urban corridors, see R. Robinson and J. Shaw, 1973).

A theoretical underpinning is needed to provide a mechanism
giving successive time stages of each density gradient. The wave
theory of H. Blumenfeld (1954) provides such a mechanism for peaks
of growth rates occurring at varying distances from the centre
through time; and R.R. Boyce's (1966) development of the theory
would even cope with urban renewal of the city centre as the next
upper wave undulation, wavelengths from crest to crest being as
long as may be fifty to seventy-five years.

TRANSPORT AND THE EVOLVING CENTRE

It may have seemed strange that transport has not been given a more

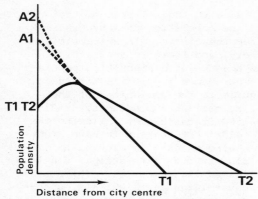

FIGURE 10   City density gradients in successive time periods
The pecked line indicates what might happen if 'central facilities'
could be measured on the same basis as population and the two added
together for a city which added facilities to its central core in
successive time periods, without any areal expansion of the core.
This is indicated by the 'tip of the crater' (solid line, population alone) being in the same position in T1 as in T2, and implies
vertical development of the core.

prominent place in this chapter. Yet within the centre the dominant
human movement is on foot both in the Greek *agora* and in the modern
downtown mall or precinct. This statement needs justification to
the observer of traffic at its densest if allowed to penetrate to
the centre. Some of that traffic should not be there at all if it
is through traffic with origin and destination outside the city
altogether. Traffic which originates at one edge of the centre, and
aims for an opposite edge should go around the centre. There
remains the traffic with destination in the centre and this is predominantly radial (via right-angled diversions in a grid lay-out).
Some transport, such as builders' vehicles, repair servies, street
cleaning, snow clearance, is concerned with maintenance of the
centre's fabric; another sector of transport could be labelled com-
misariat supplies, and a good lay-out provides back of building
unloading bays for such vehicles to avoid double parking or techni-
cally illegal but normally 'blind-eye' parking. Yet another sector
of traffic to the edge of the centre is tidal because the non-
camping army has to be taken in and out each day.
     The remainder of traffic actually within a centre is: taxi-
type, or walking avoidance: off-duty, time-saving, labour-saving
(parcel burdens), or climate evasion. All these are impossible if
a centre is pedestrianized. 'Off-duty' window shoppers do not
require to be whizzed around the centre. Time-saving can be
achieved by the telephone or by the elevator and escalator, with
pedestrian movement as feeder. Parcel burdens are avoided if the
shopping is high value per unit of weight. Subsequent delivery can
assist those unable to carry even small weights, but the infirm find
the centre a burdensome place anyway. Climate evasion can be assisted by covered malls above or below ground and bridges between
buildings.

Of course, a factor such as the break of transport may have been the most powerful cause of the initiation of a centre (see above, p. 40; and R.E. Murphy and J.E. Vance, 1954, 334). Changes in inter-city transport have affected not only the links between the centre and the non-urban area it could serve efficiently, but also helped to establish its position within a hierarchy of centres through competition. The extent and shape of a continuous urban area served most efficiently from one centre has altered with different forms of transport. J.S. Adams (1970) has distinguished between those modes of transport that provide a pan-movement service (such as walking, private car) with those that are highly structured, with a network of distinct nodes and channels (electric tram (street-car), rail, freeway). The first type tends to initiate an ever-widening circular shape, while the second may set up tentacular development along channels and sub-centre growth around nodes. A point to remember is that a centre needs movement of the first type to function within itself, whereas movement of the second type enables a specialisation within a hierarchy of centres (inter-urban and intra-urban), so that one centre can serve all the people some of the time for highly specialized services and experiences. Table 11 sets out some of the relationships between transport developments and city centre evolution in the United States. Date corrections in the form of time lags after the first eras need to be applied to fit the situation in other countries.

TABLE 11   Changes in transport technology - the United States case

Approx. dates	Inter-urban[1]	Intra-urban[2]	Contemporary developments in the city centre
1790-1830	Sail-wagon	Walking-horsecar	Initiation
1830-1870	Iron horse		Horizontal elaboration
	1885		Functional segregation with vertical expansion
1870-1920	Steel rail	Electric streetcar	
1920-present	Auto-air-amenity post-1945	Auto-recreational Freeway	Above continues with out-of-town centre competition

1   J.R. Borchert (1967).
2   J.S. Adams (1970).

CHANGING ATTITUDES TO THE CITY CENTRE

The idea of the city has provoked ambivalent reactions summed up in 'a great city, a great solitude' (from a Latin proverb, itself translated from the Greek). An anthology of quotations under the subject heading 'city' will parade a great variety of view (see

D. Seamon, 1972, 7-1-4). Sometimes the author is referring to
residential or industrial areas of a large city rather than to the
idea of a city as a central meeting-place. In a survey of European
thought C.E. Schorske (1963) classifies three broad types of evaluation. Many writers have considered the city as a virtuous agent -
Voltaire, Adam Smith, and Fichte; but ranged against writers of
this persuasion are those that have seen vicious influences emanating from urban centres. Goldsmith, Wordsworth, Blake, and Engels
prove to have been anti-city. But if the view is taken that the
city is part of society and not some autonomous by-product of it,
then attitudes take on a more stand-back quality.

Baudelaire seems to have needed to 'bathe himself' in the city
crowd at some times and developed the idea of the interchangeability of multitude and solitude (1869, 'Les foules', xii). For
him the animation of a port gave a 'mysterious and aristocratic
pleasure...in contemplating...movements of men' (ibid., 'Le port',
xli). An archetypal Bohemian poet did not spend all his time in a
garret; the boulevard and cafe gossip were also a necessary part of
his outer world. Baudelaire seems to have been the first to capture
this diagonal idea, again expressed by J.E. Burchard when he noted
the first inherent advantage of the city as being 'the only place
where true diversity can thrive and where specialism can reach its
apogee' (discussant in R.M. Fisher (ed.), 1955, 376). This in turn
recalls J. Jacobs's (1961) idea of 'exuberant diversity' as a
quality to be sought in the central city, although this does omit
the other characteristic of extreme specialization practised by many
a profession in the heart of cities. Schorske concludes with yet
another kind of detached view of the city which sees it as a mechanical agent of the modern urban state, the philosophy of the German
National Socialists, with the example of squares built not for the
enjoyment of crowds but for their manipulation (see also H. Capel,
1975, 79-80).

If society is analysed into three groups: middle-class, lower-
class, and upper-class, D. Prokop (1967, 31-2) believes that the
city centre is most frequented by the first group who can afford
the services of the centre and use it for 'an improvement of prestige and upward mobility'. Lower classes are less able to afford
the centre's services and to manipulate their socio-economic status.
Upper classes are not so bound to specific places because they have
the means to conduct their affairs at places to suit themselves.
Examining this set of deductions, one result that emerges is that
the functioning and vitality of a centre would depend on the social
structure. Taking the inhabitants of any one city, omitting visitors for the moment, the upper classes can be ignored because their
absolute numbers are small. If Prokop is right, the centre would
become more important with the rise in the general standard of
living and with a telescoping of income levels between the salariat
and the wage-earner. In western democracies, where these tendencies are in evidence, the usage of central areas should increase.
But each city has another population, the transient businessman and
tourist. In these categories the wealthiest are well represented
alongside the middle class. This transient class makes intensive
use of the centre; it lives there. With an increase in international trade and tourism, such use of centres is likely to increase.

There must be many a businessman and tourist who knows more of
foreign city centres (but indeed little else of such places) than
he does of his home downtown. For these reasons, even if Prokop's
view of the socially segmented use of the centre is correct, the
evolving use made of it will trend upward, even if it does suffer
competition from other sub-centres for 'home' use, in a city evolving into a city region.

When architects enter area design, they are sometimes inclined
to treat cities as organisms. An example of this tendency is
R.J. Neutra (1955) and an extreme manifestation is Chandigarh,
following the master plan of Le Corbusier. In this plan the head
is the capitol complex (in the extreme north), the heart is the
commercial centre (one kilometre north of the geometric centre),
the hands are the industrial area (to the east), the brain is
represented by the university and the museum (to the north-west) and
the lungs are formed by Leisure Valley (running north-south through
the city). But today the city does not function as a single
organism and a comment by R. Khosla (1971) on the Chandigarh High
Court might stand synecdochically for the city: 'The grandeur and
finality of the conception of the building prevents it from res-
ponding to its changing uses' (p. 683). (For another critique of
Chandigarh, see N. Evenson, 1966, Chapter XII).

The spatial pattern of a city is a composite result of social and
economic systems (R.A. Murdie, 1969, Fig. 1). The combination of
the two systems, and their multiple sub-systems, is what differen-
tiates a city from other human groups, as suggested in Table 12.

TABLE 12   Bisociation of social and functional (economic) systems(1)

	few functional parts	sum of many functional parts
single social unit	family	medieval castle, monastery
sum of many social units	village	city

	small city	medium-sized city large city
social centre functional centre}	the same	- -
separate social areas separate functional areas}	} -	} separate centres separate centres of each, but with separate centres one common social and functional centre

1   The first part of this table is based on a suggestion by H.
    Blumenfeld (1949, 8).
Note: This table also illustrates the 'gemeinschaft / gesellschaft'
dichotomy of F. Tönnies (1887). 'Gemeinschaft' represents close-
knit social relationships with common goals (e.g. medieval castle,
monastery, family and village life). This is contrasted with 'gesellschaft', a more impersonal functional grouping (e.g. in trade
unions, business associations, and in the non-social functions of
cities).

This chapter has considered just a few of the changes that have taken place in city centres. The way the centre evolves is conditioned by what is there already, and any cross-sectional examination at a particular time must recognize that the system will contain vestiges of past states and leading parts as anticipatory symptoms of future states. When the observer has his feet firmly planted in the heart of modern downtown, the past and the future are present in the ever-changing scene. There is one ray of reassurance in all this complexity. As a city grows larger, so the area that can command a consensus as being central, grows more legible, if it is realized that the focal scene stands written diagonally in more than one language.

CHAPTER 3

IN DOWNTOWN (1): THE FRAMEWORK OF ORDER

Downtown is an American term not much used in the Third World or in
Europe (it is difficult to translate), yet is useful because vague
enough to cover the CBD, the urban core, and the inner city (where
this exists); and, in addition, the word offers a suggestion of
relative distance from a periphery towards an urban centre. Perhaps
it is wise to start by defining the terms just mentioned, and even
wiser to follow the lead of H.W. Ter Hart (1967), who took advantage
of an Amsterdam study week on the urban core to produce a list of
multi-lingual equivalents. The definition of the CBD is however
taken from the pioneer paper which initiated much geographical work
in this area.

urban core: hard core area and core fringe; or inner core area and
             outer frame (this is more extensive than the CBD) [all
             variously delimited] (cf. J. Rannels, 1956)

CBD: central business district. 'Here one finds the great-
             est concentration of offices and retail stores reflec-
             ted in the city's highest land values and its tallest
             buildings' (R.E. Murphy and J.E. Vance, 1954, 189).
             The definition adumbrates the Murphy-Vance delimitation
             method based on an intensity index and a height index
             (see below). (Note: V. Gruen, 1965, 47, feels that
             the term is misleading in that it implies that the
             heart of the city is meant only to serve business. It
             is perhaps rather the district of centralized business,
             but it is too late to change the name now.)

inner city: part of the town formerly enclosed by walls. If this
             has 'significant architectural qualities' and 'a con-
             tinuing social life', A. Papageorgiou (1971, 28) would
             use the term 'historic urban centre'. Other types he
             recognizes under this heading are: (1) independent
             and monumental groups of buildings which resemble
             settlements; (2) small rural historic centres; and (3)
             medium-sized towns which reached a peak of growth in
             the past such that the past pattern has not been
             greatly affected by this century's explosive phases of
             urban growth (idem, 32-34).

downtown: central zone [= vague, from the location of Wall
              Street near the southern tip of Manhattan Island;
              perhaps could be defined as the original urban core,
              based on commerce, plus any urban core encroachment
              over areas originally wholly residential.]

FUNCTIONAL ORDERING IN THE CENTRE

The major functions of the urban core are offices, public buildings, and shops; with industries, residences, transportation
depots, and warehouses occurring towards the core fringe, perhaps
as vestiges of former patterns. As far as the CBD is concerned,
Murphy and Vance particularly excluded industries (except news-
papers), residences, vacant lots, and wholesaling (p. 204). Even
public buildings were considered as 'neutral' and included in the
CBD only if they met certain contiguity criteria with reference to
office and retailing functions (p. 219). Any survey for CBD delimitation will encounter a cross-section of an evolving phenomenon,
which J.E. Vance (1966, 115) called a cell-by-cell replacement by
exclusion based on the rent gradient steepening from the centre; and
J. Allpass et al. (1967) even started a paper on urban centre
structural change with the headline: 'A C.B.D. Function: A Function Which Has Not Yet Left The Central Business District.' The
functions of the core separate out into a geographical pattern, in
clusters or sets, much like the process of crystallisation; in
crystallography. There is another term for the process - centro-
symmetric ordering.* This is a particularly appropriate wording
because it includes both relationship to a centre and the tendency
to order through an evolutionary process. There are many explanatory variables involved in producing this order, and their combined
effect is stronger than an entropy-maximizing process. Before these
variables are reviewed, it must be repeated that because centro-
symmetric ordering is an evolutionary process, it will tend to be
more in evidence as the centre grows in size.
     The question naturally arises as to the threshold of settlement
size at which the process begins. Theoretically, if a central function was exercised in just two separate establishments, and if the
settlement were linear, and its tributary population spread along a
line, a not impossible state of affairs, then there would be economic advantages for the two establishments in being located back-to
back at the centre, as in H. Hotelling (1929). This solution has
come under criticism (see W. Isard, 1956, 162 ff.) but in the case
of our linear town there can be added in the desirability of establishment cluster. Then it could be envisaged that in a nodal
settlement with n radial approaches, if there were n functions of a
similar type, they could locate in the centre at the points where
each approach road joined the centre. When the $n+1$ function

*The analogy from crystallography is suggestive rather than exact.
 Symmetric ordering of functions in cities around a centre is a
 tendency towards an ultimate state that never arrives; but then
 the idea of crystal as a regular repetitive array of atoms is also
 an idealisation in some respects.

arrived, it can be randomly assigned to a point alongside any of
the pre-existing establishments, always bearing in mind the given
desirability of propinquity to establishments of a similar type.
When the *n+3* function arrives, location near *n+2* is more attractive than anywhere else. This simple example merely demonstrates
that the threshold for clustering could be quite low. In a small
centre the function with the most individual establishment units is
retailing. R.J. Johnston and C.C. Kissling (1971) showed that
retail segregation can occur in quite a small suburban centre. The
Gardenvale shopping centre of Melbourne with 93 shops did display
four segregated patterns of linked use; whereas the 21-shop Fend-
alton suburban shopping centre of Christchurch, N.Z. was a single
organizational structure. These are only indications of threshold
level in the case of low-order establishments. Perhaps the threshold can never be determined exactly because when there are so few
retail outlets, nuances of shopping centre lay-out could override
tendencies for centro-symmetric ordering. But it seems safe to say
that when a centre has grown large enough to be called a town or
city, the process is already well under way.

REASONS FOR CENTRO-SYMMETRIC ORDERING

The reasons for centro-symmetric ordering are analysed below, but
the point must first be made that the process is the result of a
combination of factors and that the mix varies for different types
of function. Historico-geographical study and one-centre analysis
can throw great light on this multivariate process. The generalized analysis below merely attempts a few insights into the triumph
of order over random location in an urban core.
    A simple idea is to note the use of urban core in preference to
city centre. Functions cannot be located at a point, and so they
are separated in space. A striking example is that of the religious function which requires a place apart, perhaps the first evidence of 'centrality' in the first centres (see Chapter 1). The
religious life and the profane life cannot exist in the same place.
If the former is to develop, a special spot must be set aside from
which the second is excluded (E. Durkheim, 1915, 422). The pulling
apart of functions can also occur if they are differentially oriented to extra-urban space. For example, in a port with an agricultural hinterland, port-oriented functions will be drawn towards
the waterfront and deeper water (see Fig. 1) while services for
farmers will be oriented towards the approach roads from the richest
farming areas and the place where they sell their produce. A modern
example is where there is planned skewed growth in a particular
direction from a centre, perhaps to correct an excessive radial
concentration upon the organically grown urban core. The pioneer
example is the Centro Direzionale on 103 hectares, relatively close
to the urban heart of Milan (J. Labasse, 1970, 16).
    Aggregation takes place through those external economies that
accrue to establishments through linkages either with other urban
functions (see P.A. Wood, 1970, 36) or because of the services provided within the urban fabric (see Fig. 11). B. Thorngren (1967)
acknowledges Alfred Marshall as the originator of the external

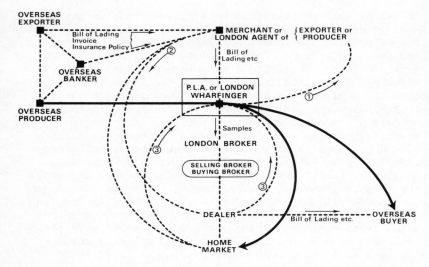

FIGURE 11 Linkages between central city functions and the port of
London
The physical movement of goods is represented by the continuous
lines; communication by telegraph, telephone and air and surface
mail are shown by broken lines. The numbered arrows show the three
main sequential movements of the dock or warehouse warrant. In the
diagram the port function is contained within the small rectangle;
the function of the commodity market, dealing with movements of
ownership is within the ellipse beneath. Each particular trade
will show variations from this highly generalized scheme. While the
principal port focus is now 40 km downstream, the commodity markets
and associated financial services are located within a radius of
1000 m from the original port focus of the Custom House (see Fig. 1,
no. 29). P.L.A., Port of London Authority.

economies concept and first explains them as side-effects. An activity producing for a market will train labour which could move to
another similar activity; will leak its acquired experience to
others (if an answer to a problem is seen to exist, this in itself
and alone makes the route from the problem to the answer much, much
easier); will use 'public' service facilities, thereby making them
more profitable (or less unprofitable); and will assist in the
sharing of indivisible resources, such as a pool of rentable spaces,
of skilled labour, and of skilled subcontractors (E.M. Hoover and
R.E. Vernon, 1959, 13). In other words, the producer of an external
economy cannot prevent its use by a nearby non-paying customer. The
only way to reduce the generation of external economies is to have
an organization so large that it generates internal economies and is
located far away from competitors and ancillary activities. But
there is a limit, and although a huge complex may even have its own
power plant, it must still make use of the public highway. When
external economies become highly important, the establishment may be
regarded as a secondary service. For example, the accumulation of
extra people ('extra', lit., 'from outside') needs all kinds of

services, like commuters being fed during the day and tourist
entertained at night, summed up in the restaurant which offers
cheap business lunches during the day and candlelit dinners in the
evening.

Offices obviously have 'human external economies' in large
centres, because there is a great deal of necessary connectedness
between individuals in different establishments. M.J. Croft
(1969, 75) concluded that compared to offices concerned with manufacturing and physical services and 'miscellaneous' offices, financial and professional offices had more ties through interaction in
the central area. B. Thorngren (1970) has usefully classified all
these interactions according to the width of the technological
environment that needs to be scanned or utilized.

I   orientation processes by highest level decision makers, policy-
     making, long-term, strategic, goal-changing, positive feedback;
II   processes towards pre-structured goals by research groups,
     management groups, intermediate term, goal-seeking, tactical,
     positive feedback to a higher level;
III control of on-going processes, day-to-day, routine, negative
     feedback (cf. S.M. Robbins and N.E. Terleckyj, 1960, Chart 1).

J.B. Goddard (1973) has used this classification in his study of
office linkages in central London and Table 13 is a summary of his
results.

TABLE 13   Central London office linkages (1)

Contacts (incl. meetings)	
80% D III (could be carried on outside a large centre	15% C I (orientation meetings)

Meetings (2)		
20% D III (similar to telephone calls)	5% D II (could be performed by telecommunications if these included document trans- mission)	75% C I (orientation meetings) (3)

1 Based on contact diaries filled in by 705 respondents in 72 firms,
   recording 5,266 telephone contacts and 1,954 meetings in a three-
   day period.
2 78 per cent of all business journeys are to places less than
   thirty minutes away.
3 Usually between a large number of relatively unfamiliar people.
Source: J.B. Goddard (1973)

The Roman numerals inserted in the table refer to the above functional classification; and C represents an activity that requires a
location in a large centre; while D represents an activity that
could be decentralized. The problem Goddard faced was the extent to

which other centres besides London could aspire to having thriving
CI-type processes in a suitable 'contact environment'. Because
the majority of business journeys in London take under thirty
minutes (a similar finding was made by Thorngren, 1970, in respect
of Stockholm and Gothenburg), it is essential that any centre with
pretensions to CI-type processes should have not only a highly
varied contact environment, but also one that is compact. If a
city office complex is dominated by DIII-type activities, an isolated CI-type of activity will wither for lack of local contact with
similarly oriented groups or even the research and management substructure of DII-type activities. There will also be few higher
status opportunities for office workers who will have to migrate to
the CI centre if the promotional ladder is to be climbed. Croft
(p. 93) mentions the social infrastructure (public transport, restaurants, etc.) necessary for office employees, and also reinforces
the conclusion that office decentralization must be on a large scale
in order that clients may make several calls in the course of a
single visit to such a 'decentralized central area' (p. 68, p. 75).

Future further sorting of office functions will occur between
the central core and favoured suburban centres of metropolitan
areas; and G. Manners (1974, 102 ff) parades the views of those who
put the emphasis on the central area of cities and those who believe
that suburbanization will be the dominant trend. Because site
problems will be greater in the centre, it seems certain that if
office employment should grow at a great rate, the central area of
a metropolis will discharge a diminished relative share, but within
this share there will be a greater proportion of CI-type orientation
functions of headquarters echelons. In this connection there are
two further pointers to centralized concentration. A. Pred (1973,
37-42) has shown how the accumulation of operational decision-making
experience positively affects the probability of further decision-
making being located in the same area (the process of cumulative
causation). R.B. Armstrong (1972, 118-a) has deduced that increased
automation and telecommunications will reduce the necessity for
large numbers of clerical workers in decentralized branch offices
and contribute to stronger head offices. Future concentration on
the CBD and those sub-centres with headquarters echelons is therefore anticipated (ibid., 124; cf F. Kristensson, 1967).

S.M. Robbins and N.E. Terleckyj (1960) in their detailed locational study of financial activities in New York added two other
factors under 'external economies' to explain clustering. One was
the idea that in any undertaking where the uncertainties are great,
'knowledge in a hurry' is vital to keep abreast of ideas among
grouped specialists; this could possibly be called 'short-term
orientation processes' in a centre which is an information capital
(P. Rendu, 1970, 20). Instant telephonic connection is necessary
besides the ability to meet frequently. An example is quoted of a
medium-sized financial house in Wall Street with 120 direct lines
to other firms; if such lines were maintained from, say, Chicago,
the telephone rental bill would increase nearly one thousandfold.
'Our first principle, then, is that clustering tends to occur when-
ever the high risk of an activity can be modified through the swap-
ping of information and ideas' (op.cit., 35). Another finding of
Robbins and Terleckyj is that the élite of the financial world play

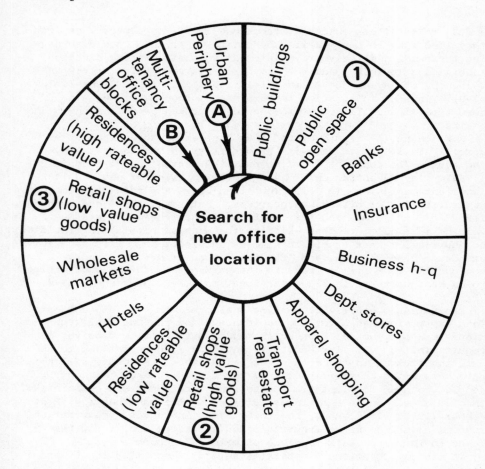

FIGURE 12 The search for new office location
Read clockwise the diagram assumes site scanning from less likely
to more likely locations as classified by current land use. Read
anti-clockwise the diagram assumes office development blocked at
most likely locations by planning or other constraints and a search
forced into progressively less suitable sites, classified by current
land use.
   A large organization which had achieved internal economies of
scale might build its own bespoke offices on a vacant lot or, alternatively start its search at A; small organizations with external
linkages might start at B.
Notes. 1 Public open space may be 'ornamental, productive, protec-
tive, or recreational' as in the classification of C. Tunnard and
B. Pushkarev, 1963, 339.
2 If in small units and combined with residences of high rateable
value, this category might be moved clockwise.
3 If in small units and combined with residences of low rateable
value, this category might be moved anticlockwise.

a dual role: their essential functions are CI-type processes; but
they also like to have their subordinates near them when discharg-
ing their administrative role internal to their own organization.
Robbins and Terleckyj admit that where this second feature is in
evidence, it may be due to inertia, tradition, or sentiment (ibid.,
42-3).   Thus an integration is maintained, though, as we have
seen type II and III activities could be broken away from the
centre.
   A.W. Evans (1973) discovered that the larger the company the
more likely it was to have its headquarters in the largest city in
the system (London), called a 'management centre' by W. Goodwin
(1965) - 'a concentration of headquarters offices of nationally
important companies' (p. 3).   Thus take-overs and mergers promote
centralization of office headquarters.   But small firms are being
formed all the time, and the location of their headquarters may
well be in smaller centres, keeping the general population of office
headquarters rather stable in numbers and location.   This is a reference to headquarters, and 'the more consumer oriented and/or
non-durable is a firm's product, the stronger is the need or desire
to be headquartered in a central location' (R.B. Armstrong, 1972,
70).
   Proximity to other like functions also brings 'psychic comfort'.
This expression can cover the avoidance of search and find techniques for optimum location which may be difficult, expensive, or
require initiative.   Instead, one can simply add oneself on to an
existing cluster in the reassuring belief that a majority will not
have been wrong in their choice of location.   Indeed, if enough
people who need to cluster make the same locational choice 'mistake',
then it ceases to be a mistake.   Expressing this another way, M.J.
Webber (1972, 275-6) shows how uncertainty increases agglomeration
economies; new firms are uncertain and therefore small; and this
tends to increase their reliance on external economies.
   In central locations A generates external economies for B, and
perhaps vice versa; and the greater the number of enterprises, the
more likely it is that some of them will have located near the
centre because of the external economies already extant.   Rent for
central locations will reflect this opportunity for external economies, and it will rise above the economic limit for those functions
that, for one reason or another, cannot derive benefit from the
external economies on offer.   There arises, through both attraction
and exclusion, a cluster of activities linked through mutual external economies.
   Rents have at last been mentioned.   They are of course high in
the urban core, the centre of which is sometimes denoted by the
peak land value intersection (PLVI).   As D.R. Diamond (1962, 535),
pointed out: 'The correlation of land values and land uses is
closest in the very centre where the competition for space is most
severe and the selection of sites for particular uses most
advanced.'   As far as retail stores are concerned, if rents rise in
the centre, productivity per lot square foot must also increase.
One solution is to concentrate on highly profitable long-term non-
bulk durables such as books, clothes, jewellery, souvenirs (serving
all the people some of the time) or to make intensive use of lot
area via the vertical development of department stores.   Both these

tendencies are in line with the constraint of a common horizontal walk distance no matter the city size. Thus as the size of the city increases the segregation of retail land use also increases (R.W. Thomas, 1972, 93).

Thorngren believes that rents, however high, cannot increase supply or reduce demand for office space in the city centre (p. 417). The reason is that rent may be a small proportion of the total financial budget of an organization which needs an office in the centre for at least some of its functions. Decentralization of functions that do not need a central location would give those in the organization that do more freedom to get close to the centre.

In the case of retail shops, K.L. Buzzacott (1972), with reference to London, has given details of how they appeared, first selling durable goods in the late seventeenth century. Gradually, during the eighteenth and nineteenth centuries, the food markets, which had become specialized as early as the sixteenth century (see Fig. 1), began to find it impossible to cope with retail outlets because of the vast quantities of food being brought into London to feed the growing population. Specialized retail outlets grew up dependent on specialized markets, which had derived their specialization from the dominant direction from which goods entered the city. By the end of the nineteenth century, the markets of central London were almost entirely wholesale, and centro-symmetric ordering had taken place in two dimensions: the specialization of wholesale markets and the segregation of retail outlets. Obviously, not every city will go through such a long evolution. A city with a shorter history will, at the time of its most rapid growth, fit into existing patterns which have perhaps painfully evolved elsewhere (D. Harrison and J.F. Kain 1970, 44). In the twentieth century, food shops have been driven from the centre of western-style cities unless they occupy temporary sites in a traditional market area (at subsidized rent); or are linked vertically (literally and figuratively) to consumer durables in a department store; or unless they achieve extremely high turnover per square foot through specialized selling, perhaps to office workers, often in tiny premises.

The edge of a shopping area is often quite sharp. Bearing in mind that the pattern is a response to pedestrian movement, it can be seen that the most effective lay-out is one which gives a contrasting scene going outwards from a start, an interesting U-turn, and return. If there can be a focus at the end of the shopping section to lure a pedestrian to it, so much the better, but this is not normally found in centres organically grown. In these cases it is remarkable how often shops of the same type end together on both sides of the street. Indeed, a gap caused by a park, a public building, a service station, or a wide intersection on one side of the street may depress the value of retail sites on the other side even if the shopping facade is continuous there. The reason for this is quite simple. Pedestrians must make a U-turn at some point along a street to retrace their steps. They may find their tendency to do so reinforced by the presence of the gap to the detriment of any retail establishments on the far side. At this point one can hear the echo of a thousand shoppers saying to their companions: 'My dear, we seem to have come to the end of the

TABLE 14   The spread of pedestrian precincts and the mall movement

Some significant dates	
1951-4	Upper precinct, Coventry, England (cruciform, see R.L. Davies 1972, Figs 1 and 2).*
1953	Lijnbaan, Rotterdam, Part 1 completed.*
1957	Vällingby, satellite of Stockholm, completed with shopping plaza.
	Ten-day trial of pedestrian mall in Springfield, Oregon, 15-26 August, called Shoppers Paradise.
1957-60	Lower precinct, Coventry.*
1959 } 1960	D.H. Lutes, architect of Shoppers Paradise and V. Gruen warns that a mall (pedestrianized street) is only a part of a necessarily integrated programme to revitalize downtown, and other measures include traffic/pedestrian separation, parking facilities, proper business location, and commercial area rehabilitation.
1959	Toledo, Ohio, 110-day mall experiment; Kalamazoo, Michigan, first permanent mall in the United States, and subsequent publicity.
1960	23 February. By this date M.C. Moody, Executive Assistant, Kalamazoo County Chamber of Commerce had given 274 presentations of his slide talk.
	Stevenage, England: shopping area completely pedestrian-based in a new town, first phase complete.
	Mall, Miami Beach, Florida; also Ottawa, first temporary experiment, later made permanent.
1961	Mall, Knoxville, Tennessee.
1962	Mall, Pomona, California; Midtown Plaza, Rochester, New York, with covered mall.
	Stevenage, completed (and other British new towns with pedestrian-free shopping areas).

*Opportunities afforded by necessity for wide-scale reconstruction following damage by aerial bombardment.
Sources: G. Lewison, R. Billingham et al. (1969); M. Meyerson et al. (1963); F.J. Osborn and A. Whittick (1963); L.G. Vincent (1960); and S.F. Weiss (1964). See also Y.S. Cohen (1972).

shops.' Even if the shops are continuous on the pedestrians' side,
the presence of a gap opposite will warn them that to proceed
further will result in retracing their steps on the same side or
walking past a 'dead area' on the other side.

A major central shopping area combines maximum availability of
choice with ease of accessibility by public transport or parking
lots, and its lay-out is based on pedestrian movement. If this
schema is interfered with, drastic steps must be taken to restore
it by such devices as one-way streets, new parking facilities, or
pedestrian preference areas. The mall movement ('pedestrianization' of a main street) appears to have begun in 1957 as a temporary experiment, but the idea soon spread (see Table 14).

The maximum availability of choice is aided by compactness of
shopping. As long ago as 1902, R.M. Hurd (see C.C. Colby 1933, 15),
pointed out that a number of similar shops close together is the
shopper's insurance against failure. R.L. Nelson (1958, 67 ff)
elevated this type of clustering into an empirically derived rule
of retail compatibility. This states that retail outlets in close
proximity will show an increase in business directly proportional
to the amount of customer interchange between them and inversely
proportional to the ratio of business volume of the larger store to
that of the smaller store. The business mutually generated will
increase as purposeful shopping increases over impulse purchasing.
Another feature leading to retail clustering is the intercept location which is sited on the route which most customers take towards
the centre of the retail shopping area. Taken to excess this is
the ribbon development on the approaches to downtown. In downtown
itself, it helps to explain the linear development of shops towards
bus stations, railroad stations, and parking lots if these are
permanent.

But a retail shopping street, even if well established, can
decline, not only through macro-changes in shopping habits or
through major changes in traffic regulations (one-way streets,
elevated throughways), but also through any process that interferes
with clustering to mutual advantage. In a perceptive newspaper
article G. Nuttall (1972) noted the features of 'airline blight' and
'tourist office fungus' which spell danger if allowed to spread:

'Airline blight' looked like being the ruin of Regent Street
[London]. Not only do all those areas of plate-glass fail to
attract the paying customers, but they actually hit the remaining
retailers in the pocket-book as well. Showplace offices are not
required to generate anything like the sort of trade on the premises which would justify the rent they pay, so lease prices
start spiralling. And because they tend to dilute the window-
shopping, impulse-buying crowds, the surviving shops have to
fight twice as hard to generate the extra sales to meet the
rising costs.

Finally, on shopping compaction, it may be noted that horizontal
extent of the shopping area is restricted by vertical developments
in departmental stores. The non-shopping distance to be walked
from the parking lot, the bus stop or railway station also affect
the shopping distance. The latter may be estimated roughly as ten
minutes in time, four blocks, or one kilometre. Impulse shoppers
promenading will walk further; purposeful shoppers and the city's

inhabitants will not walk nearly as far, particularly with young
children and heavy parcels or in inclement weather. Offices also
often cluster together because of the prestige originally attached
to a location leader. A street name can awaken prestige overtones
(Harley Street and Carnaby Street, London; Wall Street, New York),
and even postal numbers or area codes can become powerfully
evocative.

A fish market, an unsightly superannuated public utility, or an
almost-abandoned factory which occupy historic central sites will
encourage development elsewhere, perhaps with enforced grouping,
maybe leading to a shift in the PLVI. They act as poles of repulsion to any establishment that has pretensions to a prestige
address or smart fashion; high chimneys and haute couture hardly
conjoin.

SOME COUNTER-PROCESSES AND SUMMARY

Not all processes work in favour of centro-symmetric ordering.
B.J. Garner (1961, 115) referred to complex patterns of different
needs and preferences as a result of different amounts of disposable income available to consumers besides their different social
and perhaps ethnic characteristics. These factors together with
different styles of products and their different mix in large
stores, are combined by Garner under the heading 'product differentiation', the term itself indicating a process working against
ordering in the centre and a neat hierarchy of thresholds for different types of goods. Units in the centre may grow so large that
external economies can be replaced by internal economies on a more
spacious site (R. Vernon, 1957, 86; R. Llewellyn-Davies, 1957, 86).
If the links of the organization achieve a wider span, with the
surrounding region rather than exclusively with the city, then a
peripheral site might be just as efficient (J. Allpass et al.,
1967, 110-13); this could apply not only to offices, of say a
regional builder, but also to the case of retailing via the concept
of the hypermarket. If there are important nation-wide or international links, a central site will remain important at least for
headquarters staff.

The initiative of a large organization may well cause a change
in the shape of the core. Many downtown ventures are destined to be
used largely by one organization, but ground-floor or basement
levels are often let off to shops and services thereby causing a
large step-like addition to the CBD almost at a stroke. L.R. Ford
(1973) quotes the two famous examples in Ohio - the Terminal Tower,
Cleveland and the AIU Citadel, Columbus. These buildings, dating
from the 1920s, 52 and 47 storeys high, were so huge for their time
that centrality became projected upon them, and they caused the
prestige office centres to move in their direction. If such
developments include shops they are more successful if there is no
appreciable gap between the new shops and the older established
shopping nexus in the originally developed core. But what if land
ownership is in many hands? L. Holzner (1970, 325) estimated that
over three-quarters of West German cities was in private hands, and
this made the rebuilding of cities on a large scale much more
difficult.

TABLE 15   Summary of centro-symmetric ordering

Processes at work in city centres, with examples (1)

1 Dissociation: religious function.

2 Directional orientation (perhaps to some extra urban attraction): port, towards deeper water, market (later specialized
   wholesale markets), towards route from source in umland;
   Centro Direzionale, Milan.

3 External economies (linkages, side-effects, services, human
   external economies in orientation processes, knowledge in a
   hurry, tradition and sentiment, consumer orientation, psychic
   comfort; impact of uncertainty): financial and professional
   offices.

4 Rent sorting: shops selling goods of high value per unit of
   weight.

5 Retail segregation (horizontal walking distance constraint):
   shopping precincts; vertical developments in department stores.

6 Decentralization sorting: head office isolated from rest of
   organization.

7 Specialization: retail and wholesale outlets (latter specialized).

8 Pedestrianization: (of some streets but not others): see
   Table 14.

9 Compaction for comparison: retail store shopping façade.

10 Intercept location: retail ribbons.

11 Prestige cluster: Harley Street, London; Wall Street, New
    York.

12 Poles of repulsion: fish market, superannuated public utility.

13 Administrative exclusiveness: exclusion of private sector.

14 Planned centre, based on any of above processes: Place Ville-
    Marie, Montreal.

1 For discussion of these topics with particular reference to newly
   developing countries see G. Breese (1966, 109-114); D.J. Dwyer,
   ed. (1971), and N.S. Ginsburg (1972, 4).

Finally, it may be noted that centro-symmetric ordering is bound to occur in the separation of the major categories of functions in the centre, because shops, offices, and public buildings have basically different internal lay-outs. Shops normally work on one level for short distances such that back and forth trips and U-turns can be made. Offices can tolerate great vertical development which can be achieved by shops only if grouped in a department store, on the upper floors of which are space-consuming units, like furniture selling, which by itself would be better located in the core margin. Public buildings such as government offices are usually places where tenant and landlord are one, and the business throughout many departments is interlinked. With the growth of government involvement in economies, it is not difficult to envisage that this function will grow at least as fast as the total urban core. Often, co-operation with the private sector is excluded, such that there are few combinations with private offices and shops. Thus public buildings (as opposed to government space rented in private buildings) provide barriers to other city functions, and an administrative precinct can easily arise simply because of its own growth and the repulsion of other uses.

The centre of a city is written in a decipherable language. In reading the language we are forced to diagonalize between the form of buildings and intervening spaces on the one hand and their function on the other, and between what can be described as central and what cannot.

Chapter 4

IN DOWNTOWN (2): MEASUREMENT, ACCESSIBILITY, CHANGE

Centro-symmetric ordering was described as an evolutionary process, but there is always a desire to go beyond description to measurement. Indices of segregation and compactness have been devised, and are discussed by R.W. Thomas (1972, 70-3). Here we are concerned with the outer limits of what could be called the centre, and if a standard methodology can be agreed, certain advantages flow: several cities can be compared, or one city can be compared with itself at different times. The spatial range of comparison is constricted by the type of data available and the mesh of the grid on which it is collected; unhappily, there is no one method of central city measurement and delimitation that is universally applicable.

CORE MEASUREMENTS: LIMITATIONS, LIMITS, AND SOME RESULTANT PATTERNS

The Murphy-Vance method of delimiting the American CBD takes advantage of the block pattern of a rectilinear grid. The rules for delimitation are so carefully defined that the method can be applied to other cities where this lay-out obtains. In surveying the method, Murphy (1972, 12) calls it 'relatively objective', but in fact the rules for calculating the two indices upon which delimitation depends have '...no inherently critical levels. To a considerable extent, such limiting values have to be based upon reasoning supported by experience from numerous field observations' (idem, 34). The CBD is an area defined in terms of both function and 'centrality'. Murphy and Vance are quite clear on what functions are and are not to be included under 'business'; and 'centrality' is then taken to be the contiguous pattern of blocks meeting the assigned criteria around the peak land value intersection (PLVI). The result need not be geometrically central in the built-up area. Indeed, it is hardly ever so in cities that began life with a dominant port function (idem, 3); but Murphy goes on to state that he is concerned with centrality, not geometrically measured, but deriving from the peak of accessibility as the chief focus of transport.
    Thus the measurement of the CBD involves two types of classification conjoined. 'Business' and 'non-business' is a nominal classification, or opposition by 'cut' in C.K. Ogden's (1932) terminology.

Centrality and non-centrality are, on the other hand, at opposite
poles of a scalar continuum, and it is much more difficult to place
a boundary upon a continuously varying relative quality. Two
indices are thus necessary, the one correcting the deficiencies
(or absurd polar cases) of the other.

Central Business Height Index:(1)	total floor area of central business uses in the block divided by the total ground floor area; critical level chosen, 1:00.
Central Business Intensity Index:(2)	percentage of floor area in central business use at all levels of total floor space at all levels; critical level chosen. 50 per cent.
Contiguity rule:	to be included in the CBD, blocks exceeding the above critical levels must also be one of a contiguous group of blocks, surrounding the PLVI. A block is considered contiguous even if it touches another only at one corner.

1 CBHI needs correction by CBII because it fails to indicate the
  proportion of total space in central business uses.

2 CBII needs correction by CBHI because it takes no account of
  the amount of floor space in central business use.

Many other methods of CBD measurement are discussed by Murphy and
Vance (1954), such as volume of trade, building heights, traffic
flow, pedestrian counts, and land valuation. They are found want-
ing on the grounds of lack of comparability between cities or
because they do not discriminate among land uses. Murphy has himself reflected upon the shortcomings of the method he advocates,
notably that block shape and size differ from city to city, even
in the case of cities with suitable grid lay-outs. The distinction
between central and non-central uses is subjective; and the defined
area is produced not only by the nature of the CBD but also by the
technique of definition (Murphy's comment, 1972, 98, on an observation by H. Carter and G. Rowley, 1966, 119). But despite these and
other shortcomings, the method has the great merit of comparability
over time and over a range of cities. There is space here to consider only four cases where the technique has been considered for
use outside the United States (see also G. Rowley, 1965).

   D.H. Davies (1959) applied the method to Cape Town and had to
modify the rules slightly because of the many tall buildings in the
city, many more than in the nine cities of an average population of
only 151,000 in 1950, which Murphy and Vance had first studied.
Second, there were three or four very long blocks, each of which
decreased markedly in CBD character from one end of the block to the
other; and these were in fact internally divided to produce the CBD
boundary. Davies (1960) went on to attempt a definition of the
'hard core' of Cape Town's CBD by stiffening the critical values.
He also excluded: all government buildings (which may be included

in the general CBD only if they meet certain contiguity criteria),
cinemas, hotels, and lower quality retail establishments. After a
visual inspection on the ground and a search for a break of slope
on the CBHI and CBII graphs, limiting values of 4.00 and 80 per
cent respectively were chosen. The result shows Cape Town's hard
core asymmetrically disposed around the PLVI and also asymmetrically located within the total CBD (Davies, 1960, Fig. 5D). This
should come as no surprise. The CBD itself is defined by omitting
certain functions that are found close to the centre, either through
inertia (establishments like churches and colleges) or most notably
through a planned decision (government property, including public
buildings like museums, libraries, and arts centres). Second, if
business functions are restricted, the tendency is to put a line
around part of a complex that is undergoing segregation in the process of centro-symmetric ordering.

W. Hartenstein and G. Staack (1967) applied the CBD method to
several German Cities. Because the height of buildings is consider-
ably lower in Europe than in the United States for cities of comparable size, the critical values were altered slightly: the CBII was
reduced from 50 per cent to 40 per cent when the height index
reached 1.5. But the greatest contrast results from their definition of the hard core compared with Davies.

	Davies	Hartenstein-Staack	
CBHI	4.00	1.50	2.00
		or	
CBII	80.00%	60.00%	50.00%

Some interesting results of the German study are that with growing
size of the hard core, retail floor area does not grow at the same
rate - a phenomenon noted in connection with the allometric growth
law. On the other hand, office use grew at a greater rate with
increase of city size probably reflecting the wider national and
international functions of big cities. Within the 'office' category, banks and insurance appeared more concentrated in area than
business organizations. The possible reason for this is that the
bank and the insurance firm could be regarded as services to other
businesses, which, as shown in the last chapter, may well move away
from the centre if they become big enough to generate internal
economies. In the very largest centres, like London and New York,
even life assurance offices have moved from the centre, which might
eventually be thought to contain ranks of banks, until it is remembered that the world's great cities will serve international trading, and the largest companies need to have headquarters in the largest cities (A.W. Evans 1973, 393).

M.J. Bowden (1971, 124-5) working in San Francisco, slightly
altered the Murphy-Vance criteria, first adopting a finer mesh than
blocks, and then he decided to include government and public land
occupance, and wholesaling if it was selling-oriented, but not if it
was a case of seller-distributors needing proximity to transport
terminals. This is a division of wholesaling suggested by E.M.
Hoover and R. Vernon (1959, 85) in their study of New York. Bowden
also adopted a slightly stricter rule for contiguity than Murphy and

Vance to counterbalance his slightly wider set of functional
categories.

In the case of a city of enormous size and highly irregular
blocks, J. Goddard (1967) was forced to use a 500-metre square
grid, superimposed on the city without reference to street pattern.
The Murphy-Vance criteria were applied and the CBD mapped, Goddard
felt that the result in no way accorded with reality. First, the
CBD concept lumps together several functions. In a very large city
each of these has its own spatial and organizational structure, via
centro-symmetric ordering. In London there are even two office
cores in the City of London and in the West End, the former concentrating on the interrelated functions of banking, commodity trading, risk insurance, and shipping (see Fig. 11). Another peak of
office use occurs around Whitehall in Westminster with ribbons to
north-east and south-west, and a gentle talus slope of office
development in the West End, where offices cohabit converted premises alongside residential, retail, and even industrial use.

Shopping is also concentrated in two areas of London, and it
might be thought they have been separated by the great parks. But
it seems unlikely that one shopping area of the combined extent of
the West End and Kensington would be attractive to the individual
shopper who must decide which part of such a vast area he will concentrate upon in any one trip (producing that non-concordance with
the allometric growth law). Goddard maps the extent of public
buildings in the central area of London, acknowledging them as
important functional units. He notes that any one such institution may dominate the ground area of a locality, that 'non-economic
values are frequently attached to these structures', and he specu-
lates on their role 'as barriers to the expansion [of other
functions] in the Central Area or as divides within it' (p. 131,
see Table 15 above).

P.E. Venekamp and B. Kruijt (1967) worked out a method for
determining the relative centrality of shopping streets in Amsterdam, using a combination of indices, perhaps following the lead of
Murphy and Vance. Once the core had been delimited, they divided
retail floor space into that selling durable goods from that selling
consumable goods, or comparison shopping from convenience shopping.
Streets were given two indices according to the average floor space
per establishment selling durable goods and the total of such floor
space in the street. To these two indices was added a third - the
so-called concentration grade in which the percentage of floor
space selling durable goods in the street of the total of such
floor space in the inner city was divided by the same percentage for
consumable articles. The concentration grade is a refinement by
which every street is related to all the others under consideration,
and is a way of weighting those streets which are more specialized
in durable goods. Even if the floor space in a particular street
remains static, its relative centrality can be affected by developments elsewhere, and this is as it should be. The three indices are
calculated for each street of the centre, the street put in rank
order, and the three ranks added. The results of the total ranking
show a coherent network of central streets, with a department store
established in each of the four leading streets (as one might expect
from the process of calculation). More revealing is the clear

indication that streets with a high relative central position contain relatively more clothing and textile shops, whereas furnish-
ing stores are in streets with a relatively less central position
(loc.cit., 234, Table 5). Perhaps the reason for this is that
textiles and clothing are highly subject to comparative shopping
(fashion), whereas furniture is more bulky, and so are the shops
housing these goods, with consequently greater distance between
areas of comparison. Another factor is that textile clothing is
more in the nature of impulse shopping, whereas the buying of
furniture is much more of a premeditated act, so that display
attraction is not so vital.

Two department stores have more than double the significance of
one, because if located sufficiently close together they generate
a 'centrality' along the shopping strip between them. This is
true not only in the western CBD, but also in the out-of-town
shopping centre (see pp. 109-12 below) and in Japanese cities
(P. Scholler, 1962, 580).

The comparative study of eight American CBDs enabled Murphy and
Vance, with B.J. Epstein (1955) to compare the land use in four
'walking zones', measured along streets from the PLVI, at 100, 300,
and 400 metres respectively. The space occupied by various types
of establishment was then plotted for each zone and ranked. Here
are perhaps the two most striking results of this exercise.

1 Zone 1 was ranked last for all uses except clothing (ranked 1),
   variety stores (1), and headquarters offices (ranked equal 2
   with Zone 2). Not only were other retail functions (food, house-
   hold, and miscellaneous) not ranked 1, but in fact ranked 4, or
   'not represented' (car sales). Yet retail business as a whole
   was ranked 1, showing that clothing and variety stores must have
   comprised big retail outlets. (A point to note is that Walking
   Zone 1 has a diameter of 200 metres along streets, the very distance that R.L. Nelson (1958, 236 ff) empirically derived as
   being the critical distance for a shopping façade based on 'North
   American' habits of pedestrian traffic in the lay-out of bespoke
   shopping centres.

2 The zone of highest buildings is usually Zone 2 or 3. Perhaps
   several reasons combine to bring this about. Financial general
   headquarters and general offices are the generators of tall
   buildings, and they are rarely found in Zone 1 (cf. Davies, 1960,
   Fig. 5D), yet their continued massive development would incline
   the location of the PLVI and the derived walking zones in their
   direction. This chicken and egg situation can be broken by
   understanding that it might not be possible to assemble a lot
   large enough right at the PLVI for a modern tall building
   development. A concentration on high-rise buildings (see P.W.
   Daniels, 1975b, 18-25, with full references) shifts the focus
   from the functioning centre towards an area of assimilation.
   High-rise is a way of providing great amounts of floor space for
   sedentary human beings in offices or bedrooms (apartments and
   hotels), based on the fact that the human body can be moved
   faster for short journeys up and down rather than horizontally.
   This is due not to a technical reason but to the power of what
   might be called the 'elevator paradigm', attested by the fact
   that, as far as I know, no 'horizontal elevator' exists within or

between buildings. High-rise peaks are just off the city centre, not only because being newer developments they could not get into the oldest part of the core, but also because their efficiency, and hence their use, is restricted to particular functions which are themselves subject to centro-symmetrical ordering.

From such detailed spatial studies of downtown it appears that 'offices' form the function 'most central' within the CBD, and that the growth, laterally and vertically, of the CBD in large cities is associated mainly with this function. Bowden's (1971, 131) work on the San Francisco CBD led to a ranking of functions according to each one's ability to displace any or all other uses. The financial nucleus was displaced by no other, and the apparel shopping district was subject to displacement pressure only from finance (see Bowden, Fig. 6, 132). The hotel district was under some pressure from finance and apparel selling, but was also subject to internal changes, and moved further over time than the other two functions. Another way of observing growth is to discuss the problem of site search. The advancing front of office growth is often towards a zone of higher class residences, which are often suitable for office conversion in the first place, pending the construction of purpose-built premises. There is also the problem of what is already there and Fig. 12 attempts a classification of land uses within the central city, according to their increasing resistance to office redevelopment (when read clockwise; see also D.C. Weaver, 1969).

Pedestrian movement is another index of CBD use, usually at its heaviest near the PLVI, except in the largest metropolises where the shopping centre is very distinct from the financial district. D.L. Foley (1952) compiled figures to show that the maximum accumulation of people in the CBD dropped proportionally with city size. In the smaller cities studied (pop. 100,000-250,000) there were about 250 destinations in the CBD for every 1,000 metropolitan residents, but for cities from 1 million to 2 million there were only 170; Foley wondered about that missing 80; perhaps they had gone to sub-centres in the larger cities. The figures of maximum CBD accumulation varied downward from 12 to 9 per cent of metropolitan population for a range of city population from 100,000 to 2 million. This suggests that the growth and use of sub-centres restrains the pressure of entry to the original CBD of an expanding city, and this is an important factor in postponing the arrival of operating diseconomies through congestion (J. Rannells, in D.A. Wallace (ed.), 1961, 18).

Many of the techniques discussed in this section turn out to be rather place and time specific, though efforts by Murphy and Vance show that it is possible to derive methods that are applicable over a number of cities. There remains the problem of adding together different functions, and it is difficult to avoid a subjective assessment in their equivalence or in assigning a ratio between them. The very term CBD excludes an important function of cities, that of administration, including civic, regional, and perhaps national. Many a classifier of the centrality of the downtown has nobly striven to include an ingredient which relates a functional unit to the urban core as a whole; but it is difficult to see how an index with such a component can be compared with a similarly derived index in another city. The striving of Murphy and Vance for a

technique as objective as possible so that the method can be replicated by other workers with comparability of results between
cities was echoed by W.K.D. Davies (1966) in his review of the
ranking techniques for service centres. The reward of those who
successfully devise such techniques is to see them applied over a
range of cities, and we, the observers, gain insights from the
further problems that such an array of studies reveal in review.

CONTRASTS IN FOCAL ORGANIZATION

Every general study of the internal structure of the city is likely
to mention the so-called 'classical' spatial explanations of city
patterns of R.M. Hurd (1903, 58-63) and E.W. Burgess (1925) -
concentric zones; H. Hoyt (1939) - *sectoral pattern*; and R.D.
McKenzie (1933, 68) and C.D. Harris and E.L. Ullman (1945) - *multiple nuclei*. Sometimes attempts are made to update these (e.g.
H. Hoyt, 1964), or combine them to produce a more 'real-life'
pattern. They have been criticized for being gross over-
simplifications (L.S. Bourne, 1967, 16 and B.T. Robson, 1975, 16),
generated as generalizations covering United States cities at specific past periods. A number of students have found it useful to
consider the models as complementary rather than exclusive. Development of the field has been concerned not only with urban sub-areas
and centres (incl. sub-centres) but also with social area patterning. Because such analysis of the total intra-urban area is somewhat marginal to a study concentrating on centrality, it is felt
that a summary of comments on the synthesis of the models is sufficient here. Table 16 is arranged to demonstrate an evolution in
these synthetic attempts.
    Somewhat at a tangent to these models are schemes put forward
by W.I. Firey (1949, re Boston) and E. Jones (1962, re Belfast)
where patterns are explained to a significant degree by the socio-
cultural values symbolically invested in certain topographical
features. In this case the idea of an original centre is not so
mechanistically required, although the symbolic values may confer a
kind of sub-centrality on selected features of the urban scene.

ACCESSIBILITY

The three classical models have proved too simple for analysis of
the modern city, but because this study concentrates on centres, the
reliance of these models on some form of focal organization can
still be a source of illumination. Fig. 13 shows how three different patterns resembling each of the classical models can be generated by applying some very simple ideas about accessibility and different foci. The notion of accessibility is itself quite complicated, but some of the complexities can be discarded if concentration
is held upon the centres rather than upon all possible points in
their tributary areas. As far as retail shops are concerned, B.J.
Garner (1965) has pointed out that some believe that accessibility
is the basis for rents, while others believe that it is related to
sales. The synthesis between these points of view offered by Garner

TABLE 16   Syntheses of concentric zones, sectoral, and multiple nuclei focal organization models in physical space and social space

[Only the essence of the contribution or comment is attempted below.]

Models considered independent and additive

R.M. Hurd (1903, 56-74)
Axial growth and central growth (pan-directional from centre and sub-centres); vital feature is additive continuity.
G.A. Wissink (1962, 42-50)
All three theories have some validity in that they direct attention to tendencies. Multiple nuclei theory perhaps best suited to deal with complex modern situations. But all three theories less adequate for non U.S. cities.
B.J.L. Berry (1965, 115)
Models are independent additive contributions to total socioeconomic structuring of city neighbourhoods.
P. Mann (1965, 95)
Burgess's scheme a starting point, and the sector and multiple nuclei theories provide more detail.`
J.W. Simmons (1965, 170)
The different models describe different elements of the land use pattern.
J.S. Adams (1970, 38)
The three models are independent and additive, as are the three dimensions of residential variation (synthetic diagram provided as Fig. 15).

Sector model preferred

F.L. Hauser (1951, 128-9)
City sections grow from a work centre. The concentric theory fails more conspicuously than the sector theory in the cases of the four cities studied (London, Paris, Stockholm, Vienna).
P.J. Smith (1962, 323, 326)
All models have some relevance, but in a city [Calgary] oriented to transportation, sector theory seems to be most meaningful, with the sector pattern breaking down in the future into the much more flexible multiple nuclei pattern.

Models considered complementary

E.E. Bergel (1955, 100-114)
'Burgess-Hoyt hypothesis' combined with W.I. Firey's (1949) theory of symbolic values and a theory based on transport models (synthetic diagram provided as Fig. 7).
L.S. Burns and A.J. Harman (1967, 78-9)
Evidence of all theories can be found in spatial distributions of Los Angeles, dependent on area scale and chosen characteristics for study.
B.J. Garner (1967, 343)
The models are not mutually exclusive and perhaps factor analysis

will enable even more general models to supplement them.
R.A. Murdie (1969, reprinted in L.S. Bourne (ed.), 1971, 283)
Burgess and Hoyt models based largely on deterministic principles,
whereas Firey and Jones (E. Jones, 1962) are probalistic.
Concentric, sectoral, and multiple nuclei models complement each
other, and further synthesis made with social area analysis (syn-
thetic diagram provided as Fig. 15)
R.A. Murdie (1970, in reply to R.J. Johnston 1970, see below)
Zonal and sector models are complementary.
C. Hamnett (1972, 61)
Use of the Burgess and Hoyt models in combination circumvents many
of the paradoxes inherent in their individual application, but this
procedure cannot correct their culture-bound nature.

Models represent different urban characteristics

T.R. Anderson and J.T. Egeland (1961)
Concentric zone and sectoral models tested in the case of four
U.S. cities of comparable size and roughly circular in shape. Concentric model supported with respect to urbanization (more apartments, less children, wife working constituted 'high urbanization'),
but not social rank; sectoral model vice versa.
B.J.L. Berry and P.H. Rees (1969, 459)
Socio-economic status varies in sectors, life cycle in concentric
zones, ethnicity in sectors for minorities, modified by concentric
life cycle zones of ethnic areas, the shape of physical growth of
the city, and existence of peripheral work-place nuclei in addition
to the original centre (see redrawn synthetic diagrams as Fig. 6.1
in B. Robson, 1973).
B.J.L. Berry and F.E. Horton (1970, 309)
Indices which measure socio-economic status of individuals or groups
vary by sector; familial characteristics and age of population vary
principally by concentric zone; and minority groups cluster.
D. Timms (1971, 248)
Social rank (sectoral), family and ethnic status, and variables
relating to community integration (zonal). But each index has a tendency towards a secondary patterning: social rank (zonal), family
and ethnic status (sectoral).
B.T. Robson (1973, 222)*
Results from a variety of cultural contexts suggest modern cities
almost invariably show two dimensions, essentially measuring
aspects of socio-economic status and age structure.
B.T. Robson (1975, 16)
Need to look at processes rather than spatial patterns in attempt to
understand intermeshing of housing and social space within the context of physical space.

Model testing procedures

J.A. Quinn (1940)
R.J. Johnston (1970, 1971a)

*With extended discussion of early ecological, social area analysis,
 and factor ecological approaches. For another more extensive
 ordered résumé see R.J. Johnston (1971b).

(p. 104) is that at the macro-scale within the city, the general
level of rents is related to accessibility; but within a nucleated
centre, the level of rents is more related to the advantages of
individual sites with respect to the known concentrations of shoppers and hence the potential sales. It is of course a little too
easy to believe that site location is directly related to an easily
determined threshold of sales, because these must vary according to
selling methods and consumer needs and tastes, including shopping
habits on multi-purpose trips. The employment by Garner of a
multi-scale approach matches conclusions drawn by industrial geographers when examining site selection by entrepreneurs, first
seeking a profitable region, then an appropriate community setting,
and finally via an available site (e.g. J. Rees, 1972, Fig. 2; and
1974, Fig. 7.1, 194-5). We might pause to remember that availability of sites might not match the time-scale of pressure of
demand, especially during periods of economic boom; and this is a
contributory factor causing functions not to be sited on 'optimum
locations', if they can ever be determined by the available
information.

Taking a more homely example, literally speaking, consider the
perhaps unconscious three-stage process in the search for a home.
The general area of choice may be determined by reference to a
centre, transmitted as an acceptable time distance for the journey
to work. Within that general constraint an area is chosen with an
acceptable level of services commensurate with income, values, and
life style through what B. Robson (1973, 222-3) has called institutional and special filters (special to sub-groups). Finally, a
home is chosen from those on the market at the time of search - the
best buy at the time. In retrospect, the home-buyer or renter, the
industrial decision-maker, and the shopper may invert this hierarchical search procedure in order of perceived importance as opposed
to the actual order of search (see R. Dewey, 1948-9, Fig. 2).

Accessibility to a centre may be a quantity that diminishes
faster for the average home-seeker compared with an institution,
where the cost involved in diminished accessibility is small relative to the cost of the large site required (J.W.R. Whitehand, 1972,
39). This is a feature which may cause some institutions that grow
large to move out of the peak area of accessibility and works in the
same direction as those changes in internal organisation which were
noted under centro-symmetric ordering.

The downtown area may also lose its quality as the peak of
accessibility for the whole city as the urban area grows larger,
a process accelerated if congestion becomes significant. A general
trend is set out in Table 17. The table points up the inappropriateness of the belief that a linear city has more people close to a
linear downtown than a circular city with a circular downtown (a
belief expressed in 'The Planning of a New Town', 1965, 29, Fig.
19). First, not all the linear downtown would be equally accessible because of its strung-out lengths, and thus it would lose one
of the features required, compact comparibility and closeness of
linkages. Second, as a city grows larger not everyone needs to
visit the central downtown for regular convenience shopping because
some degree of decentralization will surely have occurred.

The systems of centres within a large urban area may be regarded
as forming a hierarchy, much as occurs in the systems of central

Concentric

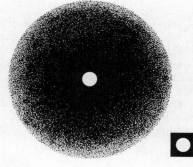

City centre with
'organic' centrality and
pan-directional
accessibility

Sectoral

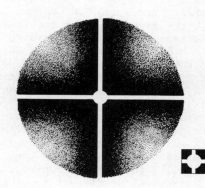

Organic central node
with canalised linear
accessibility

Centro-Symmetric Ordering
or City Region with
Planned Sub-centres

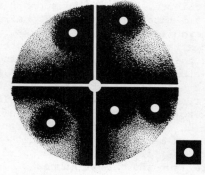

Nodes with
special or planned
accessibility

Maximum accessibility   Decreasing accessibility

FIGURE 13   Three different types of accessibility
Note how the simple shading technique implies a concentric pattern
in the top diagram and a sectoral pattern in the middle diagram.
    The multiple nuclei of the bottom diagram could be held to be the

result of centro-symmetric ordering of functions close to downtown, as each function develops its own centre within a specialized
precinct. On the other hand, the nuclei could be planned centres
such as in order of historic time, a cathedral with its close, a
market square, an artisanal quarter, an administration complex or
sub-centres further out within a city-region system. In the latter
case the scale of the bottom diagram should be thought of as smaller,
so that the diagram represents a wider area.
Reproduced from 'Geography', 1973, 58, 107, by permission of the
editor.

place theory (W. Christaller, 1933; and H. Carol). 'We conclude
that the hierarchical nature of intra-urban retail structure may be
attributed to the same process that generates systems of central
places. The primary difference is the high density of households
within cities' (B.J.L. Berry and F.E. Horton, 1970, 456). It is
fascinating to see the germination of the idea of the necessity for
three different systems within cities arising in the work of B.J.L.
Berry in 1959, where he first mentions the idea (also citing W.
Bunge, 1958), and then it blossoms into a typology in 1963. This
typology includes first the hierarchy of centres which has grown up
organically within the city, from the corner or convenience stores
that serve some of the people all of the time to the more specialized stores in compact groups for comparison. Second, there is the
hierarchy of centres developed as ribbons planned or unplanned.
Last, there are those highly specialized functional precincts only
found in the larger centres. In summary, one recognizes organic
centres, linear centres, and special centres. Thus there are different types of centres with different types of accessibility:
organic centres (tend to develop where there is ease of movement
over an area based on pedestrian, horse, or local automobile movement); linear centres (based on buses and trams aiming at a node);
and special centres (arising offset from organic centres because
of some added attribute, but needing support by a large population).
It appears that all three concepts are required as basic models for
intra-urban patterns (J.S. Adams, 1970, esp. p. 38), and from these
three ideas of centrality and associated accessibility, one can
easily adumbrate the concentric, sectoral, and multiple nuclei
models of intra-urban morphology (see also R.L. Davies, 1972a).
   If these three definitions of intra-urban centrality and accessibility seem overly deductive, experiment would consist of a decep-
tively simple exercise - the determination of the centre of a settlement, from which accessibility is measured. It would seem that
even a layman should be able to establish the centre of a town, but
as a settlement grows larger, it becomes harder to fix on a point as
the unique centre (see the modest number of four central symbols in
Fig. 15). One method might be to tackle the problem from the other
way around and agree that if in every direction one attempts to
turn, a move is palpably made towards the periphery, then one must
be at the centre, just as one must be at the North Pole, if south is
faced in every direction. In quantitative terms, if in every direction one moves, the land value per frontage foot declines, one is at
the centre. Fortunately, the gradients between the highest and
lower land values are usually steep, and the slopes are often

similar on both sides of streets, unless there is something
unusual to prevent this.   In a small town, the centre might well
be represented by the highest land values - the PLVI.   But as a
town grows larger, its individual functions must occupy more space
close to the centre, and in a large metropolis there is pattern
resulting from centro-symmetric ordering where the original centre
has been replaced by an urban scene of immense functional contrast.
One of the resultant problems that arises is how to measure distances to the so-called centre of a large metropolis.   Distances to
London are usually measured to Hyde Park Corner, which is not even
in the City of London and is certainly not the centre for most
visitors to London on business or pleasure.   Each function there
has its own focus.   For London shopping or theatre-going the 'West
End' is the central attraction; yet the term which is now in
itself a centralizing magnet, was obviously anything but that when
it was first literally applied to the west end of the city.

THIRD WORLD VARIATIONS

The extent to which the foregoing remarks are applicable to cities
in the Third World is perhaps proportional to the extent of the
adoption of a western-style economy, perhaps as the result of former
colonialism.   Sometimes a form of dual economy is in existence
(T.G. McGee, 1971, Figs 3 and 7), and this may disperse the concentration upon a single centre.   Ethnic precincts each with their own
focus may be thought of as a special form of centro-symmetric
ordering leading to the special centres of Fig. 13, bottom (see also
G. Breese, 1966, 63 ff).   There are however many students who
believe that different spatial models are required for each culture
(see the comments of C. Hamnett, 1972, 45).   Certainly there are
fierce variations in population density profiles between western and
non-western cities, and great contrasts in spatial arrangements of
classes.   Societies which have progressed directly from walking/
animal haulage to some form of reliance on the internal combustion
engine are bound to show forms of incremental growth very different
from those where, for instance, the railway played an important part
in areal spread.   The focus on an intra-city centre is stronger in
the less mobile societies of the Third World, and there are several
processes at work resulting from competition for locations within
the city (Breese, op.cit., 109 ff).   The way this focussing operates depends on the way the world is seen.   This is a subject which
returns in the last chapter, but it may come as no surprise to learn
that it will be argued here that in this respect the dichotomy between western and non-western societies disappears at some point
within the progression: spatial pattern; behaviour; values and
attitudes, motivation, beliefs; psychological drives; brain processes (see Table 6).   This will be briefly discussed again below
(see p. 149 and Fig. 26).

LOCATIONAL CHANGE OF THE CENTRE

Considering the great investment locked into city centres, any

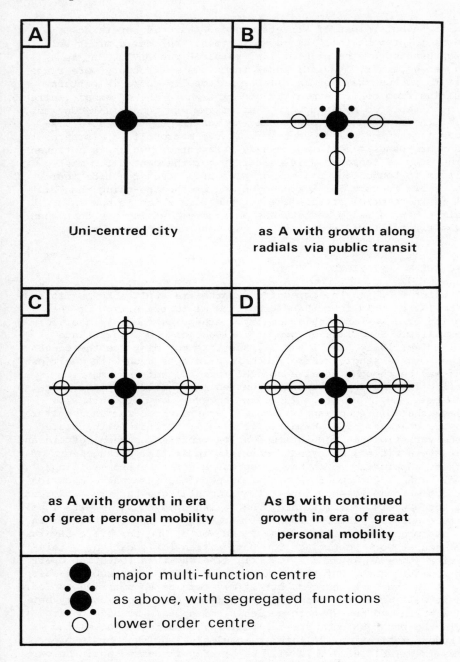

FIGURE 14   Some simple variations of intra-urban pattern with various types of transport development

locational change of the PLVI, if by only a few blocks, causes immense problems. In many cities there can be identified a frontier of central area advance and a frontier of retreat; and their passage

TABLE 17   Limitations on centralized focal organization with city growth and growth of personal transport

	All people all time	All people some of the time	Some of the people all time	Some of the people some of the time
Small city:				
Downtown	✓	✓		
Medium city:				
Downtown		✓		
Neighbourhood centre			✓	
Large city region*				
Downtown		✓		
Neighbourhood centre			✓	
Planned out-of-town centre			✓	✓

*Variations in the relationship between the three types of centre depend on the way transport has developed, see Fig. 14.

Note.   This table might be compared with J. Labasse's (1970, 11-12) spatio-temporal hierarchy giving degrees of centrality:

elementary centrality - daily or more than once a week visits (measured in hundreds of metres) to centre;

average centrality - monthly or less than weekly visits from anywhere in the city region;

higher centrality - specialized functions used a few times a year by a clientele originating from within the area of maximum extent of the city's umland influence.

This is a nested hierarchy in that functions appropriate to each kind of centrality are often located within one another in what is loosely termed the central area of the city, though as cities grow larger, functions of 'higher centrality' progressively dominate the 'centre'.

is marked by the presence of two areas called by Murphy, Vance, and Epstein (1955), the zone of assimilation and the zone of discard (loc.cit., Fig. 16).   These zones are included in the core-frame concept of E.M. Horwood and R.E. Boyce (1959) and were studied in detail by R.E. Preston (1966), who called them a 'transition zone' after the term in Burgess's original model (1925).   Murphy (1972, 112-20) has given a critique of these attempts, stressing particularly that Horwood and Boyce provided no delimitation technique and that this also applies to the Griffin-Preston concept (D.W. Griffin and R.E. Preston, 1966).   Moreover, the dichotomous classification of transition zone functions and non transition zone functions

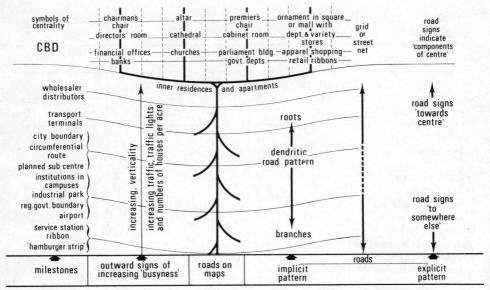

FIGURE 15   The approach to centrality in an urban centre of the western world

The approach to the CBD is dominated by the *flat principle* (I), whereas the closer one gets to 'the centre of the CBD', so the dominating principle should be that of '*static, modelled form*' (II).

I, *flat principle* (or, more explicitly, the principle of space seen as if projected via perspective on to a vertical plane), based on an observer's view, producing an imaginary plane of projection, which because of binocular vision and the laws of perspective is 'seen' by the mind as three-dimensional. This gives rise to axial type developments, 'Roman' type vistas and facades; motorway route views of distant skyscrapers and the North American 'strip' are modern manifestations (for a description of an archetypal form of the latter see R. Venturi, D. Scott Brown, and S. Izenour, 1973).

II, *static, modelled form,* based on the ability of an observer to enter *into* urban space, leads to a free and asymmetrical grouping. This gives rise to a Greek-type style and occult balance. Most cityscapes contain a mixture of styles though, as the diagram suggests, Style I is often more dominant on city approaches and Style II ought to be dominant near the centre.   (Style distinction based on A. Papageorgiou, 1971, 56 ff.)

[Note. I is equivalent to *route* images of city taxi-drivers; II is equivalent to the aerial *survey* view of student pilots training near a large city; see report of an empirical survey in G. Rand, 1969.]

ultimately rests on an arbitrary basis. As far as this context is concerned, the interest in these zones attaches to the extent to which they provide evidence as to why the centre is moving, and for distinguishing, if possible those characteristics of a zone of assimilation from those of a zone of discard.

When a centre moves, there are obviously a number of concomitant

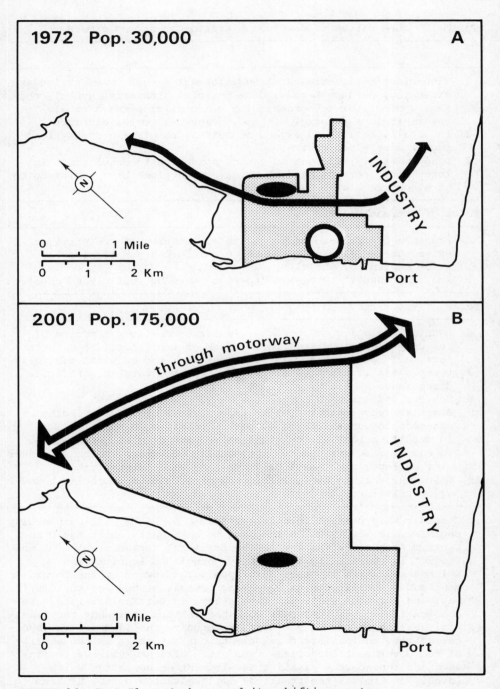

FIGURE 16 Sept-Iles, Quebec, and its shifting centre
The small settlement, port dominated, had its centre near the
waterfront (A). The peripherally developed centre on the Avenue
Laure subsequently finds itself more 'central' in the expanded city
(B).

TABLE 18   Some causes of downtown migration or skewed growth

Latent centrality

1   High-class residential areal development skewed in a particular
    direction, perhaps because of a powerful attractive symbol, phy-
    siographical, or topographically planned; or perhaps merely
    enshrined in a prestigious name, or even a postal district.
2   In detail, ability to expand on both sides of main routes lead-
    ing from original centre.
3   Land ownership adjacent to centre conducive to development in
    large lots, perhaps because existing functions have a site to go
    to elsewhere. (1)

Poles of attraction

4   Presence of cross-route to wealthiest suburbs of the city, or
    extra sub-radial giving access, via a forked junction, to a
    wider segment of the city.
5   Public transport terminals (towards these but not beyond them).

Poles of repulsion

6   Decline (relative or absolute) in former dominant function of
    the city (religious; military, break of transport, (2) e.g. the
    port, a function which also migrates from the original centre).
7   Lower class residential areal development skewed in particular
    directions.
8   Noxious industry.
9   Barriers (physiographic, like impossible slopes for building;
    man-made topographical, e.g. parks, public open space).
10 In detail, a barrier to retail shops extending at ground level
    in one or more directions (e.g. public buildings, monument, inner
    city college, or a particular busy and wide intersection).
11 Land ownership in small lots, or administrative or zoning bound-
    ary peculiarity.

1   Consider this passage in a letter from C.G. Hands, the Durban City
    Engineer, 16 May 1972, in response to an enquiry about the Durban
    Centrum project. 'The key to the practical implementation of the
    Project is the ability of the City Council to acquire land on
    which the Centrum is to be developed...land owned by the Govern-
    ment and South African Railways and presently used for the City's
    gaol and terminus station. The latter, in particular, is a vast
    complex including ... repair workshops. Thus it is not the finan-
    cial ability of the City Council to acquire the land or its physi-
    cal ability to initiate development, but rather it is the ability
    of the Government authorities and South African Railways 'to fin-
    ance and replace the existing development on new sites which
    largely determines the practical implementation of the Centrum
    proposals.'
2   Conversely to note 1 above, and a caution to railway buffs: his-
    toric railway stations near a city centre are ripe for demolition
    or conversion to something else.

processes in action, and the mix will vary from city to city. The simplest approach will be to list some of the characteristics of a centre in motion. It is useful to think of the zone of assimilation as having some latent centrality whereas the zone of discard may mark a retreat from a pole of repulsion or is on the distal flank of a pole of attraction. In many cases these two ideas are linked. For example, a high-class residential area adjacent to the CBD is ripe for takeover by offices, which can easily convert the premises to the new business function. Such a residential area can be said to possess latent centrality. Alternatively, it may be that in every other direction, save the one occupied by the high-class residences, there is a pole of repulsion, in the form of some kind of barrier (physiographic; or man-made, such as noxious industry, railway yards, or public open space).

The zone of discard is often an area of blight caused either through structural changes in urban technology or socio-economic organization, or through what L. Wingo (1966, 147) called 'externalities effects', whereby properties are caught in an interdependence trap. Investment in property improvement yields an acceptable return only if others follow suit, whereas a free extra return may be acquired if the property owner does not invest but his neighbour does. The neighbour who decided to invest risked not achieving a full rate of return if *his* neighbours did not also improve their properties. There is thus a state where a net disinvestment or blight is likely to arise and be self-perpetuating:

> In short, both are trapped by the uncertainty of the other's behaviour into the position where the optimum strategy for each independently produces lower returns than in the case in which each was required to follow a strategy which would maximise the yield to both. (Wingo, loc.cit.)

Net disinvestment might be thought of as a combination of physical and frictional blight in B.J.L. Berry's fourfold typology of commercial blight (1963, 179-81). Other categories in this typology are economic blight when there is a loss of demand in the service area of centres; and functional blight refers to technological obsolescence. These last two forms of blight are more likely to occur with respect to retailing in suburban or ribbon centres than in connection with functions still active in the central downtown area.

Centre mobility has been quite a feature of Japanese cities according to P. Schöller (1962), in cases where there was an absence of an underground net of public utility services. Conversely, the advent of the elevator and bye-laws permitting tall buildings enabled the centre to become more concentrated around a location even with growth.

THREE CURRENT BASIC PROBLEMS OF CITY CENTRES

Two basic problems of city centres derive from the process of growth. However much vertical development takes place, there is the fundamental problem for any central function in a growing metropolis - the sites available around a unique centre cannot grow in proportion. Indeed, accessibility may even deteriorate. Perhaps

this problem can be most vividly demonstrated by the difficulties
faced by centrally located markets (J. Bird, 1958; K.L. Buzzacott,
1972, 347-57) which, with general city growth, have to serve more
customers on progressively restricted sites. Second, for every
organization that grows and outgrows the centre by means of its
own internal economies, for every flight to the suburbs, there is
a rate reduction for the central municipal government, if regional
government is not established.

Last, any decline in public order reduces the attraction of the
centre, particularly in respect of those human external economies
to be obtained there. The big city may well become the home of big
crime (K.D. Harries, 1973, 5). We may recall S.L. Thrupp's (1963)
concept of city as 'an idea of social order'. Consider the social
order implicit in a pioneer example of traffic segregation from the
plan for Central Park, New York (F.L. Olmsted and C. Vaux, 1858)
with its

> ...system of independent ways; 1st for carriages; 2nd, for
> horsemen...3rd, for footmen; and 4th, for common street traffic
> requiring to cross the Park. By this means it was made possible
> to go on foot to any district of the Park without crossing a line
> of wheels on the same level. (F.L. Olmsted - quoted in C.S.
> Stein, 1966, 44.)

Because of changed social conditions the idea of the segregation and
isolation of pedestrians has deteriorated into the basis for a joke
in a 1974 television comedy series, possibly funny, certainly
frightening.

Maude: Cheer up, I know where we can get a cheap vacation,
         where there is walking, riding, boating - you'll get
         a magnificent suntan.

Walter: Gee, honey, where?
(husband)

Maude: Central Park.

Walter: Oh, fine!

Maude: And at night, there are beatings, muggings, stabbings....

Chapter 5

CENTRE-PERIPHERY CONTRASTS

One of the most deductive statements ever made about contrasts
between town and country is to be found in the course of C.K.
Ogden's (1932) linguistic and psychological analysis of opposition.
He recognized three types: opposition separated by a *cut* (such as
right/left); by a *scale* (such as top/bottom), where there is a continuous scale from one pole to another, its opposite; and by *definition* (see his diagram, p. 16). For an example of the last type,
Ogden took the pair of town/country. His amplification is deductive as far as urban geography is concerned because he was interested
in town and country only to the extent that they were exemplary
opposites; yet it is remarkable how his argument penetrates to their
essence.

> Town and Country. If this is taken as a typical case of opposi-
> tion by definition (based on statistical density of population,
> houses, etc.), the value of the opposition in practical applica-
> tion is relative to the growth of suburbs. In due course the
> distinction might vanish altogether throughout the entire sur-
> face of an urbanized planet. An opposition originally created
> by definition (in response to factual requirements on the basis
> of a cut) is thus shifting to a scale whose extremes are being
> gradually obliterated by the expansion of its middle (suburban)
> range. A temporary stage is thus reached where semantic compli-
> cations are produced by legal definitions in terms of difference
> rather than opposition. Finally, in such cases, the oppositional
> definition may retain historical significance only. (p. 78)

Here is emphasized the temporary nature of the boundary between town
and country, or between city and tributary area, or umland - a term
first coined by A. Allix (1914). The pair centre/periphery form an
opposition by scale because there can be a double comparison between
the two poles (the true opposites) or between any position on the
scale between them and any other position, including either of the
two poles. The expressions 'inside the centre' (city)/'outside the
centre' (city) form an opposition by cut. They are correctly used
only when cities are in fact bounded by cuts (walls, administrative
boundaries), often the first attempts to organize space. But the
mismatch of municipal government areas and the extension of the
built-up landscape had become evident in Brtiain as early as 1835

(W. Ashworth, 1954, 71), yet as late as 1961 a study for a new town
in Britain was designating as a major aim the fact that the town
should stand out distinctly from the countryside ('Planning of a
New Town', 1965, 17). Modern transport networks blur former
boundaries, and the resultant 'transition zones' are characteristic of scales. Recognition of them may also indicate the change
from a cut boundary to a less easily determined gradation within a
scalar continuum. Thus Ogden's elegant deductions are matched by
a problem familiar to urban geographers:

> Where does the city end? Certainly the municipal boundary has
> little significance as denoting any sort of closure, except for
> administration and statistical space, which thus gives a false
> image because of its non-correspondence with the real world.
> (A.E. Smailes, 1971, 12)

H.G. Wells (1902) saw that this was going to happen.

> ... old 'town' and 'city' will be, in truth, terms as obsolete
> as 'mail coach.' ... We may for our present purposes call these
> coming town provinces 'urban regions.' Practically, by a pro-
> cess of confluence, the whole of Great Britain south of the
> Highlands seems destined to become such an urban region, laced
> all together not only by the railway and telegraph, but by novel
> roads such as we forecast in the former chapter, and by a dense
> network of telephones, parcels delivery tubes, and the like
> nervous and arterial connections. (pp. 61-2)

And so if the focus is shifted from the city centre, to the city
as centre, or central place, the boundary of that central place is
bound to be one that shifts under the hand. Consequently, the
academic literature also changes its stance in an attempt to keep up
with this fringe chameleon.

THE CHANGING URBAN CENTRE-RURAL PERIPHERY BOUNDARY

The urban fringe has provided a problem area for geographers, and
sociologists, and D. Thomas (1972) and R.E. Pahl (1968, 263-97)
provide overviews of the respective literature. Table 19 illustrates Ogden's deduction that even as the problem was first being
recognized as lying between two polarities, there were changes in
the ideas about the polarities because of the growth of the middle
range (suburbs and fringe). The social distinctiveness of the
fringe is now attenuated, but there remains the problem of the
relationship to pre-existing centres or to any new types of centre
that may be erected to deal with spatial difficulties. Of the six
problems concerning the fringe, recognized by Thomas (op.cit.,
84-5), five are dominantly spatial: scattered, piecemeal development; intermixture of conforming and non-conforming uses; the protection of agriculture; the protection of recreational land; and the
high cost of serving scattered settlements. The sixth problem concerning the intermixture of social groups is 'the only one of the
six which shows any signs of abating'. The fringe arises and then
gets caught up in the expanding urban pattern (J.W.R. Whitehand,
1972), remaining as fossilized strands produced by former expansion
waves - to borrow R.R. Boyce's analogue approach, which even
includes an analogue to explain the analogue (1966, 106), a doubly
diagonal approach.

TABLE 19   The rise and transmutation of the urban centre-rural
periphery boundary (the rural-urban fringe) as perceived in the
literature
(Note: There are three caveats: the list of studies is subject-
ively selective; the arrangement of the studies and the sub-
headings are of course designed to illustrate the table heading;
and the abstracts describing each study are so brief that the
studies themselves rather than the abstract of them justifies the
progression here suggested.   Sadly, the only true test of the
table's thesis is to read all the literature.)

The rural-urban fringe recognized

T.L. Smith (1937)
First use of the term, signifying the built-up area just outside
the corporate area of the city.
G.S. Wehrwein (1942)
Identified as less than the trade area and the commuting area bet-
ween well-established urban land uses and farming.
W.I. Firey (1946)
A marginal area.   'Social utility' of residential land use dimini-
shes with decreasing accessibility to the centre.   Urban fringe
located where farms and residences have equal social utility, with
residences tending to gravitate towards the lowest class status.
A. Hawley (1946)
Prefers economic explanation to concept of 'social utility'.
G.A. Wissink (1962)
Firey's theory sounded like the aftermath of depression and war and
related to a specific situation round a specific city.   [Flint,
Michigan.]

The fringe as a zone

S.W. Blizzard and W.F. Anderson (1952)
Broader definition than Firey - a zone of unsettled and marginal
conditions - an intermediate area of lower socio-economic status
between town and country.
R.A. Kurtz and J.B. Eicher (1958)
Summarizes confusion of concepts to date, including their variations
in spatial width and proposes 'the mixed rural and urban area outside the city'.

The fringe - good description, less good as a basis for raison
d'être

R. Golledge (1960)
A geographical no man's land, delineates seven features, including
'constantly changing pattern'.
G.A. Wissink (1962)
An area of mixed urban and rural land uses; characteristics somewhat
similar to those of Golledge.

Urban and rural worlds as dichotomous typologies

P. Sorokin and C.C. Zimmerman (1929)

Against the fringe as lying between social dichotomies

L. Wirth (1938)
Society not dichotomous (urban/rural), instead two poles in refer-
ence to one or other of which all human settlements tend to arrange
themselves.
L. Reissman (1964)
Sets out previous attempts at urban/non-urban dichotomies to dismiss
them.
O. Lewis (1965); P.M. Hauser (1965) [successive articles]
Also dismiss dichotomies, with a citation of other critics.
(Note 2)

The fringe as a continuum

T.L. Smith (1947), V.H. Whitney (1948), S.A. Queen and D.B. Carpenter (1953)
Supported continuum; V.H. Whitney believed that urban and rural are
points along a line drawn from the most isolated farmstead to the
mass of the megalopolis.
H. Miner (1952)
The linear continuum will evolve into a more complex and insightful
construct, and ideal types are useful as a basis for such development.
R.J. Pryor (1968)
A continuum between a growing urban centre and its rural hinterland
- fringe as residual between two more readily defined poles. States
that the fringe need not be a continuum, but see his Fig. 1.

Against the continuum

O.D. Duncan (1957)
Theory depended upon what variables were chosen to judge whether
population is urban or rural. Continuum uni-dimensional and there-
fore not totally realistic.
C.T. Stewart (1958)
Continuum rejected. Societies in transition, but difficulties of
cross-cultural comparisons.
R. Dewey (1960)
Too many heterogeneous items believed as the basis for distinguish-
ing ruralism and urbanism. Lack of consensus remarkable.
L.F. Schnore (1966)
The notion is an over-simplification. Rural-urban divergencies in
the U.S. still substantial though diminishing. Dialogue between
urban and rural sociology should be continued.
E. Reade (1968, 426)
Theory may well have the effect of limiting what we are able to see
(cf. T.S. Kuhn, 1970, 24).
R.E. Pahl (1968)

Against the continuum

A false continuity - overlapping of different meshes invalidates the
continuum.
H. Carter (1972), E. Jones (1972)
Urbanization of society much more extensive than previously thought,
and tendency towards M.M. Webber's non-place urban realm (context
mainly England and Wales, and U.S.).

Wave theory of urban expansion

H. Blumenfeld (1954)
Tidal wave of metropolitan expansion.
F.S. Chapin Jnr and S.F. Weiss (1962)
Expansion like ripples from pebbles dropped in a pool which bump
into one another, but this simple pattern becomes more complex
because affected by private and public decisions.
R.R. Boyce (1966)
Expansion sometimes channelled (e.g. transport routes), barriers
(e.g. physiographic), a series of induced waves, successive wave-
like veneers, and each wave's progress affected by what there was
before.
P. Korcelli (1972)
Although the intricacy of social phenomena cannot be matched by
those of physical phenomena, the wave analogue approach offers
certain advantages, but utmost care must be taken.

Source: I am indebted to A.W. Keir for permission to use a reading
orientation erected by him, in an unpublished M.Sc. dissertation
(1973) for the University of London, on the rural-urban fringe, but
the summaries and author-ordering in Table 19 are my responsibility.
The table can be compared with the summary provided by D. Thomas
(1972, 81-5). See also J.H. Johnson (ed.), 1974.

CENTRIFUGAL AND CENTRIPETAL TRENDS

Centrifugal trends in cities were recognized much earlier than is
generally realized. H.G. Wells (1902, 48-55) was the first to discuss twentieth-century centrifugal attractions and centripetal
forces. He used these very terms, and his essay in forecasting has
stood the test of time. The impact of the railroad had produced
the first satellite settlements, and the process was well under way
before the First World War.
    Many reasons are readily apparent for the location of these new
    industrial communities. The impulse towards cheap land, low
    taxes and elbow-room throws them out from the large centres of
    population. These are the centrifugal forces. The centripetal
    forces are equally powerful and bind them as satellites beyond
    the outer ring of the mother city.... Through switch-yards and
    belt lines, practically all the railroad facilities developed
    during years of growth, which are at the disposal of a downtown
    establishment, are at the disposal of the industry in the
    suburb. (G.R. Taylor, 1915, 1-20)

TABLE 20   Centrifugal and centripetal urban force indicators (1)

Centrifugal (Push) Force Indicators (refers to central areas of cities)

1   Increasing land values and high tax rates. (High taxes are partially due to the high cost of improving city services, e.g. drainage and sewage, and providing for access by a vast army of commuters who pay no local taxes. These tendencies are well exemplified in U.S. cities, but just beginning in parts of Britain, e.g. Glasgow. (2))
2   Traffic congestion and resultant high cost.
3   Difficulties of horizontal expansion.
4   Avoidance of nuisance complaints by industries incompatible with other city functions (e.g. the eventual removal of the paper mill on the Hull riverfront directly opposite the Canadian Federal Parliament Buildings, Ottawa).
5   Impossibility of acquiring sites near the city centre with specialized facilities (e.g. with deep water access).
6   Legal restrictions.
7   Decline of social importance of inner suburbs.
8   No general provision for the recycling of land in central areas when initial development obsolete; thus a transfer to a new site is often the easier alternative. (3)

Centrifugal (Pull) Force Indicators (refers to areas on or formerly on the periphery of central urban areas)

9   Large parcels of land available at relatively low costs (allows flow-line techniques for small firms spawned near the centre who wish to expand to achieve economies of scale). (4)
10 Circumferential or axial transport arterial development brings greater relative benefit to peripheral areas compared with central areas. (5)
11 Attractive site qualities, level, good drainage, water frontage, perhaps made available by cheaper and more effective methods of drainage and flood protection (also applies to inner areas).
12 Lower taxes.
13 Desire for a place of one's own (nostalgic frontier heritage in U.S. and Canada);(6) better for children (cleaner, more space). (7) Formerly plentiful supply of land was permissive and great value placed on freedom of individual to do what he wants (8) (cf. planning constraints in Britain via 'Town and Country Planning Act', 1947 and national green belt policy since 1955 (9)).
14 Modern equipment makes homes more independent of outside service (e.g. deep-freeze, television); (10) and factories more self-contained (e.g. grid supply, lorry fleet, cafeteria, self-service factory shop).
15 Anticipation of development at the margin may depress the value of the land for agricultural purposes, (11) and thereby make the expansion all the more likely in a free planning situation.

Centripetal Force Indicators (refers to central areas of cities)

---

1 Site attraction (prestige), and long-standing permanence of the central sites.
2 Functional convenience: (i) metropolitan - access to all parts of the city; (ii) regional - terminus of regional communications; (iii) inter-regional, where city is nodal point between two or more regions.
3 Functional magnetism (see centro-symmetric ordering, Chapter 3 above).
4 Improved ability to grade formerly 'poor' (i.e. sloping) central sites and protect other adjacent areas from flood. (12)
5 General increase of office functions (12) and all forms of quaternary industry.

---

1   The basic reference is C.C. Colby (1933).
2   W.F. Lever (1972).
3   J.R. Borchert (1967).
4   R. Vernon (1957, 309).
5   M.H. Yeates (1965, 70).
6   G.A. Wissink (1962, 296).
7   R. Dewey (1948-9).
8   G.A. Wissink (op.cit., 297) and H. Brodsky (1973, 165-6).
9   D. Thomas (1970, 88).
10 C.B. Wurster (1963, 80).
11 R. Sinclair (1967, 78).
12 E.L. Ullman (1962, 599).

A.F. Weber (1899) in his pioneer study of the growth of cities in the nineteenth century recognized the human needs involved in this push, quoting C.H. Cooley who was writing at about the same time:
   Humanity demands that men should have sunlight, fresh air, the sight of grass and trees. It demands these things for the man himself, and it demands them still more urgently for his wife and children. ... Industry says men must aggregate. Humanity says they must not, or if they must, let it be only during working hours and let the necessity not extend to their wives and children. *It is the office of the city railways to reconcile these conflicting requirements*. (op.cit., 474; italics in original)
Since then many students have recognized centrifugal and centripetal forces at work, the classic paper being that of C.C. Colby (1933); and the forces recognized are summarized in Table 20, where the analysis is for convenience only. Colby (op.cit.) is careful to point out that an important factor is the social evaluation of the advantages of the periphery against the centre - a diagonal appraisal - and that in any one migration attraction and repulsion forces are quite mixed up.

CENTRES IN THE PERIPHERY

Under such an antithetical title some important and diverse subjects

appear to nest: new towns, growth poles, and out-of-town centres
(including hypermarkets, industrial estates, and office parks).
These have in common the idea of exporting some form of centrality
into the periphery of an existing centre, or sometimes way off into
what has become to be regarded as a peripheral region. Often there
is explicit acknowledgement of dependence on the original centre as
in the expression 'satellite town'; less frequently in modern times
is the attempt to start a large-scale independent development in a
peripheral region on a greenfield site (e.g. Canberra, Brasilia).

TABLE 21   Centres in the periphery

Work-centre (1) and services to a surrounding area	Services to a surrounding area	Work-centres
new towns planned growth centres	out-of-town shopping centres hypermarkets	industrial estates office parks

1 Similar to the idea of 'zone of conflux' in J.E. Vance (1960).

The reader can relax. There is no intention of plunging into
the ample topics of new town and growth pole development. Even if
new towns were to be included, the theme of this book would con-
strain the treatment to a concentration on their centres. Each of
these tends to make manifest a version of an 'ideal arrangement' for
existing centres, current at the time of planning and construction.
Some of the latest ideas about centre lay-outs, and of what they
should consist, can be included in considering out-of-town shopping
centres. These are perhaps the latest form in the long-evolving
succession of ideas about centres traced in Chapter 2. (For convenience, a select new town bibliography is here provided: L. Rodwin,
1956; R. Llewellyn Davies, 1966; F.J. Osborn and A. Whittick, 1969;
F. Schaffer, 1970; P. Merlin, 1971; H. Evans (ed.), 1972; C.E.
Smolski, 1972; J.E.Y. Hawkes, 1973; R. Thomas and P. Cresswell,
1973; and F. Butler, 1975, esp. 40-8).
The concept of growth poles exhibits the strange fact that its
originator, F. Perroux (1950) first conceived of them not as centres
in the real world but as arising in abstract economic space defined
as a field of forces (loc.cit, 94-5) - hence growth *poles*; by 1955,
however, 'territorial agglomeration' had appeared to add its 'specific consequences' (Perroux, 101, in 1970 reprint). And so in 1958
A.O. Hirschman was able to say that 'pôle de croissance' was used
both for regional and sectoral growth leadership (p. 183, n.3).
From the outset Perroux had insisted on the exogenous nature of
centrifugal and centripetal forces engendered by growth poles in
geographical space conceived as regions or national territories, and
this theme will be elaborated in this next chapter (for bibliography
of growth poles see O.P. Mathur, 1973; and M.J. Moseley, 1973 and
1974).
The push factor of centres into peripheral regions is fairly
simple to understand. Fear of overgrowth in the main centres and
consequent imbalance stimulates attempts to 'pump up' the economic
structure of lagging regions. Referring to office centres,

J.B. Goddard (1975, 55) has usefully written of a desirable public
policy of concentrated decentralization. Concentration of
development funds in specific centres selected for growth may be
politically attractive, giving positive visual results in place of
the dispersed and slow-maturing effects of blanket investment, in,
say, infrastructure developments over wide areas (see Fig. 17). If
the proposed centres are where the government derives or hopes to
derive electoral support, the match between practical politics and
regional planning is brought closer still. On a micro-scale, the
promotion of small centres near the advancing fronts of large city
regions is held to be one answer to the ill-effects of unplanned
sprawl. Those in the 'ecological lobby' are new recruits to the
ranks of opponents of sprawl, attacked via the promotion of discrete centres near the advancing suburban growth.

OUT-OF-TOWN CENTRES

This expression is not very exact. It is an 'away from the CBD
new-type shopping centre' that is usually involved here. Causes of
the phenomenon are a rising standard of living, leading to increasing car ownership, altered shopping habits, and decreasing toler-
ance thresholds of discomfort. Thus only relatively affluent societies are in question. It has been estimated that 8,300 such
planned shopping centres were opened in the United States alone in
the period 1946-64 (H. Hoyt, 1964; p. 86 in 1971 reprint). In some
cases the 'centrality' inherent in these centres is reflected in
surrounding land values, which if added together with those around
the city's other out-of-town centres might well rival the effect of
what is hopefully only an apparent tautology - 'the central centrality of the CBD' (see M.H. Yeates's conclusions relating to Chicago,
1965, 70). Car ownership involves the feasibility of considering
round-trip journeys of ten miles or more if parking is free and many
needs can be satisfied in one multi-purpose trip. This reduces the
contrast between convenience and comparison shopping, the latter
itself being reduced by the increasing standardization of goods,
even between competing manufacturers. Altered shopping habits
include the presence of the husband alongside the wife on the major
shopping trip. The effect on the shopping centre is to increase its
size, both in respect of the car park and the size and variety of
the shopping area. Early lay-outs, as an evolution of the conventional shopping street, included a façade of shops facing the car
park, with pedestrians perhaps protected just by a canopy. Three
disadvantages of this lay-out are: (i) the shopper is not protected
from the weather; (ii) the lay-out is effectively that of a one-
sided street, a grave disadvantage in organically-grown centres
because it conflicts with 'compaction for comparison' (see Table
15); and (iii) the attraction and information of the shopping façade
is more easily apparent to the user in the car rather than when he
or she is a shopper.
    In later centres, the whole lay-out is turned inward, and this
gives two advantages: a mall, with shops on both sides, protected
from the weather. An intriguing problem is to decide where is the
'centre of the centre', or the centre of the mall. The clear answer

is to ensure that there is no clear answer; every effort must be
made to disperse any idea of a central point, or there will be a
distance decay of interest along the line of the mall to its
extremities or to the upper floor, if this is provided. This dispersal of centrality is achieved by placing department stores as
'anchors' at each end, visible along the mall, and equally available for entry via the upper floor, which is in effect a double
balcony, visible from the floor of the mall, and easily accessible
via escalators or the upper level of a car park. Extra attractions,
such as the supermarket, restaurants, can be provided at branches
along the mall's length. An associated cinema is not a good idea.
A popular film will clog the car park and make the centre less
attractive for shoppers. The basic focus is the tension of interest
along the mall subtended between the department stores. If the mall
is the 'centre of the centre', then one ought to be able to discuss
it in the same terms as the essence of organically-grown historic
city centres. So here is the appropriate passage repeated from
Chapter 2:

> the centre as a 'functioning symbol within a contrasted frame
> focussing upon it'. Any central symbol gains in power by being
> set among other city functions which are separated from it, yet
> look towards it. The symbol gains additional sway, if when
> approached it can actually be entered, so that the feeling of
> centrality recedes further into the interior.

In an artificial environment adorned with indoor plants and air-
conditioned, the shopper can forget the heat, the dust, the humid-
ity, or the raging blizzard and the unspeakable slush outside.
Instead of a battle against the elements, carrying awkward weights,
shopping becomes a more civilized activity, a welcome result of the
effort to bring a little centrality out-of-town. All this was anticipated in 1902, and if many city centres do not yet live up to this
description, the modern out-of-town centre sometimes comes near it,
as do the best of the CBD renewal projects.

> And so, though the centre will probably still remain the centre
> and 'Town,' it will be essentially a bazaar, a great gallery of
> shops and places of concourse and rendezvous, a pedestrian place,
> its pathways reinforced by lifts and moving platforms, and
> shielded from the weather, and altogether a very spacious, bril-
> liant and entertaining agglomeration. (p. 55)

H.G. Wells, of course.

The hypermarket is different from the category of centres just
described in two main respects: (i) it is smaller in total selling
area; (ii) often it is a one-store operation, offering discount
trading - in its most primitive form a 'shed in a field'. Discount
trading is a necessary attraction if the store does not offer a full
range of goods. An unfortunate social consequence is that those
able to afford cars and reach the site can shop at lower prices than
the poor and the infirm (A.J. Parker, 1975, 122-3).

Out-of-town trends may be at the expense of conventional shopping
centres or an addition to them in a situation of growth, perhaps
even contributing to general decongestion (M. Fainlicht, 1970, 23).
In the case of a city that achieves its major period of growth in
the last quarter of this century, the former out-of-town shopping
centre may find itself the new focus of the city as the original

TABLE 22   Some dimensions of shopping centres

Lijnbaan, Rotterdam, from 1953

Longest distance of mall:	320 m
Width of mall (long mall):	21 m
(short mall):	15 m

Problem (1) of width

Narrow:	to stimulate impulse shopping *across* the mall
Wide:	to accommodate fountains, mall furniture, and decorations leading to a 'pleasant place to be in' atmosphere
Compromise:	range- 6m to 26m, but tendency towards narrower end of range (see below)

Width of malls

13m - 10m	in many U.S. centres before 1969 (2)
6.7m	Place Ville-Marie, Montreal, 1962
6.3m	Place Victoria, Montreal, 1965 (a few areas only 4m wide)
14.4m	Vélizy 2 (13 km south-west of Paris), 1972 (3)

Shopping area

Average supermarket:	350 m sq.
Hypermarket:	2,300 - 6,000 m sq. (4)
Vélizy 2:	80,000 m sq.
Hypermarché Laval (opened in 1944 as first such store in North America)	24,700 m sq.

---

1   R.L. Nelson (1958), 240.
2   'Shopping for Pleasure, etc.' (1969)
3   B.A. Smith (1973)
4   A.J. Parker (1975, 122); or '...at least 2500 square metres selling area situated on one level.'   J.A. Dawson (1975, 118)

tiny CBD fails to compete.   What was formerly on the edge of town becomes more geometrically central with areal expansion, particularly if this occurs dominantly in one direction - a process that certainly occurs in a rapidly developing port (see Fig. 16).

In Britain, with tight planning controls and a well-established net of conventional shopping streets, the out-of-town centre and hypermarket have been slow to develop.   For example, the shopping policy in Leeds cannot accomodate a hypermarket in its three levels of shopping - local centres, district centres, and the city centre where nearly half the trade is carried on (A.S. Ray, 1973, 560-2). It is certainly more difficult to predict the effect of new developments on existing facilities in the close-knit British context.   The effectiveness of hypermarkets is reduced if they are not allowed to

open for long hours; otherwise, traffic congestion at peak periods
is bound to occur.   In 1972 the official British policy was that
out-of-town centres and hypermarkets should receive planning
permission only where they could be shown to have no harmful effect
in existing centres, where there was rapid growth in demand, or
where there was chronic lack of shopping provision in an area; and
at the same time the following advertisement appeared in 'The
Times', 30 March 1972:

> Tesco has 800 town-centre stores already serving pedestrian and
> public transport borne customers, but continually receives
> complaints from car-shoppers that they cannot park near enough
> to the stores where they buy their heaviest weekly purchases....

Do you have a Superstore site for Tesco?

> If you have an 8-15 acre site on the edge of a major town that
> might be suitable anywhere in Britain, Please contact:

One situation that met the 1972 British planning policy criteria was
where permission was granted for a superstore development for the
centre of Telford new town - perhaps a neat superimposition of two
types of centre upon the same location in the periphery.   In 1974
the anti-hypermarket policy was relaxed because of a hoped-for
lowering of food prices by stimulating competition.

Not all out-of-town centres are based on shops.   Industrial
estates are often sited out of town, but not too far away from suburban areas or they will be cut off from a source of labour and
their ability to 'sting' a close compact market as well as 'fan' out
to other markets via regional communications radiating from the
centre (for demonstration of the 'sting' and 'fan' idea, see
J. Bird, 1973b, 264-5, Fig. 3).   From the 1950s office parks have
been in evidence, for example Oak Brook, twenty-four km west of the
Chicago CBD, or twenty-five minutes in time (D.B. Knight and T. Ito,
1972).   We have noted the attractions of peripheral sites for
offices under certain conditions, but the chosen location should
have good circumferential access to the rest of the city, and be
near high-class residential suburbs, the major autoroutes in and
out, and the airport, which if very busy may well itself act as a
generator of office growth (see G. Manners, 1974, 96 ff;
P.W. Daniels, 1974, 1975a, and 1975b, 200-1).

FRIEDMANN'S CENTRE-PERIPHERY MODEL

Peripheral regions are consistently underestimated by innovating
entrepreneurs, just as they tend to overestimate the centrality and
consequent advantages of cities, consistent with the findings of
adaptation level theory (see pp.20, 29 above; see also P.R. Gould,
1966, 216 in 1973 reprint).   Often the manifest success of similar
operations in and around an existing centre seems to dispense with
the need for locational research; perhaps new enterprises are of
insufficient scale to launch all the necessary infrastructure works
in a peripheral location.   Industrial estates and other incentives
may be promoted by governments to meet these deficiencies.   Existing
centres may succeed on a nothing-succeeds-like-a-successful-centre
basis, but they can be parasitic on the peripheral regions

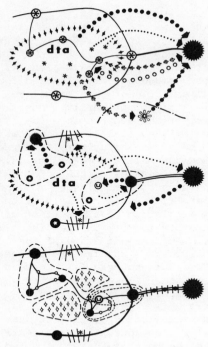

—— Transport network	Downward transitional area
●●▶ Capital	Core region
·●·▶ Foreign capital	Foreign market
····▶ Population migration	Regional sub-centres
◀◀▶ Primary products	Other urban places
○○▶ Finished products	Rural villages
	◇◇ Park reserve

FIGURE 17   Stages in the development of downwards transitional areas [lagging peripheral regions]

U = establishment of a regional university [The largest new city development in the United States at Irvine, California began when 'the Company donated 1,000 acres of land to the regents of the University of California to build a brand new campus at Irvine ...' ('Irvine - the Genesis of a New Community', 23; see a convenient summary in T.J. Ashley, 1972.)]

Note.   The core region (a gateway city, far right) is replicated by the concentration of development on small gateway centres on the borders of the dta, with asymmetrical umlands penetrating into it (cf. Fig. 18a).   For explanation of the gateway concept see pp. 115-7 ff.

Source: Redrawn from 'Regional Development Policy: a Case Study of Venezuela', p. 90, by John Friedmann by permission of the MIT Press, Cambridge, Massachusetts.   Copyright 1966 by the Massachusetts Institute of Technology and the President and Fellows of Harvard College.

(B.F. Hoselitz, 1960), from which there may be an outward migration
of people and resources to a central city with its wider opportunities for growth and propensities for innovation. All this was
clearly discussed by J. Friedmann (1966), following T.W. Schultz
(1953, 147). Schultz based his hypothesis about divergencies in
the location of economic development on the emergence of centres
which he called specific locational matrices, primarily industrial-
urban, and these were the forerunners of the centres in
J. Friedmann's centre-periphery model (1966, 11-12). This shows
how a single strong centre ought to be augmented by vital centres
close to lagging regions, which Friedmann called downward transitional areas (see Fig. 17). In the final stages of the model
there is 'a functionally interdependent system of cities' (37 and
Fig. 21.). The argument here is that Friedmann's model is valuable
because it offers a remedy based on a polarity of a kind that gave
rise to the initial problem - it attempts to work in the direction
of the pre-existing spatial rhythms. But the end stage of the
model is not the disappearance of peripheries as his text suggests
and his diagram explicitly shows (Fig. 2.1, pattern 4). Instead
there will supervene a new pattern of centres and peripheries which
for a time is more socially and economically desirable than the
old, and one that enables the country to work within the wider
world system. Here is foreshadowed a discussion of the city not
merely as a centre *in* a less central region, but also as a centre
for its region - as an ambassador to the rest of the country and
the outside world.

Chapter 6

THREE THEORY TYPES AS VARIATIONS OF CITY CENTRALITY

THE GATEWAY CONCEPT

A prime function of seaports is to act as ambassadors of their
hinterland to the outside world. They differ fundamentally therefore from the classical central place of W. Christaller, who himself recognized this basic difference at the outset of his famous
monograph when he distinguished three major types of settlement:
(i) central places whose chief function is to serve a surrounding
region; (ii) areally bound places - 'Those settlements the inhabitants of which live on their agricultural activities, which are
conditioned by the land area surrounding them...' (1933, transl. by
C.W. Baskin, 1966, 16); and, most significant for this discussion
(iii) point-bound ones - 'those settlements the inhabitants of
which make their living from resources found at specific locations
... especially harbours' (idem). Christaller immediately went on to
say that very often harbours simultaneously become central settlements, but this seems merely like an attempt to sweep them under the
carpet of central place theory. This can be done until one is confronted with the outside stimulus for the origin of the port and
the outside connection for its continued function.
        Fascinatingly enough, this fundamental difficulty arose for
Christaller, and it can be demonstrated that he ignored it, rightly
so in his context, in order to make his theory more pure. At the
beginning of his discussion of central places he quotes with appro-
val a statement by his former teacher, R. Gradmann (1916): 'The
chief profession of a town...[is]...to be center of its rural
surroundings and mediator of local commerce with the outside world'
(idem). This combines the seed of Christaller's concentration on
centrality with the second idea of the outside connection, which
henceforth can be called the gateway concept. But in the paragraph
following this Gradmann quote, Christaller writes as follows: 'we
can broaden and generalize Gradmann's statement in this manner:
The chief profession - or characteristic - of a town is to be the
center of a region' (idem). Christaller has generalized Gradmann's
statement - yes; but he certainly has not broadened it. He has now
omitted the gateway function, perhaps rightly in order to advance a
purer form of the deductive theory with which he was particularly

concerned. J. Gottmann (1974, 9-10) ascribes the preoccupation of
Christaller and Lösch with closed units of space to the 'locked in'
feeling prevalent in Germany when each was writing. In the whole
of the central place literature that followed Christaller's seminal
work, ports or gateway cities are hardly ever considered, a good
example of the blinkering effect produced by a powerful paradigm
(see p. 3 above). Sometimes ports are even treated as exceptions
or 'special cases' (e.g. W. Alonso, 1964, 86). A. Lösch, originally
writing in 1939, certainly refers to 'transport points' and 'gateway
points' as important (pp. 187-91), but ports still creep in under
'special cases' (ibid., 82-3), and the gateway concept is not
developed.

But this concept adumbrated by Gradmann has never been utterly
overshadowed. Curiously enough, in 1933, the very year in which
Christaller's central place monograph was first published, R.D.
McKenzie brought out his study of the metropolitan community in
which there are scattered references to the idea of gateway cities -
the freight-rate breaking points of the developing United States
midwest (p. 140). But although he coined a name which was far
removed from Christaller's idea, McKenzie's gateway cities do seem
to have a lot in common with central places:

the city was for the most part the child and servant of the
expanding rural settlement; it followed rather than directed
population spread. *Gateway cities* arose at entrance points
to producing regions and *functioned* as collecting centres for
the basic products from surrounding settlement and *as distribut-
ing points for manufactured goods brought in from outside
territory.* These gateway centers maintained contact with
tributary territory through a community hierarchy of villages,
towns, and cities established on the basis of railway transportation. Thus the basic pattern of modern American settlement
was formed. (4-5, italics added)

Only through the italicized words above does the idea of the gateway exterior connection really shine out. McKenzie's ideas may
have been true of the central United States gateways, but further
west: 'The towns were the spearheads of the frontier. Planted far
in advance of the line of settlement, they held the West for the
approaching population' (R.C. Wade, 1959, 1; see also B.J.L. Berry,
1967, 108-11). These are examples of gateway cities in a new world
context, but gateway locations for cities have always been important. J.C. Russell (1972, 26, 231-3, and Fig. 1) discovered that
gateway (or portal) cities were of 'unexpected importance' in
medieval Europe, 'somewhat surprising' in view of the great concentration on cities central to regions in theoretical study.

During the 1960s several theorists recognized the importance of
the outside stimulus to settlement generation and growth. The
Taafe-Morrill-Gould (1963) model of transport and settlement evolution in a developing country requires ports to play a leading role.
R. Murphey (1964) pointed out that Asian port cities were rare
before the advent of the exotic European. And in a paper on the
conception of cities, E. Smolensky and D. Ratajczak (1965) find
themselves forced to modify their Löschian landscape. 'The advantages of water-transport and proximity to the transport net outside
the region shift the larger cities from the centre of the region

to...points on the periphery' (p. 101).   In an Australian context,
A.J. Rose (1966) traced out an answer to his question:
     ...will...a pattern [of central places]...prevail if the
     central point is created at the outset? Will it occur if,
     instead of being fundamentally a response to the needs of a
     rural population, the urban centres act as a springboard from
     which the pioneer makes his attack on the wilderness...? (p. 5)
His answer is that metropolitan primacy is the normal state, and
that if his theoretical 'isolated continent' has been developed
from an overseas base, the metropolitan nodes will be the pioneer
seaports. W.R. Black (1967) experimented in generating the railway network of southern Maine from 1840. He found that the most
important hypotheses were: (1) nearness to a point at which the
network began; (2) a gravity model formulation; and (3) closeness
of route link orientation with regional orientation. In a region
with important overseas trading links, regional orientation is
channelled through relatively few coastal locations. One can then
imagine the implications for the development of nodes and routes in
the transport network of the hinterland - leading to the idea of
spatial organization based on geometrically 'excentric centres'.
The foregoing references were used as support for the arguments in
a 1970 paper which attempted to show that seaports played an important part in the development of settlement hierarchies and were not
to be regarded just as aberrant to central place theory (J. Bird,
1970).

GENESIS AND DEVELOPMENT OF GATEWAYS

The gateway concept embraces both the functions of ports and the
long-distance exchange functions of inland cities. In cases where
settlement hierarchies are generated from outside, there is the
problem of the nature of the motive power leading to settlement
generation and maintenance. Adopting an 'historico-inductive
approach' J.E. Vance (1970, 8, 101,) concentrated on trade, and in
particular upon the role of the merchant wholesaler. In the ambit
of port study, I have always believed that the correct sequence is
that trade stimulates port and shipping developments. In economic
terms the hinterlands and forelands are pacemakers for ocean
carrier developments; though in technical terms ships make demands
which ports struggle to fulfil (J. Bird, 1971, 17, 126, 194). Trade
appears to be a good fundamental motor inducing exogenous* change
in post-medieval spreads of settlement via, in Vance's vivid
phrasing, the push of abundance and the pull of scarcity (p. 5);
but we must remember that a surplus is not sufficient unless it be
institutionalized (see p. 39 above). This process is incorporated
in Vance's mercantile model, and his discussion is so interesting
that it deserves the compliment of a critical exegesis (bracketed
numbers below refer to pages in Vance, op.cit). The main theme
here will be that the Vance model takes us a long way in the right
direction but that no one model can take us far enough.

*Exogenic, exogenetic, endogenic, endogenetic are other possible
  formulations.

A focus on trade forces a focus on exogenous forces in contrast
to the dominantly endogenous mechanism within Christaller's central
place theory (5).   Indeed, Vance rejects the general applicability
of central place theory which he dubs as a 'paradigm for a special
case' (5), requiring a closed economic and geographical system (9).
Yet his mercantile model (diagram, 150) allows an endogenously-
settled landscape to have an exogenous development (e.g. western
Europe), and the reverse could happen (e.g. North America).   In any
exogenous model there must be room for two-way trade, so that
Vance's term 'unraveling point' (82) seems too inductively derived
from the role of the merchant-wholesaler in satisfying consumers,
which he can accomplish at a distance by quantity price adjustment.
The choice of the term 'unraveling point' is surprising when Vance
is obviously aware that wholesaling involves collection (ravelling)
as well as dispersal (154), and that we are concerned with the
farmer's exports as well as with his consumption (162):   in which
case ravelling/unravelling points are in question.   At a later
stage his exogenously-derived settlement pattern develops its own
commercial structure via the internalization of wholesaling (103),
i.e. the emergence of central place infilling (151, Fig. 18, bottom
left).   Vance just barely mentions (143, n.) the industrial roles
of cities as gatherers of raw materials and suppliers of manufactured products, sometimes to distant wholesalers, but sometimes via
semi-processed materials to other manufacturers.   As we shall see
shortly, the idea of agglomeration and scale economies is a deductive device for incorporating past development into current functions.   Because Vance adopts his avowed historico-inductive approach,
he obtains fine insights into the development of the United States
systems of cities (85 et seq.); but the absence of agglomeration
and scale economies robs him of the chance of explaining the permanence of the original gateways he has recognized, if not by that
name.   For example, having demonstrated that Winnipeg has become
the 'true archetype of the unraveling point' (99), he is rather at
a loss to explain its continued pre-eminence now that its umland
settlement fabric has expanded greatly and disposable income grown
on an even larger scale - bringing more and larger trading towns
into being (98; and 163, Fig. 19, bottom).   Vance is therefore
forced to conclude that the port alignment, the river alignment,
and the regional boundary site of cities (100), which are all gateway locations, will be perpetuated through historical-geographical
forces (96), tradition (159, italics), or inerta ('be perpetuated
even after the forces that made the site distinctive may have ceased
to operate', 100).
    The permanence of such settlements is chiefly due to improvements
in transport and its progressively lower relative cost, partly
brought about by the existence of the gateway settlements themselves in their successful functioning as nodes within networks.
These transport improvements not only help people to agglomerate, by
making it possible to amass resources and distribute products at a
distance, but also enable them to remain, if they wish, in the location of first settlement choice, where perhaps the projected images
of settlement history and centrality are also strongest.
    We must remember that Vance was aiming to understand wholesaling
rather than retailing, and he appears justified in believing that

the mercantile model (akin to the gateway concept) is more successful with the former's resultant spatial patterns and central place
theory with the latter's, although the 'use of either model alone
produces a simplistic abstraction' (165).

In 1971 a study by A.F. Burghardt advocated the hypothesis of
gateway cities, impelled towards that aim by a detailed study of
Winnipeg. Here is Burghardt's comment on his diagram of a mid-
continental gateway linked to a national core area (redrawn here as
Stage I of Fig. 18): 'If my diagrams were moved to the coast, then
clearly the sea routes would be the heavy lines and the "national
core area" be changed to overseas markets' (Burghardt in correspondence, 3 November 1971). Burghardt gives a valuable insight into
the sequential development of gateway cities on a pioneer frontier
and the subsequent rise of central places. As the moving frontier
crosses a region, gateway cities are spawned along its edge to serve
the pioneer area beyond and link it back to the national core area.
When the frontier has passed by, the formerly exclusively gateway
settlements become more and more equipped with central place functions serving an area more equally poised about them. Burghardt is
careful to point out that should these 'relict gateways' have particular transportational importance they will tend to maintain it.
Interestingly enough, Winnipeg was not a gateway city created by
the Canadian Pacific transcontinental railway. It had begun as a
gateway settlement at the confluence of the Red and Assiniboine
Rivers when the fur trade had a total dependence on water transport.
The railway was in fact diverted to Winnipeg, when engineering considerations alone would have caused the railway to cross the Red
River at Selkirk, twenty-five miles to the north ('Trans-Canada
Field Excursion Guide Book', 1972, Winnipeg section). It is too
easy to dub this persistence of Winnipeg from water to rail transport eras as inertia. Rather it is a fact that a gateway once
successfully established provides per se an advantage for transport
by being a population focus with basic service facilities and
possessing a psychological centrality. These advantages offset what
would appear to be 'natural' advantages ready to be projected on to
other sites.

If the settlements which opened up a country are ports, they can
indeed be hardly called 'relict gateways' if the pioneer ports have
blossomed into major cities with the modern port function there to
attest the continued gateway feature. L.S. Bourne (1974) builds on
this type of urban system evolution (pp. 153-4) to compare Australia
and Canada, providing an excellent example of diagonalism when he
superimposes one national system upon the other (Fig. 6, p. 166).

It appears that there are two kinds of gateways - pioneer gateways where there is a hinterland predominantly in one direction -
and exchange gateways where there is mature exchange of products in
two or more directions. A city may well develop from one type of
gateway into another and acquire central place functions on the way
(Fig. 18, Stage III). This appears to be so common in tropical
Africa that B.S. Hoyle (1972) has generalized the sequence in his
'Cityport' model. The key to the measurement of this change would
be the amount of manufacturing carried on in the city and its type,
together with the importance of the employment in transport
functions.

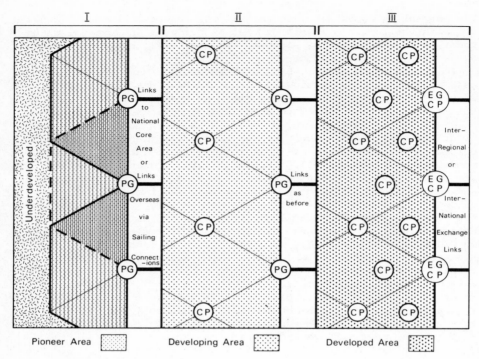

FIGURE 18   Relationships of gateways to central place in three
stages of regional development
The first stage is adapted from A.F. Burghardt (1971, loc.cit.,
Fig. 3, top). The key to places in each stage is as follows:

I PG	Pioneer gateway (inland or seaport)	Raw materials exchanged for manufactured goods; little or no manufacturing industries
II CP	Central place (grows in former pioneer service area or port hinterland)	Non-basic (i.e. non regional-exporting) service industries, and collecting and distributing node to and from PG
III EGCP	Exchange gateway and central place (develops out of former PG)	Basic industries well represented alongside other industries attracted due to agglomeration and scale economies

Cross shading (inserted only on Stage I) represents service area
(or hinterland), and areal or functional overlap. Note how service
areas tend towards a semi-hexagonal shape (see J. Bird, 1971, 125,
and 134 ff.)
Note. No account is here taken of inter-gateway (or inter-port)
competition and selective gateway success. For this see the compatible Taafe-Morrill-Gould dynamic model (1963, 304), adapted by
J. Bird (1971, 131) incorporating ideas from P.J. Rimmer (1967).
Reproduced from 'Geography', 1973, 58, 113 by permission of the
editor.

An example of the gateway concept in action is provided by one of the remedies proposed by J. Friedmann (1966, 89-98) for what he calls downward-transitional areas (*dtas*), with a rural economy either stagnant or in relative decline; *dtas* form part of the periphery, exporting more to centres than they get in return (Fig. 17a). One possible remedy is to upgrade settlements which show potential for growth on the edge of the *dta*, so that they act as gateways for growth factors into the *dta*, just as the organically-grown major core area acts as gateway for the whole territory (Fig. 17b and c, where some of the recommended concomitant financial and land resettlement measures are also shown). It might be added that D.C. North (1955) stressed the importance of the export sector as a development motor, though he was not concerned with the associated city development.

H. Carter (1972, 130-1) did propose a system of cities in which technical and organizational change and 'exogenous interpolations' are included. Moreoever, he recognized that the system in question was an open one. In his scheme, however, exogenous forces do not seem to be present at urban genesis and are allocated a minor role until such time as they pose problems for an established urban net (see also ibid., 38 ff). In other words, Carter's system is rather a set of developmental variations on the theme of the city as a central place and, significantly, appears towards the end of a chapter entitled 'Some Problems associated with Central Place Theory' (pp. 115-32). The theme stressed here is that alongside a dominantly endogenous route for city system development there is also a dominantly exogenous route (see below, Fig. 21; and the reference to C. Renfrew (1975) in Table 7, note 4, p. 32   above). From the approach of the development of regional economic structures this double viewpoint receives emphasis as the heartland/hinterland paradigm in B.J.L. Berry et al. (1976, 256-67).

AGGLOMERATION AND SCALE ECONOMIES

Industrial geographers have also found central place theory rather constraining, exemplified by G. Alexandersson (1967, 19) who noted that in the real world central places often seem to have a rather excentric location, and he too cast a wistful eye towards a hoped-for development of the gateway concept. In fact central place theory as expounded by Christaller explicitly disregarded industrialization (198 in C.W. Baskin, 1966, translator). 'Agglomeration and scale economies' is a phrase used by industrial geographers as an umbrella to cover mass production and specialization effects (for scale economies see J.S. Bain 1954); external economies, including linkages between industries which specialize; the impact of uncertainty on locational choice; reduced transport costs to favoured sites; and rural migration to urban areas: all these are interlinked (see A. Pred, 1962, 6-7; M.J. Webber, 1972, M.J. Moseley, 1974, 90 ff; and also the discussion in O.D. Duncan et al., 1960, 80-1). It may be that this very interlinkage of factors is the source of growth, in which case the expression 'agglomeration economies' is particularly apt (J.M. Gilmour, 1974, 362). E.S. Dunn (1970) also refers to central place theory as having insufficient

breadth to stand as an urban meta-theory and adds the concepts of
tree networks (transformation systems comprising linked transformation and transfer sub-processes sharing a common transformation
objective, e.g. production processes and industrial system complexes); and circuit networks-functional systems with process flows
sharing common transfer channels. As I understand it, his tree
networks might be held to subsume agglomeration and scale economies
and the circuit network idea is akin to central place theory and the
gateway concept. This would lead to urban structures being viewed
as the synthesis between phenomena in tree networks on the one hand
and circuit networks on the other (see Table 3, above).

Recently, some progress has been made with a technique for measuring the effect of agglomeration and scale economies (J. Bergsman,
P. Greenston, and R. Healy 1972). One of the major agglomeration
economies according to J. Friedmann's (1972) general theory of
polarized development is the propensity for existing centres to
undergo the cumulative effects of successive innovations in
'enclaves of accelerated change' (loc.cit., 86-7); and the wheel is
coming back to a fundamental theme, because one of Friedmann's
basic conditions for innovation is the probability of successful
bisociation (88, 2.3.2, A. Koestler, 1964, cited). The very
existence of an industry may be a 'resource' capable of generating
nearby development through agglomeration and scale economies,
leading through the process of cumulative causation ('nothing
succeeds like success') to the generation of large manufacturing
complexes (A. Pred, 1965 and 1973) and preferred transport axes
(D.G. Janelle, 1969, 353-4 steps, 6, 1-3 in his basic model of
spatial reorganization).

THREE THEORY-TYPES OF SETTLEMENT LOCATION AND FUNCTION

At this point we have arrived at the necessity for three types of
theory with regard to the generation and maintenance of settlements:
central place theory; the gateway concept; and agglomeration and
scale economies. For convenience, henceforth these will be called
the 'three theory-types'. It is possible that other major concepts
will be thought necessary to get us closer to the real world, but
there must be a cut-off in the number of theoretical ideas, or
we shall lose simplicity. It is possible to consider all settlements in the light of only one of these concepts, as is the case
with classical central place theory. But if this is carried out,
'noise' occurs with those settlements and functions that do not
'fit in'. For example, seaports and mining-based settlements can
be incorporated into central place theory only with a good deal of
discomfort. Similarly, the gateway concept is inefficient at
explaining a hierarchy of hamlets, villages, and market towns in
a highly developed agricultural area.

The best way to illustrate this argument about three theory-
types is by a triangular explanation map (Fig. 19). At the apices
of the triangle are the places or functions where each explanation
works perfectly, and the territory of the map indicates a distance
decay of explanatory ability towards the centre and the other
apices. In the central place theory sector of the 'map', that

particular 'explanation' works best for hamlets (*h*), agricultural villages (*v*) and agricultural market towns (*t*) in that order, as suggested by the practical fieldwork of M.F. Dacey, (1962). If these build up towards a regional centre with some manufacturing (*c*), we shall probably have to make use of agglomeration and scale economies equally as well as central place theory to explain the city functioning.

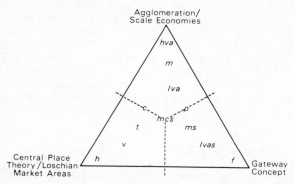

FIGURE 19   Triangular explanation map for three theory-types of settlement location and functions
See text for explanation of settlement types and their location on the map where the best fit of settlement type and theory-type is at the apices of the triangle.
Reproduced from 'Geography', 1973, 58, 114 by permission of the editor.

The gateway concept would work very well for a ferry port (*f*) and for a seaport with low value-added manufacturing, necessitating vast tonnages of raw material imports to a seaboard location (*lvas*). If secondary industries occurred, perhaps based on the primary port industries (*ms* - a manufacturing seaport), or if the seaport (*p*) had a wide range of manufacturing types, then the explanation would need to be a combination of the gateway concept and agglomeration and scale economies. These certainly apply to settlements with high value-added industries which rely so heavily on the external economies provided within the urban, industrial structure (*hva*), and this also applies but with diminishing force to those inland cities with a wide range of manufacturing types (*m*), but perhaps least well to low value-added industries exemplified by a simple processing of inland mined resources (*lva*).
    The metropolitan capital city seaport (*mcs*) might be explained only by a combination of all three theory-types; and this might be expected, because this is the most complicated type of settlement.
    The three theory-types should each be regarded as embracing a family of theories closer to each other than to those in the other theory-types. For instance, 'central place theory' includes the Christaller and Lösch formulations. In the Christaller version the order of entry requirements specified force the aggregation of functions, whereas the Lösch theory deals with functions independent of other similar enterprises,

with the most critical locational factors involving centrality
with respect to markets, transportation routes, and raw
materials. Thus, for secondary industries, the Löschian system
appears to be more appropriate than that of Christaller
[,more appropriate for tertiary activities]. (T.L. Bell,
S.R. Lieber, and G. Rushton, 1974, 214)
Putting this another way, in the ternary diagram, Fig. 19, the
Christaller version copes better with places and functions lying
in the 'north-east' of the central place segment. Bell, Lieber and
Rushton conclude that we must study a process that accommodates a
trade-off between centrality advantages and agglomeration advantages
(idem, 224). Agreed. The ternary diagram is an attempt to provide
co-ordinates in respect of which any trade-off between three theory-
types can be mapped. (For an alternative path to a hoped-for synthesis see P. Claval's (1973) review of central place theory with a
more general unitary theory hinted at on the penultimate page.)

THE THREE THEORY-TYPES AND METROPOLITAN AREAS

In 1970 R.L. Forstall and V. Jones surveyed the metropolises of the
world, and attempted a functional classification of the largest
metropolitan areas. With some preliminary comments, guarded use
can be made of this survey to see what light it throws on the relative standing of the three theory-types.
1 'As in any classification, certain decisions and allocations
   are essentially arbitrary but it is hoped that in this instance
   they are reasonably consistent' (ibid., 30).
2 The classification recognizes seven different types of function,
   and these have been 'assigned' to one of the three theory-types
   as follows:

   region serving   central place theory
   port function   gateway concept
   manufacturing
   administration
   seat of government   agglomeration/scale
   special service function   economies
   original mining base continuing as very
   important (only example Johannesburg)

3 The port function is under-represented in the Forstall-Jones
   classification, because the authors do not designate cities as
   ports (a) unless the port is within the metropolitan area (e.g.
   Manchester is not classified as a port); and (b) 'Some cities
   that are incidentally ports have not been so designated because
   the role was not felt to be of sufficiently great importance
   [e.g. all the Great Lake ports]' (idem). Nevertheless, it is
   true that as a port town grows into a metropolis, the port function becomes *relatively* of less importance compared with the
   days when it was the settlement's raison d'être. But of course
   the gateway function could be represented by the proportion that
   is basic (i.e. region-exporting), and this also is not
   considered.
4 The classification deals with the world's 100 largest metropolitan areas as they were in 1964. Because these are the very

largest cities, it is not surprising that every one of them has a
central place function as 'the commercial focus and chief manufacturing and service center of a region (greater or smaller)...'
(ibid., 29).

Summarizing these points, it must be remembered that this is a
subjective classification, so the tendency must be to look at
broad indications of resultant figures rather than absolute
results; the gateway function, represented by ports, is certainly
explicitly underweighted, and also because the 'region exporting'
role of cities is not accounted for; and, last, since this is the
top rank of the settlement hierarchy, it would be unthinkable if
such great masses of population did not have considerable effect on
the local region. 'Among cities of less than 1,000,000, some
undoubtedly have so little regional significance, that they would
be classed as wholly manufacturing, port, or mining cities or the
like' (ibid., 30). Fig. 20 shows the results of this imperfect
exercise. '...every one of the 100 cities has been recognized as
having...regional importance...' (idem). Hence the score of 100 in
the 'central place' sector of the triangle. Secondly, 95 of the
cities had some other function (see 2 above) due to agglomeration
effects, most commonly in manufacturing. If this could have been
shown to be regional-exporting manufacturing, as most of it probably
is, this could have been held to be a gateway function; but in the
absence of input-output statistics for world metropolitan areas, it
is difficult to recognize the gateway function of inland manufacturing cities. Even so, and perhaps surprisingly, 44 of the leading
metropolises of the world have significant seaports within their
boundaries, surely justifying the statement that seaports are not
aberrant cases in settlement study (J. Bird, 1970). Thirty-nine of
the 100 leading metropolitan areas in 1964 had all three functions:
central place, some form of agglomerative effect, and a seaport gateway. This justifies the position of *mcs* (metropolitan capital seaport) on Fig. 19, at the geometric centre.

The datum year for the Forstall-Jones classification is 1964, but
the passé date of the survey may involve more than the mere passing
of years and the fact that the cities will have grown absolutely,
and in many cases relatively, compared with other settlements in
their nation states. Perhaps the mid-1960s may have been the latest
date for an attempt at such a comparative survey. Classical central
place theory and the gateway concept depended on links between the
city and a separate type of non-city realm. The distinctions between these two types have become blurred into the conception of city
regions. Agglomeration and scale economies rely heavily on the
advantages of concentration and specialization that the city region
can promote. But they also require for their effect either central
locations or very large units drawing their workers from a wide
catchment area. Centralization and urban mobility to central areas
become more difficult as cities grow to enormous size. New systems
within the city grow up which do not need the historic centre for
their day-to-day functioning. As mentioned above, central place
theory has been extended to deal with this hierarchy of centres
within an urban area. There is thus a hierarchy, leading to a
'central centre', a 'downtown', a 'CBD', which have in the largest
cities not one centre but several functional centres crystallized

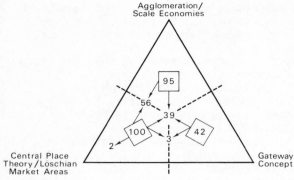

FIGURE 20 Simplified classification of the functions of the
world's 100 largest metropolitan areas, 1964
The totals boxed in each sector of the triangular explanation map
(cf. Fig. 19) represent numbers of the world's metropolitan areas
and are built up from numbers in the direction of relevant arrows.
These unboxed numbers represent combinations with one of the other
two three theory-types, or, in the case of the figure 39, of all
three theory-types. The figure 2 in the central place theory sector
represents two cities in the Forstall-Jones classification which
were assigned a region-serving function and nothing else: Edmonton
and Nanking. Curiously enough, A.F. Burghardt, 1970, loc.cit.,
276 specifically mentions Edmonton as having maintained its gateway status - another indication that the Forstall-Jones classification underscores the gateway function of inland cities.
Source: Based on data in R.L. Forstall and V. Jones, 1970, loc.cit.
Reproduced from 'Geography', 1973, 58, 116 by permission of the
editor.

out in that process of centro-symmetric ordering. The ultimate is
the street of one specialized function; but the Tin Pan Alleys,
Savile Rows, and Wall Streets, occur only in the largest cities of
the world, where centro-symmetric ordering may extend over wide
areas.
   At first sight it seems likely that the gateway concept, concerned as it is with inter-regional exchange, would not have much
to contribute to the internal pattern of city regions. Yet one
could observe that the explosive growth of cities into city regions
is only possible where transport improvements permit massive inter-
regional and international exchanges. Second, D.G. Janelle, (1968,
Fig. 3) has demonstrated how transport improvements cause the significance of distance to decline more rapidly for longer journeys
(loc.cit., 9). He thus expects that the declining significance of
intervening space to impinge more significantly on those relatively
long distances between the largest centres than on the 'closer-
together' smaller places in a 'nothing-succeeds-like-success'
syndrome. Within the city region linear accessibility along lines
of transport towards nodes is often easier than pan-directional
movement (which obtained for instance in the walking/horse transport
era up to about 1890 in the western city J.S. Adams, 1970; see also
Table 11, above). Linear accessibility to a node begins to look

like the gateway concept on the intra-regional scale. Indeed,
inhabitants of city regions have been shown to have a rather sectoral view of one part of the city, a wedge narrowing in width from
the residential area towards the downtown area with which all citizens are familiar (J.S. Adams, 1969, esp. Fig. 3 and 323; D. Mercer,
1971, esp. 141; and W.A.V. Clark, 1972).

The ternary diagram (Fig. 18) has been subjected to critical
comment, notably by D.R. Ingram (1974, in correspondence). Two
points have been made: first, the top section of the 'explanatory
map' does not build up settlements towards the metropolitan middle
as do the central place and gateway sectors. My reply to this
point is as follows. Whereas, on the one hand, central place theory
and the gateway concept are concerned with functional types of
settlement recognized in everyday language such as hamlet, village,
port transhipment, point, on the other hand, agglomeration and scale
economies refer to the enlargement, elaboration, and specialization
of functions already implanted by other means.

The second point of criticism is that the diagram is qualitative;
the data from Forstall and Jones is really only a justification of
the central part of the explanatory map. This criticism is well
founded, and it is to be hoped that someone will devise a method of
providing a quantitative illustration. The following is merely a
suggestion. Let a region with a well-developed settlement hierarchy
be in question. Take data referring to the largest settlement, e.g.
employment figures. Assign categories of these figures to 'central
place' (e.g. retailing, services), 'gateway concept' (e.g. wholesaling, transport, and transport-oriented industry) 'agglomeration
and scale economies' (e.g. high value-added industries, sub-assembly
type manufacturing, quaternary office employment). (This type of
procedure, not the one detailed above, was first carried out by D.R.
Ingram in respect of Ontario cities in 1974.) Whatever figures
result under these three heads, make them equal by weighting factors, so that the major city is in balance at the centre of the
diagram. Apply the same weighting factors to the same data for the
other smaller settlements in the hierarchy, and having found the
relative strength of the three theory types, plot the settlement on
the explanation map. It would be interesting to see if the settlements fall on or near the two types of path indicated on Fig. 21.

It is important to realize that the above procedure, which may be
called the combinatorial method, involves at least two assumptions,
but then so does central place theory and the gateway concept, if
used alone.

combinatorial method:	1	assumes largest settlement is in balance;
	2	assumes one can find the best data mix by correct assignment of data to one of three types and by weighting factors (the available data may never be detailed enough):
central place theory:	1	assumes that the system is closed - outside influences not only ignored but actually wrongly included as part of the closed system:

2   assumes that service function of
    settlements can be correctly
    measured by available data e.g.
    number of employees, sales, floor
    space, etc.

gateway concept:

1   assumes that a boundary can be
    drawn between endogenous and
    exogenous spatial links, but the
    balance between the two depends
    upon where that boundary is drawn:

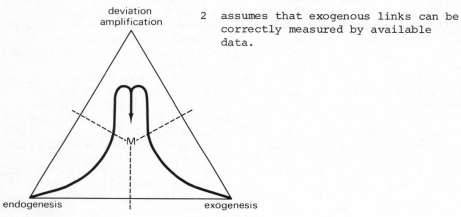

2   assumes that exogenous links can be
    correctly measured by available
    data.

FIGURE 21   From centre genesis to major metropolitan area
The solid lines show two possible routes to metropolitan size (M).
The endogenous route is from a beginning based on local regional
resources, helped along the way by the region's links with other
parts of the world (indicated by the curve to the right), with
agglomeration and scale economies (deviation-amplification - the
deviation is a centre in an area previously without centres)
becoming more important in the later stages. But as size increases
so greater impact is made on long-distance transport links, and at
metropolitan size the three families of influencing factors may be
said to be in balance. The route from endogenesis follows a mirror
image path in the diagram. Here the curve to the left represents
the change from pioneer gateways to exchange gateways with central
place functions (see Fig. 18) before agglomeration and scale
economies set in. The reason why the lines return upon themselves
towards the centre is the fact that large centres have further
impacts on their umlands and trading links simply because they are
there as mass markets and suppliers. Endogenetic and exogenetic
cities should be compared with, respectively, orthogenetic and
heterogenetic cities in the classification of R. Redfield and M.B.
Singer (1954, 59), see p. 41 above.

Assumptions like the above must be made if we are ever to contem-
plate the quantified study of that quivering mass we call the city,
where every functional development causes repercussions on other
functions within the city, on its region, and even on distant

regions with which it is connected and which affect the city in their turn. Of course, we can proceed a long way with statistical techniques if the city is treated as a system of disorganized complexity (see p. 23-4). But this is another assumption, because cities are organized, in toto, and in their component sub-systems.

METROPOLITAN DEVELOPMENT AND VARIATIONS UPON A THEME

Central place theory has little to say about the functioning (other than retail) of built-up city areas, and does not deal with regions as systems open-endedly connected to other regional systems in the world economy. Fortunately, the explanatory powers of agglomeration economies and the gateway concept are particularly strong in these two areas respectively. Only in combination do the theory-types provide a sufficient framework for understanding total centrality in a scheme like this (see frontispiece):

		explanation via theory-type of...
total centrality	endogenous centrality	central place theory
	in situ or internal centrality	agglomeration and scale economies
	exogenous centrality	gateway concept

Occasionally, one can cite cities that have followed one developmental route on Fig. 21 rather than another: perhaps Madrid, Milan, and Moscow have followed a dominantly endogenous path, whereas Sydney and Vancouver had exogenous beginnings. Generally, there is some more complicated form of route combination than is shown in the alternatives of the diagram. The routes should be regarded as describing types of city development: each vital stage in the growth of an individual city has to be validated by some form of proclaimed impulse (see pp. 36-7).

Several students have noticed the tendency for the end product of these processes to be aligned in some way. This is especially true where development is channelled along river axes, but corridors also develop where there are no morphological barriers (see P. Pottier, 1963; and C.F.J. Whebell, 1969). The Rhine, Rhône, and lower Seine are obvious river-based examples (see R. Brunet, 1973, esp. Fig. 1). Axial development between independently developed centres has been recognized, for example between London and Liverpool-Manchester (E.G.R. Taylor, 1938, 23, 24, Fig. 6), and between Toronto and Stratford, Ontario (L. Russwurm, 1970), a concept now expanded to embrace the axis between Quebec city and Windsor, Ontario (M.H. Yeates, forthcoming). Such axes consist of nodes separated by less central areas (see recommended type of development for these in I.R.W. Miller, 1972, 103); all function together by means of express forms of communication. Central place theory can contribute to an understanding of the emergence of the league table leaders, represented by the nodes within the axis, the development of which allows agglomeration and scale economies to be canalised across a wider area. The gateway concept has much to contribute to the under-

standing of how the axial nodes relate to less central areas within
the national territory and to international trade patterns.

Geographical studies of the city and the evolving city studied
may be brought closer together. Central place theory, agglomeration and scale economies, and the gateway concept have been put
forward as generic names for families of deductive schemes or theory
types. All three depend on the idea of a 'centre', either as 'area
serving', or as an 'agglomeration', or as a 'gateway for inter-
regional exchange'. Until this century the evolving city just grew,
and somehow geographers and others, including its inhabitants, just
had to make some sense of its growth. Today there are few of the
world's metropolitan regions that are not being consciously planned.
Even socialist and free enterprise societies may be alike in this.
A student of Warsaw, A.H. Dawson (1971), suggests that any differences in the future reaction to similar developmental problems may
be due to a different mix in the determining variables rather than
having different variables altogether (p. 112).

In urban planning, systems of centres and sub-centres and lines
of accessibility are needed, not only so that the city region will
function more efficiently, but so that the mind of the individual
human inhabitant can comprehend that part of the city machine which
he needs to use at any one time. The idea of 'centrality' may be a
basic psychological human need in this connection - a diagonal image
connoting not only the centre itself but at the same time embracing
the idea of accessibility to the area served. If this idea is so
basic, it would help to explain the power of the three theory-
types if it is realized that they are but variations on an immanent
theme of city centrality.

Chapter 7

CENTRALITY, PERCEPTION, AND THE FUTURE

This study has attempted to demonstrate the relationship between centrality and cities in several dimensions: (1) the genesis of centres; (2) the idea of the city; (3) the central area of the city; (4) the city as a central place; (5) the city as a gateway; (6) the city as an agglomeration. Attempts to measure the central area have been described in Chapter 4, and measurement of the city as a gateway can be approached via transport data. Measurements of the city as an idea, as a central place, and as an agglomeration, likely to undergo further development simply because it is there, are more difficult.

ATTEMPTS TO MEASURE ASPECTS OF CENTRALITY

One of the first attempts to measure centrality was that of W. Christaller (in translation by C.W. Baskin, 1966, 18).

centrality (surplus, or relative, importance) = $B - B_2$

where B = aggregate importance or absolute importance

B_2 = town's population

R.E. Preston (1971b) refines this to:

$C = N - L$

where C = centrality of a place

N = nodality

L = local consumption of central goods and services by functions in central place

Here nodality is distinguished from centrality in that N consists of the importance of a place plus its services to a complementary region, Christaller's absolute importance. Christaller used the proportional number of telephone subscribers as data to fuel his equation, but with the more widespread use of the telephone in the western world, other data must now be used. Preston's formula is activated by sales data and is designed to isolate the influence

of the region served; 'instead the fraction of nodality attribu-
table to non-residents is established specifically for each
settlement' (loc.cit., 303):

C = R + S - a MF

R = total sales in retail establishments

S = total sales in service establishments

a = average percentage of median family income spent
    on retail items and selected services by families
    in a central place

M = median family income for a central place

F = total number of families in a central place

(for another index, of retail centrality, see G. Curdes, 1967,
based on a combination of four ratios: shops per inhabitant,
employees per inhabitant, sales per inhabitant, and sales per
employee).

R.L. Davies (1973, 142 ff) compares various indices of service
centrality in the same area, even providing a table of rank correlation coefficients, and concludes that no single index was particularly superior to all others.

There are some indices of centrality which are based on the
positive deviation from an average in a data universe, e.g.:

$$\frac{\text{employment in wholesale trade}}{\text{employment in wholesale and retail trade}} \times 100 = 18.8\% \text{ (U.S.1950)}$$

The index of centrality is then scored above the base datum of
18.8 (W.R. Siddall, 1961). The use of the same word 'centrality'
for the different functions of services to a contiguous area on the
one hand and the wider ramifications of wholesaling on the other
suggests that these approaches ought to be labelled as measuring
some qualified form of centrality.

There are, indeed, even other types of centrality. For example,
J. Campbell (1972) has used an 'Index of Relative Centrality'
derived from graph theory in order to assess the functional centrality of industries based on input-output data (formula and explanation, p. 84). Another 'centrality' formula based on graph theory
referring to road connectivity will be found in W.R. Stanley (1970,
545-6) where the relative centrality of a town is an expression of
its 'centralness' to the entire road network. If a route network
is converted into nodes and edges (straight paths between nodes)
then a König number (developed by D. König in 1936) may be calculated as an index of centrality for each node; the König number is
given by the maximum number of edges to any other node via the
shortest available path. The lower the König number for each node,
the greater the degree of centrality (see P. Davis, 1974, 44).

The Murphy-Vance delimitation of the CBD (see above pp. 81
ff) and the Venekamp-Kruijt index of retail centrality (see above,
p. 84) are attempts to measure internal centrality, as is the
rate index of D.T. Herbert (1961), where gross rateable values are
divided by units of ground floor space - the higher the values, the
more 'central' the establishment within the core. At this point it

might be useful to summarize the attempts to measure centrality so
far mentioned in order to sort out some confusion in nomenclature.

TABLE 23 Aspects of centrality

| Author (1) | Nomenclature | |
	Previous suggestions	Suggestions here
Christaller	nodality-absolute importance	endogenous centrality
Christaller, Preston, and Davies	centrality-relative importance	relative retailing and service centrality (2)
Siddall	centrality	relative wholesaling centrality
Campbell	relative centrality	relative industrial functional centrality
Stanley (and König number)	relative centrality	relative route centrality
Murphy-Vance	CBD, PLVI (peak land value intersection)	CBD, PLVI ⎫ aspects of internal centrality
Herbert	rate index	rate index ⎭
		exogenous centrality (importance of all links, not just those with contiguous umland); imagined, or subjective, total centrality (3)

1 Authors cited in text above, Davies excepted, see below.
2 These are aspects of endogenous centrality as in the equation:
   total centrality = endogenous centrality + internal centrality +
                      exogenous centrality
   (While it is conceivable that one index could cover endogenous
   and exogenous centrality, internal centrality appears to be in
   another dimension.)
3 A second equation: total centrality - imagined total centrality
   = cognitive dissonance.
Note. A method of distinguishing internal from endogeneous 'relative-
commercial centrality' (sic) is offered by J.-B. Racine (1973). And
recent Japanese experience calls for a multi-dimensional view of
centrality (Y. Watanabe, 1975, 184).

W.K.D. Davies (1967) wished to find an index that was objective,
testable, comparable in any area, and incorporate all the central
functions of a place (idem, 61; and 1966, 51). Not surprisingly, he
derived a measurement of centrality values from the family of location coefficients used in industrial geography. Three steps are
required:

1 location coefficient: $C = \dfrac{t}{T} \cdot 100$

   where C = location coefficient of function t,
         t = one outlet of function
         T = total outlets of function t in whole system
2 centrality value: this is obtained by multiplying the relevant
   location coefficients by the number of outlets of each functional
   type present in the settlement in question.
3 functional index: this is derived by adding the centrality
   values in any one settlement.
The data used were confined to retail and service functions (explicitly, idem, 78, n.4), and because the technique has to assume that
the system under study is a closed one, the gateway function of
settlements cannot be considered.

The agglomeration aspect of internal centrality is measured by
J. Bergsman, P. Greenston, and R. Healy (1972) via the correlation
coefficient between the number of people employed in two activities.
Factor analysis is necessary as is some correction because of the
skewed nature of the data: 'a few large cities have a large share
of the total employment in several industries' (idem, 266). Of
course, one must not forget that the regional multiplier (change in
total employment divided by change in basic employment), the
economic base, and their various sophisticated derivatives could
also be said to measure aspects of agglomeration and scale economies of centres (for a discussion of these concepts with particular
reference to seaport cities, see J. Bird, 1971, 84, 200-1, 211).

The dream of a total centrality index, objective, testable, and
comparable may be in vain. It would have to include the power of
the central pull of a large city - in short its attractiveness.
There is a qualitative approach which does attempt to score the
relative central attraction of great cities. J. Burchard (1971)
produced an urban amenity score sheet. This consisted of '24 things
generally of the high culture' (loc.cit., 496-8); and cities can be
scored 1 if they possess the quality, and $\frac{1}{2}$ if there is room for
doubt. The reader can look up the scoring to see if he agrees
(Burchard's leading cities are Paris $20\frac{1}{2}$, Rome 20, London and New
York, 19); and comparison of personal scores makes quite a good
party game. It is perhaps more instructive to take Burchard's
'things' and score *them* as to whether they derive from either (1)
non man-made attributes; or (2) continuance of successful (i.e.
still functioning) emanations from the past; or (3) attributes
solely due to the activities of the current citizens. Bear in mind
that this is subjectivity compounded: the list of amenities is
subjective and the assignment to one of the three categories is
also subjective.

Even allowing for all the subjectivity, the results are rather
striking. So let us throw qualitative caution to the winds and
interpret Table 24 as if the data had been objectively collected.
Only one-eighth of the attractions of a large city are non man-made,
and less than half are the results of the direct creation of the
current inhabitants as opposed to the successful maintenance of
what is there already. This would suggest that centrality depends
upon a spatial dimension combined with a temporal dimension; a truly
great central city is what it is combined with what has been for a
long time.

TABLE 24   An urban amenity score sheet itself scored

Burchard's amenity or 'thing generally of the high culture'	1 Non man-made attribute	2 Successful emanation from the past	3 Attributes solely due to activities of current inhabitants
1 Fine river, lake, etc.	½*		½*
2 Great park(s)		½**	½**
3 Distinguished buildings		1	
4 Distinguished museum(s)		1	
5 Readable plan		1	
6 Great university		½	½
7 Diverse neighbourhoods		1	
8 Great eating			1
9 Fine music			1
10 General boscage		1	
11 Glamorous site	1		
12 Great sports			1
13 Great avenue(s)		1	
14 Fine squares		1	
15 Important visible past		1	
16 Good air	½***		½***
17 Fine libraries		1	
18 Exciting shop windows			1
19 Generally pleasant climate	1		
20 Fountains		1	
21 Theatre			1
22 Art in the streets			1
23 Private galleries			1
24 Many opportunities for participatory recreation			1
	3	11	10

*Division because rivers and lakes need to be successfully
embanked and 'waterscaped' and maintained via pollution control.
**Division because, as every park superintendent and gardener
knows, the secret of a successful park or garden is constant
maintenance of past plantings and replacement where necessary.
***Division because depends on clear air measures.
Source (for amenities): J. Burchard (loc.cit.)
Note. Burchard's scheme is an international metropolitan version
of subjective indices for shopping centres where each shop is perhaps scored 1, variety stores weighted as 2, and department stores,
3 (e.g. in the 'Haydock shopping model', see 'Urban Models in
Shopping Studies', 1970, 38). Another 'centrality index' where 'the
number of non-food shops was weighted by a score derived from the
presence of three particular types of trader' is given in D. Thorpe
and T.C. Rhodes (1966, 56)

THE CENTRE AS A PROJECTED ORIENTATION

Perception studies in geography have mushroomed. In a flush of
growth between 1968 and 1972 no less than eleven 'overviews'
appeared (D.J. Walmsley and R.A. Day, 1972, 11, 40). If the
bibliography is sectionalized such that 'urban perception' is a
separate category, then K. Lynch's (1960) 'The Image of the City'
is seen as a seminal inter-disciplinary work (e.g. J. Kameron, 1973,
162; see R.M. Downs and D. Stea, 1973, 84-5 for a tabular summary
by R.W. Kates of Lynch-inspired studies). B. Goodey (1971, 23)
picks out the following as a key phrase from an earlier essay by
Lynch and L. Rodwin (1958, 201): 'A systematic consideration of the
interrelations between urban forms and human objectives would seem
to lie at the theoretical heart of city planning work.' As far as
the city centre is concerned, these interrelationships are through
a projection of human objectives on to urban form. If the image of
the centre is affected by feedback from the observation of structures inherited from the past, nevertheless the new information is
still filed according to a centre-periphery programme. Lynch's
classification of five types of elements of images in urban perception are highly significant for the student of the centre, with his
centre-periphery programme:
  paths   -   can lead to or from a centre;
  edges   -   the recognition of the edge of an area deemed
                central;
  districts -   a central district, or an area with a centre;
  nodes   -   centrality with regard to routes;
  landmarks -   every city centre must have its quota of these
  The idea of the interrelationship between man and environment
seems so obvious that it is not easy to insist on the dominance of
the concept over the observation. This is certainly the conclusion
of D. Lowenthal and M. Riel (1972, 45):
    Judgements about places may be based rather on specific or
    experiential preconceptions than on objective observations
    and comparisons. This is not a new discovery but our data
    indicate that the effect is far greater than is commonly
    realised.
One recalls T.R. Lee's (1968) concept of a socio-spatial schema
with reference to his work on urban neighbourhoods in Cambridge
(see p.22).   Ideas about neighbourhood may be projected on to
the proximate urban environment. Emile Durkheim was on the track
of this idea in 1915:
    ... a society is not made up merely of the mass of individuals
    who compose it, the ground they occupy, the things which they
    use and the movements which they perform but above all is the
    idea which it forms of itself. (p. 422)
    This is not to say that 'seeing is believing' has been replaced
by 'believing in a centre is seeing a centre', nor that behaviour
takes place in a centres-peripheries environment, but rather that
environment is an integral part of behaviour (H.M. Proshansky,
W.H. Ittelson, and L.G. Rivlin, 1970, 102, 278). If satisficing
man has replaced economic man, L. Curry (1966, 49) went further and
developed satisficing man into summation man who makes decisions
randomly within the matrix of decisions made by a group. In this

context it is suggested that one matrix is that of diagonalism
with its inbuilt propensity for centres. Centres of cities do
not channel our thoughts into a diagonalism between centres and
peripheries, but our ideas about centres channels us into thinking
about city scenes in this way. City centres, even if rarely
visited, are nevertheless 'there' as psychological points of
reference (R. Neyret, 1970, 39). We also are aware that the city
is more than what we see and enshrines values that we need.
J. Hudnut (1949, 160) argued somewhat along these lines.

> Beneath the visible city laid out in patterns of streets and
> houses there lies an invisible city laid out in patterns of
> idea and behaviour which channels the citizen with silent
> persistent pressures and, beneath the confusion, noise, and
> struggle of the material and visible city, makes itself known
> and reconciles us to all of these.

This subconscious pull of an invisible city may explain the power
of the self-conscious pull on the city dweller towards the contrast
of a visible rurality and a wildscape.

The discussion of centres as projected orientations is one facet
of the links between different psychological schools and various
planning philosophies; Table 25 and its glossary are offered as a
comment upon such links.

The citizen's idea of the location where he feels he enters the
core area of a city was termed by W.F. Heinemeyer (1967, 87) 'gate-
consciousness'. He provides evidence that the distance of the gate
from the core centre is positively correlated with the distance
between the respondent's home and the core (95). Perhaps the older
residents nearer the core have a lesser appreciation of the city's
growth to its current size than the newer residents further out.
We also have evidence that the mental images of suburbanites in
large cities are wedge-shaped, narrowing towards the centre (J.S.
Adams, 1969, esp. Fig. 3 and 323; and D. Mercer, 1971, esp. 141
and W.A.V. Clark, 1972; see Fig. 23). The shape of the wedge might
tend to pull the location of the gate towards the wider section.

H.-J. Klein (1967, 306) believes that the locational relationship between the residential quarter and the town centre is perhaps
decisive in structuring the image of the latter. He produced a
telling diagram (redrawn as Fig. 22) in which were contrasted the
extents of the linear centre of Karlsruhe (the east-west Kaiserstrasse) in the answers of respondents living in eastern and western districts of the city. Notice also that while the measured
centre of the city has shifted from C1 to C2, the average focus of
the images will be at C3, if total city area growth is to the west.
This leads Klein to believe that eventually the facts (i.e. retail
location) will respond to the image ('wishful thinking') of the
inhabitants.

At this point it is quite reasonable to object that amid all
this concentration on the city centre, and the city as centre,
there must be some city-dwellers who hate the whole idea of the
central buzz. They appear as 'abstainers' in the classification
by W.F. Heinemeyer (loc.cit.) A key word in Table 26 is 'when'
under 'enjoyers'. The fact is that no modern city centre could
survive if all those who wanted to frequent it did so at the same
time. The 'enjoyers' of an urban core could not enjoy it all the

TABLE 25   Perception and planning

System	Relation between concept and percept	Planning philosophy	Example(s) (see Glossary)
I*	'seeing is believing'	in extreme form - laissez faire; disjointed incrementalism; adaptive approach; problem-oriented (towards Dionysian end of continuum, see Table 4)	cities of heterogenetic change, 'natural' cities
II*	'believing is seeing'	in extreme form - master plan; normative planning; unitary planning; goal-oriented (towards Apollonian end of continuum, see Table 4)	cities of orthogenetic change, 'artificial' cities, 'trees'
III	two-way relationship between phenomenal and behavioural environments (continuous diagonalism)	structure plan with opportunity for continuous positive feedback	many structure plans believed to be of this type, but impractical
IV	belief/observation/positive feedback/perhaps modified belief/observation/positive feedback-etc. (successive diagonalisms)	structure plan with opportunity for continual positive feedback (Popperian philosophy, see p. 9)	plans containing 'seeds of fulfilment', 'semi-lattices', *sprezzatura, sfumato*

*For problem-oriented/goal-oriented types of System I and System II considered as a dichotomy, with planners more inclined to the former and architects to the latter see C. Alexander, 1969. That this dichotomy is real see J. Friedmann (1966, 255-6); and B. Needham (1971) pro problem-oriented approach, who is countered by R. Gutch (1973, 1-10, esp. 4-6). pro goal-oriented in a system like that of IV below. See also the discussion in A. Faludi (1972), pro goal-oriented in a system like that of IV below. See also the discussion in A. Faludi (1973, 1-10, esp. 4-6).

In Britain one can trace the move away from comprehensive development planning towards a problem-oriented approach in spatial planning, although the planning process itself has been caught up in the comprehensive administrative idea of corporate management (T. Gregory, 1973; P. Hall, 1974, 269 ff; G.E. Cherry, 1974, 2-4; and W. Solesbury, 1975, esp. 248-9). In the specialized area of city centre redevelopment, I. Alexander (1974, 70) advocates a combinatorial approach, including piecemeal private sector action and comprehensive control by the public sector. This table, without examples and glossary first appeared in J. Bird (1975).

Glossary for Table 25

disjointed incrementalism: For a comparison between this form of
problem-oriented planning compared with goal-oriented planning see
R. Gutch (1972).
adaptive and unitary approaches: The adaptive* approach 'focuses
on process....Planning...would seek to influence various of the
development forces at work rather than aiming for a future metropolitan form as a goal' (D.L. Foley, 1964, 57).   The unitary
approach - 'In short, a future spatial pattern is proposed as a
goal.   The traditional means for communicating this future goal is
the general plan, comprehensive plan, or master plan' (Ibid.).
cities of heterogenetic and orthogenetic change: In the classification of R. Redfield and M.B. Singer (1954; see p.   41, above).
'natural' and 'artificial' cities: see C. Alexander (1966).
'trees':   Hierarchies, with no overlaps (as in many 'artificial'
cities):   'A collection of sets forms a tree if, and only if, for
any two sets that belong to the collection, either one is wholly
contained in the other, or else they are wholly disjoint' (C.
Alexander, 1966, 206).   This is a restricted form of semi-lattice.
'semi-lattice';   Hierarchies with overlaps (as in 'natural'
cities):   'A collection of sets forms a semi-lattice if, and only
if, when two overlapping sets belong to the collection, then the set
of elements common to both also belongs to the collection (idem).
structure plan: The 'South Hampshire Plan' (1972) had a more
ambitious programme of public participation and feedback than any
other previous planning exercise.   The plan turned out to be based
mainly on long-term public expenditure planning (P. Self, 1972),
and the opportunity for further feedback at later stages is not
clear.   This type of planning process is one advocated by R.G.
Studer (1971, 327-8).
positive feedback: The degree to which a belief or orientation is
subject to positive feedback is dependent, among other things, on
age, sex, type of personality (incl. native or nonnative, see
Table 5), perhaps revealed by the pattern score on the Allport-
Vernon Test of Dominant Values (see below).
'seeds of fulfilment':   Quoted by F. Jutheim (1963, 110); the
phrase appears to originate with M. Hoppenfeld (1962).   I take the
phrase to have two associated meanings: (1) a plan with the seeds
of fulfilment is an open-ended plan, which adumbrates rather than
determines the later stages; (2) the seeds sown by the artist and
designer are fulfilled only when observers and users themselves
find fulfilment in 're-creating' the design (see also below, pp.
145-8).
sfumato: Invented by Leonardo da Vinci.   A deliberately blurred
image or veiled form cuts down the information on a canvas and
thereby stimulates the process of projection (based on E.H.
Gombrich, 1960, 194-5).
sprezzatura: This is where the possibility occurs of projecting

*Foley's adaptive/unitary dichotomy should not be confused with the
 adaptive/adoptive dichotomy, where adaptive signifies active decision-making as opposed to being passively 'adopted' by the
 environment (see references above, Table 3, note 24).

Glossary for Table 25 continued

one's own imagination into the brushstrokes of a picture in order
to reproduce a pattern (idem, 194-5).

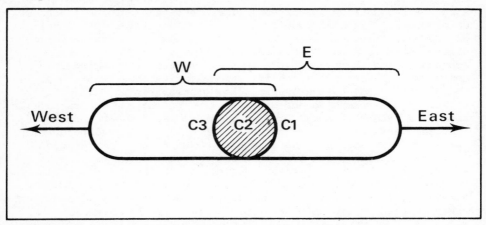

FIGURE 22 Centres and perception of centres in Karlsruhe
The diagram refers to the east-west linear centre along the
Kaiserstrasse. C1, the earlier city centre; C2, the present city
centre; with the diagonally ruled circle as the image of the city
for inhabitants living in all parts of the city (1118 interviews);
C3, the average imagined centre given a dominant westward growth
of the whole city; W, range of city image for people living in
western quarters; E, range of city image for people living in
eastern quarters.
Source: H.-J. Klein (1967, 304).

TABLE 26 Urban core-mindedness

		urban core-mindedness	
		high scores	low scores
urban ⎫ core use ⎭	high scores	enjoyers	users
	low scores	sympathizers	abstainers

enjoyers:	like the centre, well acquainted with it, 'make the most of their time when taking an active part in urban urban life'.
sympathizers:	lack leisure time, frustrated in not taking an active part, perhaps because in charge of young children; older people who have had their day
users:	work in the urban core, but not emotionally involved there
abstainers:	turn their back on the central area; perhaps strong neighbourhood orientation

Source: paraphrased and adapted from W.F.Heinemeyer (loc.cit.).

time, and when they are not enjoying it, they are equivalent to
abstainers.

Suppose we just take the idea of city centre usage. The
'users' will use it, and the 'abstainers' will abstain, by definition of course. The 'enjoyers' and 'sympathizers' seem to be
distinguished only by their opportunity, or lack of it, for visiting the centre. But there is another dimension. Supposing among
the users there is a category of people who feel forced to use the
centre daily; their tendency would be to want to flee the centre at
every opportunity (category I in Table 27), unless they subjected
their wishes to the desire of someone who is normally deprived of
visiting the centre (category II). The example is of the downtown
businessman who stays on to meet his wife, normally enforced to stay
in the suburbs, and go dining and to a theatre during a precious
evening when a suburban baby-sitter can be found. Thus if a person
falls into one of these 'enforced' categories, his orientation
towards the city centre would tend to operate in the reverse direction from the enforced category (see last line of Table 27).

TABLE 27   Role of a city centre enjoyer in different opportunity
categories

Type of opportunity for enjoyer	Use	Non-use
Opportunity	enjoyer	
Prolonged opportunity	enjoyer	sympathizer (alternating)
Non-opportunity		sympathizer
Prolonged non-opportunity		non-user (enforced, if basically enjoyer or sympathizer)
Desire, if person feels in enforced category at head of column	non-use(I)	use(II)

Using the city centre as a change from a more private life at home,
even though perhaps remaining anonymous, while feeling part of a
bigger social world seems to be the meaning of H.P. Bahrdt's
Öffentlichkeit, untranslatable by one English word or simple phrase
(W.F. Heinemeyer, loc.cit., 90-1; neither can the idea be easily
expressed in French, but it is discussed by A.A. Moles and E.Rohmer,
1972, 52).

Some of the above material, derived from Heinemeyer, seems close
to the work of the psychologist, K. Lewin (1936 and later) with his
idea of an individual's 'life space' within the general concept of
hodology (*hodos*, the way). D. de Jonge (1967-8) attempted to find
applied aspects of hodology in recreation. The most important aspect
of K. Lynch's work (1960) seemed to reside in the 'edge' effect. A
popular sedentary location for recreational visitors appears to be at an

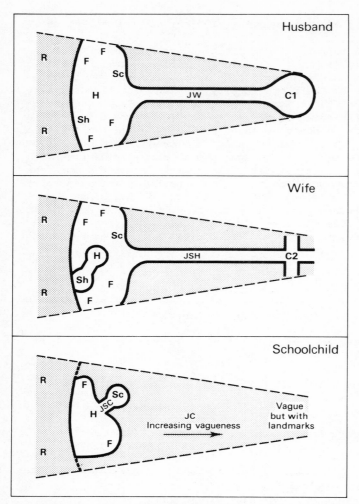

FIGURE 23   Possible variations of home-city centre territories
within a wedge-shaped orbit for members of a suburban family
C1, city centre, most likely the office functional area of the CBD;
C2, city centre, seen as a gallery forest of shopping facades along
streets or malls; F, homes of family friends; H, home; JC, journey
to centre; JSC, journey to school; JSH, journey to shops; JW,
journey to work; R, recreational areas; Sc, school; Sh, neighbourhood shops.   For the concepts of territory and orbit see A.E. Parr
(1965).

   The wedge shape can also be conceived as a biased mental map, or
image, aligned with the sectoral social structure of the city (see
J.S. Adams, 1969; and W.A.V. Clark, 1972, 179).   For contrasting
'life-spaces' for inhabitants near the centre of an agglomeration
(Paris), in a residential suburb, and in a new town see A. Metton
and M.-J. Bertrand, 1974).

edge between different homogeneous spaces such that one gives a
screening effect (back), while the other affords a wide view - the
crescentic beach beneath a cliff is an archetypal example (and
this is close to the prospect and refuge concept of J.H. Appleton,
1975). A diagonalism implied in this edge effect is obvious, yet
there is a further diagonalism between the choice of recreation
location and the habitual 'closed-in' life-space of perhaps factory,
office, or apartment. By contrast, the owner of a country estate
might base his recreation from a town house, and those characters
in Chekhov yearning for distant Moscow would fit into this example
if they only could. In highly built-up congested areas of Delhi,
G. Breese (1966, 64) notes that residents may achieve some needful
contrasted privacy by facing on to internal courtyards rather than
the throng of the thoroughfare. One might imagine, as does your
English author, that a house and an ample garden might be the perfect diagonalism on one spot. But we must remember that these
spaces can be rendered almost homogeneous if they are lonely during
the day, so that a diagonalism may be necessary between the dreaming
but deserted suburb and the place where the action is - the city
centre, especially as it appears in the sympathizer's heightened
perception.

If the image of the city centre must somehow embrace the necessity of contrast for an individual, the attractive pull may yet be
continuous for a social group as a whole. The power of this central pull was vividly demonstrated by L. Rodwin (1970) in respect
of that most magnetic of cities - Paris. Rodwin noted the ironical
fact that the 'central power' had appeared to confront the problem
of the central power when the French government campaigned to
establish more autonomous regional authorities. He went on to make
the point that the one function which if it moved would transfer a
substantial élite from Paris would be a migration of the central
government itself - involving a shift of the French capital: 'But
to mention such a move, even as a remote hypothetical possibility,
sounds too absurd, too much like the kind of suggestion only someone alien to the traditions and attitudes of the country would pre-
sume to propose' (p. 216).

D. Harvey (1973, 280-1) relates the present attraction of city
centres for individuals and for firms back to the symbolic mores of
a rank society as recognized by P. Wheatley (1971) in the case of
the first cities (see Chapter 2, pp. 33, 39ff above). Both then and
now the centre represents an axis mundi for society. Harvey finds
this type of explanation 'closer to the truth' than the 'heartless
and cold analytics' of the bid-rent curve where firms are supposed
to compete for relative locational advantage at the centre. But
Harvey goes on to appear rather heartless and cold himself. He
clearly understands that people project different psychological
values on to locations that market forces have rendered rather
homogeneous.

> Hence the urban space economy is replete with all manner of
> pseudo-hierarchical spatial orderings to reflect prestige and
> status in residential location [and presumably organisational
> location too]. These orderings are very important to the self-
> respect of people, but are irrelevant to the basic economic
> structure of society.

For Harvey phenomena like 'self-respect' (taken literally as well as
a synonym for self-esteem), 'prestige', and 'psychological projection' are superstructures in his schema of the structural evolution
of societies and their cities (see Table 8 above). Here the view is
taken that if centres as projected orientations are 'very important
to the self-respect of people', this will provide a conceptual
orientation that will precede even the perception of space and
help to prove that man cannot live on the bread of spatial homogeneity alone.

A SOCIOLOGICAL APPROACH

Even if agreed that a city centre is something perceived by the
individual in response to an inner orientation, a sociological
approach would probably work at the meso- or group scale. D.
Prokop (1966, 22) uses the concept of social space, the structure
of man's relations with his spatial environment due to the structure of society, with its cultural, behavioural, and institutional
patterns. He would no doubt attack as 'unnecessary and useless'
some of the deductive propositions in the Introduction, adjectives
he applies to instinct-like residues of the relation between man
and space which are implanted in man as 'group persistences'
according to V. Pareto (1935, vol. 2, paras 991, 1042, 1065). In
discussing social space, Prokop is referring to social imagery of
space, which it is necessary for a group to erect because a large
city is not easily legible; and he makes the point that social
groups have the strongest images about the areas their group
occupies, such that the boundaries of spatial images can be distinguished sociometrically (cf. T.R. Lee, 1968).
   This involves a difficulty in connection with the city centre
which all social groups use at one time or another; the centre
becomes the 'market place of social activities' (Prokop, 29, quoting G. Simmel). Through this orientation, we see the centre as
the shaded overlap area of as many Venn diagrams as there are social
spaces in the city (see Fig. 24). In this overlap area of the
social 'market place', groups are seen as affirming, comparing, or
exchanging their status symbols. Justification for calling this a
meso-scale approach comes from consideration of the analysis of
psychological elements regarding space made by A.A. Moles and E.
Rohmer (1972, 60):
1 power over physical environment,
2 ability to make cognitive representations of the environment,
3 awareness of others,
4 cost of effort to go and carry out some functions in a place
   distant from home base.
Moles and Rohmer find that (1) and (2) decline as the areas in
question get larger, i.e. with decreasing scale; (4) increases with
increasing distance, i.e. with decreasing scale; and (3) is at a
maximum in the centre of the city, where all the others are in
balance (idem, Fig. 17).

FIGURE 24   Social areas and the city centre
Top: The city centre as 'market place' of social areas. Interaction between areas, symbolized by double-headed arrows, takes
place in the city centre, here bounded by the presumed overlap of
social areas in the centre (indicated by stipple). For the concept
of social space, see P.-H. Chombart de Lauwe (1952, vol. 1, 24,
243-4; 1963, 95-7; and 1965, 21-30: and for social space in inter-
disciplinary perspective, see A. Buttimer (1969).
Bottom: The centre providing compact common public space (Öffentlichkeit) is contrasted with private space (Privatheit) around
dispersed points at homes in various social areas.

THE SEEDS OF FULFILMENT (see Table 25, system IV and glossary)

If we turn the discussion towards the future, the next three sections of this chapter are designed as attempted answers to three

rather difficult questions:

1 Are there some basic principles in attempting to design a
   successful central area?
2 As far as city centres are concerned, should planning rely on
   disjointed incrementalism (Dionysian) or goal-oriented (Apollonian) approaches?
3 How does the centre-periphery orientation underly the change
   from uni-centred city to city region?

Discussion of the problem of central area design might begin
with a concrete problem. Rarely is there opportunity to start with
a tabula rasa. In regard to old buildings and their restoration,
there are basically two possibilities: try to restore them to
their original design; or preserve a palimpsest of styles, as
exemplified by Romanesque cathedrals, often completed several centuries after they were begun (A. Papageorgiou, 1971, 137).
Neither course can be pursued as a rule of thumb; it depends on
whether inferior additions are to be stripped away or an opportunity
afforded to demonstrate a continuity of style. Continuity is a key
idea, when a new building is to be placed among much older ones.
Difficulties may well arise if the evolution of styles between
adjacent buildings is too abrupt, such that any diagonalism between
time and vision is being assaulted. Juxtaposed buildings of very
different styles in which the architect has made an effort, however
subtle, to bridge the gap in time, such that the effort can be
recreated by the beholder, is a way of retaining a diagonalism between the epochs through which a centre has passed (Papageorgiou,
brilliantly illustrates this point with the juxtaposition of his
Figs 74 and 75). This accords with the Gestalt Law of Closure, a
secondary law predicted from the Law of Good Figure:

Law of Good Figure: one perceives a pattern in such a way as
                     to make the best pattern possible;

Law of Closure: a figure (or pattern) which is incomplete
                     is perceived as if it were complete, as in
                     reading the following type called

ANTIQUA

The idea is perfectly expressed by Papageorgiou when discussing
restoration work at Delphi: 'This kind of partial restoration is
highly effective. It provides the observer with certain basic
points of orientation, and then leaves it to him to complete the
townscape by means of his historical knowledge and imagination'
(p. 121).

A further step brings us to the concept of a centre considered
as a labyrinth, as suggested by A.A. Moles and E. Rohmer (1972; see
also B. Bogdanović, 1975, 142). According to them, the labyrinth
in this context can be a 'canned desert' (p. 97), i.e. render the
individual isolated within a great density of individuals. A labyrinth can be disturbing as in mythology, when the traveller faces
disorientation. But a labyrinth which contains a pleasurable
number of violated expectancies (or 'micro-events' in the terminology of Moles and Rohmer) can be exciting even reassuring if the
user has a firm idea that he can grasp the Ariadne thread and solve

the puzzle even as he uses it (p. 154).
     To modulate from form to function, we can see that there should
be an optimum level of complexity or functional mix. A. Rapoport
and R. Hawkes (1970, 107-10) believe that complexity of the urban
scene is a function of violated expectancies (see Fig. 25).

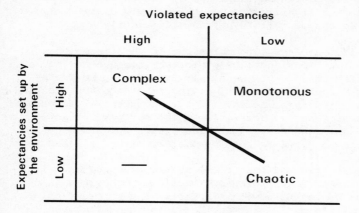

FIGURE 25   Designer's route to desirable complexity
This scheme is from A. Rapoport and R. Hawkes (loc.cit., 111).
The diagonal path for a designer creating desirable complexity out
of chaos, yet avoiding monotony has been inserted. The importance
of diagonalism, referred to as ambiguity in its restricted duplexity
of meaning sense, is stressed in the conclusions of empirical work
reported by D. Lowenthal and M. Riel (1972, 44); and also in the
conclusion of fieldwork in the Parisian agglomeration reported by
A. Metton and M.-J. Bertrand (1974, 146).

If the number of expectancies set up by the environment is low and
few are violated, a chaotic environment results. If the number of
expectancies is high, but few are violated, then the environment is
monotonous. Imagine travelling towards a city centre and then dis-
covering that the centre was merely a wide boulevard, with buildings all of one style and height and the whole thoroughfare dominated by the stream of traffic. Social homogeneity may be monotonous if spread over wide areas as in the gigantic one-class suburb
(e.g. the London County Council inter-war estate at Becontree and
Dagenham, east of London). According to R. Sennett (1970), homogeneous social polarization ('monotony') prolongs a 'purified
identity' (an adolescent self-image); diversity and conflict ('complexity') are more adult (op.cit., esp. pp. 71, 82, 97, 141).
     The diagonal line in Fig. 25 shows the path from a central
chaos to a successfully functioning city centre, where perhaps
some buildings function differently by day and night, where there
is not only a mixture of functions but where some of these overlap.
Overlap is the quality possessed by those kinds of hierarchy called
semi-lattices, but not, by definition, possessed by that kind of
hierarchy called a tree (C. Alexander, 1965; see Table 25 above).
J. Jacobs (1961, 150), A.E. Parr (1964-5, 16), and S. Carr (1967,
23) have expressed these ideas of functional diversity as a

desideratum. But it is important to stress that the complexity
be such that the user is capable of recreating the underlying
pattern by his own projection of a centrality-periphery framework
on to the central area and its surroundings.* K. Lynch (1960, 2)
concentrated on the legibility of the cityscape in his book on
'The Image of the City' (cf 'the landscape of the centre must be
legible, structured and significant', J. Labasse, 1970, 17).   The
stress here is on *latent* legibility, via a sufficiently strong
stimulus field (Parr, loc.cit.).

'Latent legibility' appears to combine two of the 'three
categories of influence' on landscape preference discovered in
experiments by S. Kaplan and J.S. Wendt (1972).   These are *legibility*, present source of information, giving coherence and identi-
fiability; and *predicted information*, a future source of information, giving complexity and mystery. The third category of influence is called 'primary landscape qualities' which appears as a
rather vague grouping of preferences for 'water, paths, and nature
in general'.

C. Steinitz (1968) stressed that there should be congruence in
the relationship between urban form and function, but warned that
congruence must not be confused with simplicity and monotony
(p. 247). He appears to imply that an ideal congruence between
form and function is one that is not immediately apparent, but one
that can be discovered by the user. Of course, if the intended
meaning of an environment proves consistently not to be the meaning
actually conveyed, the 'effectiveness' of the environment is
reduced by an amount inversely proportional to the cognitive dissonance (as suggested in idem, 246). A city, or a personality, or
a picture, that can be understood at a cursory glance will barely
escape that square of monotony on Fig. 25. The spatial complex of
the city must possess the seeds of centrality to fulfil the
expectations of the users. Such a statement would no doubt be
dubbed 'centrist' by N. Low (1975) who uses the term 'centrism' to
cover the planned provision of shops and other public services
(sic) in centres arranged in a hierarchy of sizes. Unfortunately,
his preferred non-centrist example of a 'directional grid',
proposed by Colin Buchanan and Partners for South Hampshire,
England, proved not to be a practical lay-out amid the patterns, all
based on some form of centrism, which later came in for detailed
study ('South Hampshire Structure Plan' etc., 1972).

An even more extreme view of the centre ought to be mentioned.
This is the notion of 'polyvalent space' in which all central functions get mixed up: 'the centre is everywhere in the new urban
fabric' (I. Schein, 1970, 28-30, 137-9, 137). The Agora of Dronten,
65 km north-east of Amsterdam, is cited as an example - a hangar-
like structure (70m by 50m) where many activities take place without
intervening partitions. But even in this so-called 'global-
anarchic space', activities have to be segregated, and the Agora is

---

*This statement might be compared with E.N. Bacon's (1974, 21) defi-
  nition of architecture in the context of city design: 'Architecture is the articulation of space so as to produce in the partici-
  pator a definite space experience in relation to previous and anticipated space experiences.'

only one building in the urban area of a planned town.   'Poly-
valency' not only denies the processes of centro-symmetric
ordering but would also deny that centres are necessary as manifestations of projected images.   In this connection the reader may
observe the progressive hostility with which the idea is received
in a round-table discussion culminating in the contribution of
J. Duboscq (1970, 139), and will have to decide whether such
hostility derives from fear of a new idea or resentment at an
attack on a basic human need.

The values or attitudes of citizens are very difficult to
measure, but progress is being made with the use of techniques such
as the Allport-Vernon Test of Dominant Values.   This measures the
relationship between six dominant values: theoretic, aesthetic,
religious, social, political, and economic.   The Dominant Values
datum is adjusted to score an average of 40 points on all six
values for the United States population.   Patterns of scores which
are high on aesthetic and religious values and low on theoretical,
political, and economic values tend to be associated with a more
conservative attitude towards environments.   Converse score patterns indicate more 'progressive' views - a readiness to accept
change (A. Waterhouse, 1971).   The spatial designer who confronts a
central site or central area must obviously pay attention to what is
there already and what are the significant associations.   But somehow he must also be aware of current values in society in order to
reach a level of violated expectancies which is exciting but not
disturbing.   The city planner must also rehearse the orientation
that makes innovation possible (see p. 11).

It is useful to consider cities in all their varied forms as
various phenotypes of an underlying genotype - the manifestation of
a projected centre.   To insist that we cannot make cross-reference
between the west European city, the north American city, the Communist city, the Muslim city, etc. is to take an Aristotelian view of
such cities merely as separate phenotypes.   The Galilean approach
via genotypes delights in finding that apparently dissimilar phenomena are subject to comparable basic laws and belong to the same
genotype - individuals 'prove to be simply various expressions of
the same law'; this is a view of science adopted by the psychologist
K. Lewin (1935, 1-42, esp. 11).   The anthropologist J.H. Steward
(1935) while being an advocate of multilinear evolution, nevertheless emphasises cross-cultural types which consist of cultural cores
with their interrelationships of regularities, while area types are
defined in terms of uniformities (p. 88).   A.H. Dawson (1971, 112)
adumbrated a rapprochement of morphological explanation of cities in
socialist and free enterprise societies, and C.S. Sargent (1972,
373) also appears to argue for a genotype approach to urban morphology based on his work in Buenos Aires.   He recognizes universal
spatial forces at work (1, transport; 2, urban lot speculation; and
3, segregation of land uses).   These he finds nesting within one
another (from the general to the particular in the order 1, 2, 3).
I would add a centre-periphery diagonal orientation as an infrastructure to Sargent's foundation frame of transport.   Throughout
this book I have been at pains to stress the cross-cultural regularities in man's concept of centrality.   But this is not to deny
that there are important cultural differences as variations on a

theme of spatial perception (see E.T. Hall, 1966, especially
p. 177). A remarkable effort showing how contemporary Western
and traditional Indian societies, so apparently different (two
phenotypes) form a part of one genotype because they result from
variations in the mix of similar elements is reproduced as Fig. 26.

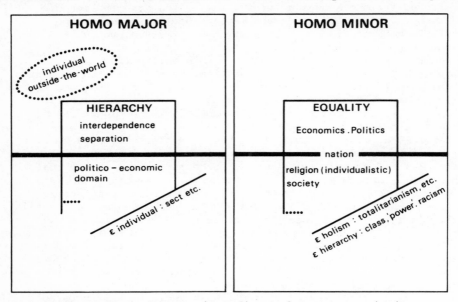

FIGURE 26   Similar elements in Indian and western societies
Indian society, left; western society, right. This 'comparative
diagram ... is only a useful memory-prop for comparison ... [and
there are] latent question marks with which it is bristling.' L.
Dumont, 1970, 231-4. 'The horizontal line can be taken as a threshold of consciousness' (idem, 232). What is placed above is *substan-
tive* and fundamental (*S*); what is below is *adjective* and residual
(*a*). In each below the sloping line are 'the existence of features
corresponding to what is brought to light by the values of the
other' (idem, 234).
(The following note is by Dumont (p. 340): The postulate for comparison used here can be expressed as follows: all societies contain the same 'elements', 'features' or 'factors', it being understood that these 'elements' can be located in each case either in
S or in *a* and are profoundly altered by their position. This last
condition naturally removes all 'reality' from the 'elements' and on
this condition $\Sigma S + \Sigma a$ = Constant. This amounts in practice to
saying that in any society there will always be found that which
corresponds to a residual way (in *a*) to what another society dif-
ferentiates, articulates and valorizes (in *S*).) Cf. W.F. Wertheim's
(1974, 113-18) counterpoints, or countervalues, to a dominant value
system.
(Redrawn and reproduced by permission of Weidenfeld & Nicholson Ltd
from L. Dumont, op.cit.)

Both have produced the same genotype of spatial centres but in
different phenotype (city) classifications.

Even those who shun these syntheses might agree on two points:
every culture has produced its spatial centres and peripheries;
today every country has its cities. In every city there are
structures and lay-outs that will endure on the ground and there
are plans on paper or in the minds of citizens, and some of these
will make significant changes to the urban fabric. Thus all
cities, in whatever culture, contain the seeds today of what they
will be tomorrow.

DISJOINTED INCREMENTALISM OR GOAL ORIENTATION (see Table 25,
systems I and II and Glossary)

The reader who has progressed this far will expect an advocacy of
a compromise between these two approaches. Much goal-oriented
planning has imposed a too rigid approach to the problem of the
city centre in the era of the master plan; even today legibility
rather than latent legibility seems to be the goal of many planners.
On the other hand, advances in building technology have enabled us
to make additions to cities by means of large indivisible projects,
each of which must be planned towards carefully formulated goals at
the outset. The downtown high-rise block and out-of-town shopping
centre, each with included mall, are often planned complete, down
to the function of each tenancy, including an a priori retail
shopping mix. Here is a clue. In the central area the goal should
be a formal and functional mix which does not run counter to the
pattern produced by centro-symmetric ordering, but which contains,
at least on the micro-scale, some violated expectancies to excite
the stranger and refresh the habitué. This makes a nice contrast
to the home environment where expectancies set up by the environment
are low and where the individual makes every effort to keep them
that way. A wife permanently in such surroundings may well develop
'home blues', and she will long to go up to town where the action of
violated expectancies lies. The goal, always subject to modifica-
tion, (Table 25, system IV) should be to obtain the complex results
formerly achieved over long periods in small step additions by historic disjointed incrementalism, avoiding chaos on the one hand
and monotony on the other (the diagonal route of Fig. 24).

Those who are busy in the centre all day often need a quiet life
at home, and this leads to a restricted view of their suburb (see
data in A. Metton, 1969). This reinforces the idea of psychological
complementarity of city and suburb for adults, who will probably
need, in addition, occasional excursions into rurality, or wildscape
if luckily nearby (cf. C. Abrams, 1965, 361-2).

In this study the discussion of centrality and cities has been
confined to spatial centrality, but E.L. Ullman (1974) has exhorted
us to think in terms of the interchangeability between space and
time. Certainly there are central moments in our lives - a night
out, a wedding, a cup final, an anniversary dinner, a conference, a
coronation (or inauguration) - and when these take place in urban
centres there occurs a diagonalism between space and time (see also
B. Goodey, 1974, 110).

TABLE 28   The city as more than the multiple of form and function

Meaning for citizen and visitor	Examples
Concrete	buildings to enter, roads to move on
Utility	city functions
Value or emotional response	architecture and lay--out considered aesthetically pleasing, invigorating, sublime; or, conversely, depressing, monotonous, ugly
Symbolic	in which the city represents more than is seen,* work of art, free and easy life, confining, a bygone era, a new world, a psychological centre ('home-base')
Violated expectancies	a functional mix which goes round corners, formal asymmetry in lay-outs thematically linked, vistas blocked off, soluble labyrinths

*Cf. D. Stea's (1967) 'invisible landscape' and J. Hudnut (1949, 160, quoted on p. 137   above); also 'the city is what people think it is; the "city of the mind"...' (D. Amedeo and R.G. Golledge, 1975, 385 ff).
Source: adapted from J. Sonnenfeld (1966), with 'violated expectancies' added (cf. perception on a hierarchy of levels in J.J. Gibson (1950 and 1968).

THE FUTURE CITY: DISPERSION OR CONCENTRATION

Dispersion/concentration constitute another of those polarities of a continuum along which analytically to arrange aspects of cities. The spread of car ownership has long encouraged some to predict a swing towards great dispersal, and Los Angeles is quickly paraded as a prototype. This reasoning forgets that Los Angeles is rather a variation of the projection of preferred spatial schemas rather than a forerunner of the form of which all other cities must tend. The 'dispersed city' hypothesis turns out to be an account of two contrasted settlement patterns, as H.A. Stafford (1962) has shown. First, it could be a description of a built-up pattern resulting from growth outwards from an existing centre (referring to southern Michigan). Second, it is a post-hoc rationalization of a group of physically discrete cities which together function as an urban unit at a higher level of organization (referring to southern Illinois).

In both forms the 'dispersed city' has very recognizable centres, and centrality and the city are still vitally linked.   I. Burton (1963, 286) put his finger on the clue to the second type of so-called dispersed city when he writes that it 'presupposes an economic base other than the provision of services for a surround-ing area'.   In other words, explanations must be sought in areas of the triangles of Figs 18-20 (Chapter 6) which are distant from the apex of central place theory.   If by 'dispersed city' we mean a city with centres dispersed within an urbanized region, then a proliferation of centres will involve much investment in traffic improvements.   The need to keep this within reasonable bounds led J. Allpass (1968) to conclude: 'The prime work for planning will be to *canalize* the dispersion to new center areas' [italics added] (p. 173; cf K. Dziewonski, 1968).

   C.B. Wurster (1963) attempted to discuss a double tendency, not only the polarization of dispersion/concentration but also that of region-wide specialization/sub-regional integration.   Her 'pre-sent trends projected' solution seemed to imply the dispersal of functions such as shops, residences, and industry, and the even greater concentration of such functions as decision-making in cen-tral cities.   These double trends are summed up in the effects of the construction of a new motorway near a large city centre: in one direction the downtown at which it aims has more centrality conferred upon it; in the other direction the urban commuter can speed to his more distant 'urban' home in a former rural scene. This scene is transformed not only functionally and visually, but also psychologically.   The big city seems near, and even if the centre is over the hill, the reflection of its lights can glow in the night-sky of one's unconscious.

   Like the rural-urban fringe, the city changes even as it is studied and the more intensive the probe, the more complicated the city appears to become; distance lends simplicity.   To someone in Europe it seems justifiable to refer to San Francisco as a city on the Golden Gate.   To an experienced student who lives in the area, it exemplifies the case of a city which has grown with all parts as siblings, such that the Bay Area is best described as a *sympolis* (J.E. Vance, 1964, 89; 1966, 130 n).   This is neither a mother city with outward growth from a centre nor a dispersed city, but a series of centres which have merged at different scalar levels: 'functional parochialism within a broad regional episcopate' (Vance, 1964, 89).   But in a broader view of California, the Bay Area, with all its internal complexity, is nevertheless a 'centre' compared with peripheral areas of the state.   J. Friedmann and J. Miller (1965) see the United States metropolitan areas and the inter-metropolitan areas fusing together as 'urban fields', a response to the fact that an individual's urban life space can be extended over a wider area.   If they are correct, centre and periphery contrasts will still occur at two levels: within the urban fields, and bet-ween the urban fields and the remainder of the national territory (as explicit in their map 3; see also E.L. Ullman, 1958).

   The ultimate in dispersal would seem to be the non-place urban realm concept of M.M. Webber (1963, 1964).   But this does not turn out to be the 'placeless place' that is mentioned by Webber's editor (L. Wingo, 1963, 19).   In fact, Webber is careful to point

out that there will continue to be a great variety of centres and
sub-centres because transport costs (and now the energy crisis)
will never permit a homogeneous dispersion. We may compare this
with the conclusions of an enquiry by M. Chisholm and P. O'Sullivan
(1971, 127) into freight flows and spatial aspects of the British
economy:

> policies designed to maintain and reinforce the major urban
> centres in peripheral locations are not likely to impose a
> significant extra long-term cost on the nation on account of
> greater aggregate transport costs, *so long as investment is
> concentrated in or near major cities.* [italics added]

When Webber introduces the non-place urban realm it is via the
extensive spatial webs traced by a specialized professional élite
in an advanced country (1964, 109 ff.). Such individuals may
certainly have much wider orbits than a single office, factory, or
local community (the cosmopolitans of Table 5). If highly mobile,
they may function in respect to many centres from a base deep in
the periphery. But even the specialist thinker in his mountain
retreat needs his publisher and printer, and the market-place of
ideas represented by a visit to a conference *centre*. Thus, while
agreeing with Webber (1968, reprinted 1971, 500) that the spatial
glue that held the city tightly together is dissolving, the new
pattern will still be one of centres and peripheries; and 'smaller
settlements will undergo a major spurt of growth' (idem). We are
here close to the paradoxical idea of the dispersion of centrality,
or, more correctly, the dissemination of metropolitan-type central
functions down the urban hierarchy. P.W. Daniels (1975b, 223)
appears to have reached this position at the end of his conclusions
about office location factors:

> Recent decentralization trends have not caused centrality to
> become less important for offices, they have simply distributed
> the demand more widely than before. There is no reason to
> believe that it will become less relevant for the future loca-
> tion of offices.

The built environment is a language that reveals our thought
processes, if we but understand the implications of what has been
written. This idea is similar to that of S.K. Langer's concept of
ethnic domain - the sphere of influence of a function (1953, 95).
Arguing antithetically, Langer gives clear illustration of the
existence of this sphere of influence, demonstrated at work divorced
from a geographical locality; the examples she uses are the ship,
and the gypsy camp and the Indian camp. The ship constantly changes
her location but is a self-contained place for her inhabitants,
often resembling a city in the case of a large passenger liner;
first came the idea of the ship, then ideas about the function each
part was to discharge. Nomadic cultures do not inscribe themselves
in fixed locations, yet a gypsy camp however temporary is a self-
contained place culturally, and it is not ridiculous to refer to
the 'centre of the camp'. The camp is different from the Indian
camp, though the gypsies may have pitched their tents where the
Indian camp used to be. Camps are manifestly sited in places, but
they are also places in themselves. This double language is the
result of ideas pursued by functions projected on to sites, via
permanent structures in the case of cities.

This language of the built environment is being continuously
redrafted as we use it and adapt it, but, nevertheless, on the
ground now are major portions of the future city (for a review of
this topic see P. Sarre et al., 1973). There is a basic continuity,
and I hope that the argument in this section has been built of
sufficient strength to support the following conclusion. Just as
we can say that the concept of centrality preceded the concept of
the uni-centred city, so centrality will survive the progressive
breakdown of what was once a city-rural dichotomy.

DIAGONALISM RESURGENT

Diagonalism is a simultaneous comparison on two or more levels
between the expected and the experienced. The cross references
to diagonalism (see p. 10ff) in the previous chapters have been
deliberately underplayed, but it has been there like a ground-bass
as 'my guide through a very varied literature' (see p. 12),
and I have tried to supply evidence from other fields of study in
the Introduction as well as from the chosen linked topics of centrality and cities. Diagonalism is basically deductive in nature;
there is always an expectation with which to compare the data
observed. P. Richards (1974) has shown how Kant believed 'that
the human mind has built into it a spatial schema which serves a
purpose analogous to that of the graticule of a map projection'
(p. 4), and this leads Richards to cite workers in other fields
who believe in innate programmes in the light of which experiences
are acquired (e.g. E.C. Tolman, 1948; and J. Monod, 1972; K.R.
Popper 1963, reprinted 1972a, 180-1, is explicitly Kantian, see the
second citation in Recapitulation II of the Envoi below).
    The analogy of a mental map projection can be pushed deeper.
It is not just a question of a graticule of squares waiting to be
filled, like the open mouths of a set of pigeon-holes. Our mental
projections are hierarchically disposed in an innate centres-
peripheries programme, in the light of which spatial information is
filed. Not only is there diagonalism between the programme and the
incoming information, but also between centres and peripheries
within the programme.
    L. von Bertalanffy (1968, 112-15) emphasizes that the evaluation
of any model should simply be pragmatic in terms of explanatory and
predictive merits, or lack thereof. For mass behaviour, systems
laws would apply, mathematized if possible; individual behaviour
can be modelled by some form of game and decision theory. In this
latter case we are dealing more closely with choices, and so we
have to know the needs which cause an individual to choose this
rather than that. One result of such processes is the appearance
of spatial coordinates, 'symbolic locales' (A.L. Strauss, 1961,
254), which heighten the contrast between centre and periphery,
between cityscape and wildscape, or, not too fancifully, between a
desirable in-scape and a necessary escape.

Chapter 8

ENVOI

(Recapitulations and exemplary quotations selected via the
orientation of diagonalism)

RECAPITULATION I (from p. 10)

The process of diagonalism *is a simultaneous comparison on two or
more levels, leading to superimposition and overlap between 'the
expected and the experienced' or between ideas.*
H. Poincaré (1908):*
   For fifteen days I strove to prove that there could not be any
   functions like those I have since called Fuchsian functions. I
   was then very ignorant; every day I seated myself at my work
   table, stayed an hour or two, tried a great number of combinations and reached no results. One evening, contrary to my
   custom, I drank black coffee and could not sleep. Ideas rose
   in crowds; I felt them collide *until pairs interlocked*, so to
   speak making a stable combination. By next morning I had
   established the existence of a class of Fuchsian functions, ...
   [italics added]
G. Wallas (1926):*
[Having proposed four stages of creative thought as preparation,
incubation, illumination, and verification, he described illumination:]
   the final 'flash', or 'click' is the culmination of a successful
   train of *association* which may have lasted for an appreciable
   time, and which has probably been preceded by a series of tentative and unsuccessful trains. [italics added]
F.C. Bartlett (1958):*
   The conditions for original thinking are when two or more
   streams of research begin to offer evidence that they may con-
   verge and so in some manner be combined. ... The most important
   of all conditions of originality in experimental thinking is a
   capacity to detect overlap and agreement between groups of
   facts and fields of study which have not before been effectively
   combined, and to bring these groups into experimental contact.
*The above three references are reprinted in P.E. Vernon (1970, 81;

156

96; and 102 and 104).

J.S. Bruner, J.J. Goodnow, and G.A. Austin (1967, 130):

he alters his hypothesis by taking the *intersect between his old hypothesis and the new instance*: those features common to the two. [italics original]

RECAPITULATION II (from p. 28)

Man projects his desired world, with its framework representation of centres and non-centres, or to the perceived world, and then organises the latter in an effort to gain the former, which itself is governed by the positive feedback of experience.

D. Lyndon (1962, 34-5):

The first, and simplest, act of possession is to establish an *inside* that is separate from the *outside*; - to set apart one section of the environment as secure against the hostile, uncontrolled *outside*. ... Being *inside* is knowing where you are. [italics original]

K.R. Popper (1972a, 180-1):

We must give up the view that we are passive observers, waiting for nature to impress its regularity upon us. Instead we must adopt the view that in digesting our sense-data we actively impress the order and the laws of the intellect upon them. Our cosmos bears the imprint of our minds.

W.T. Powers (1973):

The brain's model of reality, as far as consciousness is concerned, *is* reality - there is nothing else to perceive. [italics original]

L. Costa (1956) [Lucio Costa was the winner of the competition for the design of the new capital of Brazil, now manifest as the city of Brasilia. He submitted his entry as merely five cards of freehand sketches and a brief statement which began as follows:]

It was not my intention to enter the competition - nor in fact am I really doing so. I am merely liberating my mind from a possible solution *which sprang to it as a complete picture,* but one which I had not sought ... the drawing of two axes crossing each other at right angles, in the sign of the Cross. The sign was then adapted to the topography... [italics added]

[The above quoted in translation by N. Evenson, 1973, 143 and 146.]

RECAPITULATION III (from p. 6)

Man's actions are not determined by the environment, physical and social, but by what he thinks the environment determines him to do....

REFERENCES

ABRAMS, C. (1965) 'The City is the Frontier'. New York: Harper & Row.

ABU-LUGHOD, J. (1968) The city is dead - long live the city, 'Urbanism in World Perspective', S.F. Fava (ed.). New York: Crowell, 154-65.

ADAMS, J.S. (1969) Directional bias in intra-urban migration, 'Economic Geography', 45, 302-23.

ADAMS, J.S. (1970) Residential structure of midwestern cities, 'Annals of the Association of American Geographers', 60, 37-62.

ADAMS, R.M. (1960a) The origin of cities, 'Scientific American', September. Freeman: Scientific American Resource Library, off print No. 606.

ADAMS, R.M. (1960b) Factors influencing the rise of civilization in the alluvium: illustrated by Mesopotamia, 'City Invincible', C.H. Kraeling and R.M. Adams (eds). Chicago: University Press.

ADAMS, R.M. (1966) 'The Evolution of Urban Society. Early Meso-potamia and Prehispanic Mexico'. Chicago: Aldine.

ALBERS, G. (1968) Toward a theory of urban structure, Town and Country Planning Summer School 1968: Report of Proceedings. London: Town Planning Institute, 14-20.

ALCHIAN, A. (1950) Uncertainty, evolution, and economic theory, 'Journal of Political Economy', 58, 211-21.

ALEXANDER, C. (1965) A city is not a tree [reprinted, with slight amendments, in 1966, 'Design', 206, 46-55].

ALEXANDER, C. (1969) Major changes in environmental form required by social and psychological demands, 'Ekistics', 28, 78-85.

ALEXANDER, I. (1974) City centre redevelopment: an evaluation of alternative approaches, 'Progress in Planning', 3, part 1, 1-81.

ALEXANDERSSON, G. (1967) 'Geography of Manufacturing'. Englewood Cliffs, N.J.: Prentice-Hall.

ALLIX, A. (1914) La foire de Goncelin, 'Recueil des travaux de l'Institut de Géographie Alpine', 2, 299-334.

ALLIX, A. (1922) The geography of fairs: illustrated by old-world examples, 'Geographical Review', 12, 532-69.

ALLPASS, J., (1968) Changes in the structure of urban centers, 'Journal of the American Institute of Planners', 34, 170-3.

ALLPASS, J., AGERGÅRD, E., HARVEST, J., OLSEN, P.A. and SØHOLT, S.
(1967) Urban centres and changes in the centre structure, 'Urban
Core and Inner City'. Proceedings of the International Study Week,
Amsterdam, 11-17 September 1966. Leiden: Brill, 103-17.
ALONSO, W. (1964) Location theory, 'Regional Development and Plan-
ning', J. Friedmann and W. Alonso (eds). Cambridge, Mass.: MIT
Press, 78-106.
AMEDEO, D. and GOLLEDGE, R.G. (1975) 'An Introduction to Scien-
tific Reasoning in Geography'. New York: Wiley.
ANDERSON, T.R. and EGELAND, J.T. (1961) Spatial aspects of social
area analysis, 'American Sociological Review', 26, 392-8.
APPLETON, J. (1975) 'The Experience of Landscape'. London: Wiley.
ARDREY, R. (1966) 'The Territorial Imperative: a Personal
Inquiry into the Animal Origins of Property and Nations'. New
York: Dell.
ARMSTRONG, R.B. (1972) 'The Office Industry: Patterns of Growth
and Location'. Cambridge, Mass.: MIT Press.
ASHLEY, T.J. (1972) Planning a new city: Irvine, California,
'Town and Country Planning', 40, 114-19.
ASHWORTH, W. (1954) 'The Genesis of Modern British Town Planning'.
London: Routledge & Kegan Paul.

BACON, E.N. (1974) 'Design of Cities', 2nd edn. London: Thames &
Hudson.
BAHRDT, H.P. (1961) 'Die Moderne Groszstadt'. Hamburg:
Soziologische Überlegungen zum Städtebau.
BAIN, J.S. (1954) Economies of scale, concentration, and the
condition of entry in twenty manufacturing industries, 'American
Economic Review', 44, 15-39.
BASKIN, C.W. (1966) 'Central Places in Southern Germany'. Engle-
wood Cliffs, N.J.: Prentice-Hall [translation of W. Christaller
(1933)].
BAUDELAIRE, C. (1869) 'Petits poèmes en prose'. Paris: Lévy.
BECK, R. (1967) Spatial meaning and the properties of the environ-
ment, 'Environmental Perception and Behavior', D. Lowenthal (ed.),
Research Paper No. 109. Chicago: University of Chicago, Department
of Geography, 18-22.
BELL, T.L., LIEBER, S.R. and RUSHTON, G. (1974) Clustering of
services in central places, 'Annals of the Association of American
Geographers', 64, 214-25.
BENTON, J.F. (1968) 'Town Origins: the Evidence from Medieval
England'. Boston: Heath.
BERGEL, E.E. (1965) 'Urban Sociology'. New York: McGraw-Hill.
BERGSMAN, J., GREENSTON, P. and HEALY, R. (1972) The agglomeration
process in urban growth, 'Urban Studies', 9, 263-88.
BERRY, B.J.L. (1959) Ribbon developments in the urban business pat-
tern, 'Annals of the Association of American Geographers', 49,
145-55.
BERRY, B.J.L. (1963) 'Commercial Structure and Commercial Blight'.
Chicago: Department of Geography Research Paper No. 85.
BERRY, B.J.L. (1965) Internal structure of the city, 'Law and
Contemporary Problems', 30, 111-19. [Reprinted in L.S. Bourne
(ed.) (1971) 'Internal Structure of the City'. New York: Oxford
University Press, 97-103.]

BERRY, B.J.L. (1967) 'Geography of Market Centers and Retail Distribution'. Englewood Cliffs, N.J.: Prentice-Hall.
BERRY, B.J.L., CONKLING, E.C. and RAY, D.M. (1976) 'The Geography of Urban Systems'. Englewood Cliffs, N.J.: Prentice-Hall.
BERRY, B.J.L. and HORTON, F.E. (1970) 'Geographic Perspectives on Urban Systems'. Englewood Cliffs, N.J.: Prentice-Hall.
BERRY, B.J.L. and NEILS, E. (1969) Location, size, and shape of cities as influenced by environmental factors: the urban environment writ large, 'The Quality of the Urban Environment', H.S. Perloff (ed.). Resources for the Future Inc., Baltimore: Johns Hopkins University Press.
BERRY, B.J.L. and PRED, A. (1961) 'Central Place Studies. Bibliography of Theory and Applications'. Philadelphia: Regional Science Research Institute, Bibliography Series No. 1.
BERRY, B.J.L. and REES, P.H. (1969) The factorial ecology of Calcutta, 'American Journal of Sociology', 74, 445-91.
BIDDLE, M. (1973) Winchester: the development of an early capital, 'Vor- und Frühformen der europäischen Stadt in Mittelalter', H. Jankuhn, W. Schlesinger and H. Steuer (eds). Göttingen: Abh. der Akademie der Wissenschaften in Göttingen, Philologisch-Historische Klasse, 3 Folge, 83, 229-61.
BIRD, J. (1952) The industrial development of Lower Thameside, 'Geography', 37, 89-96.
BIRD, J. (1957) 'The Geography of the Port of London'. London: Hutchinson.
BIRD, J. (1958) Billingsgate: a central metropolitan market, 'Geographical Journal', 124, 464-75.
BIRD, J. (1963a) 'The Major Seaports of the United Kingdom'. London: Hutchinson.
BIRD, J. (1963b) The noosphere: a concept possibly useful to geographers, 'Scottish Geographical Magazine', 79, 54-56.
BIRD, J. (1964) The growth of the Port of London, 'Greater London', J.T. Coppock and H.C. Prince (eds). London: Faber & Faber, 202-24.
BIRD, J. (1965) The foundation of the Australian seaport capitals, 'Economic Geography', 41, 283-99.
BIRD, J. (1967) Seaports and the European Economic Community, 'Geographical Journal', 133, 302-27.
BIRD, J. (1968) 'Seaport Gateways of Australia'. London: Oxford University Press.
BIRD, J. (1970) Seaports are not aberrant cases, 'Area', 4, 65-8.
BIRD, J. (1971) 'Seaports and Seaport Terminals'. London: Hutchinson.
BIRD, J. (1973a) Of central places, cities, and seaports, 'Geography', 58, 105-18.
BIRD, J. (1973b) The long-term impact on south-east England [of the Channel Tunnel], 'Geographical Journal', 139, 261-6.
BIRD, J. (1975) Methodological implications for geography from the philosophy of K.R. Popper, 'Scottish Geographical Magazine', 91, 153-63.
BLACK, W.R. (1967) Growth of the railway network of Maine: a multivariate approach, 'Discussion Papers', 5, University of Iowa, Department of Geography.
BLIZZARD, S.W. and ANDERSON, W.F. (1952) 'Problems in Rural-Urban

Fringe Research: Conceptualization and Delineation'. Pennsylvania:
Agricultural Experiment Station, State College Progress Report
no. 89.
BLUMENFELD, H. (1949) Theory of city form past and present,
'Journal of the Society of Architectural Historians', 8, nos 3-4,
7-16.
BLUMENFELD, H. (1954) The tidal wave of metropolitan expansion,
'Journal of the American Institute of Planners', 20, 3-14.
BOGDANOVIĆ, B. (1975) Symbols in the city and the city as symbol,
'Ekistics', 39, 140-6.
BORCHERT, J.R. (1967) American metropolitan evolution, 'Geographi-
cal Review', 57, 301-32.
BOSERUP, E. (1965) 'The Conditions of Agricultural Growth'.
Chicago: Aldine.
BOSKOFF, A. (1962) 'The Sociology of Urban Regions'. New York:
Appleton-Century-Crofts.
BOURNE, L.S. (1967) 'Private Redevelopment of the Central City'.
Chicago: University Department of Geography Research Paper no.
112.
BOURNE, L.S. (ed.) (1971) 'Internal Structure of the City'. New
York: Oxford University Press.
BOURNE, L.S. (1974) Urban systems in Australia and Canada: compara-
tive notes and research questions, 'Australian Geographical
Studies', 12, 152-72.
BOWDEN, M.J. (1971) Downtown through time: delimitation, expansion,
and internal growth, 'Economic Geography', 47, 122-35.
BOYCE, R.R. (1966) The edge of the metropolis: the wave theory
analog approach [reprinted in L.S. Bourne (ed.) (1971) 'Internal
Structure of the City'. New York: Oxford University Press,
104-11].
BRAIDWOOD, R.J. and WILLEY, G.R. (1962) 'Courses Toward Urban Life'.
Edinburgh: University Press, 330-59.
BREESE, G. (1966) 'Urbanization in Newly Developing Countries'.
Englewood Cliffs, N.J.: Prentice-Hall.
BRIGGS, R. (1974) A model to relate the size of the central business
district to the population of a city, 'Geographical Analysis', 6,
265-79.
BRODSKY, H. (1973) Land development and the expanding city, 'Annals
of the Association of American Geographers', 63, 159-66.
BROWN, A.J., SHERRARD, H.M. and SHAW, J.H. (1969) 'An Introduction
to Town and Country Planning'. Sydney: Angus & Robertson.
BRUNER, J.S., GOODNOW, J.J. and AUSTIN, G.A. (1967) 'A Study of
Thinking'. New York: Wiley.
BRUNET, R. (1973) Structure et dynamisme de l'espace français:
schéma d'un système, 'L'Espace Géographique', 4, 249-54.
BUNGE, W. (1958) 'The Location of Population Demand, Purchasing
Power, and Services and Highways'. Seattle: University of Washing-
ton, Department of Geography.
BUNGE, W. (1966) 'Theoretical Geography'. Lund: Gleerup.
BURCHARD, J. (1971) The culture of urban America, 'Urban Studies',
L.K. Loewenstein (ed.). New York: Free Press, 476-501.
BURGESS, E.W. (1925) The growth of a city: introduction to a
research project, 'The City', R.E. Park, E.W. Burgess and R.D.
McKenzie (eds). Chicago: University Press, 47-62.

BURGHARDT, A.F. (1971) A hypothesis about gateway cities, 'Annals of the Association of American Geographers', 61, 269-85.
BURNS, L.S. and HARMAN, A.J. (1967) 'The Complex Metropolis: Profile of Los Angeles Metropolis, Part 6'. University of California: Graduate School of Business Administration, Research Report No. 9.
BURTON, I. (1963) A restatement of the dispersed city hypothesis, 'Annals of the Association of American Geographers', 53, 285-9.
BURTON, R. (1955) 'Personal Narrative of a Pilgrimage to Al-Madinah and Meccah', 2 vols. [Republished 1964, New York: Dover.]
BUTTIMER, A. (1969) [Sister Mary Annette, O.P.] Social space in interdisciplinary perspective, 'Geographical Review', 59, 417-26.
BUTTLER, F. (1975) 'Growth Pole Theory and Economic Development'. Farnborough: Saxon House.
BUZZACOTT, K.L. (1972) 'London's Markets: their Growth, Characteristics and Functions'. University of London: unpublished PhD thesis.

CAMPBELL, J. (1972) Growth pole theory, digraph analysis, and inter-industry relationships, 'Tijdschrift voor economische en sociale geografie', 68, 79-87.
CAPEL, H. (1975) L'image de la ville et le comportement spatial des citadins, 'L'Espace Géographique', 4, 73-80.
CAROL, H. (1960) The hierarchy of central functions within the city, 'Annals of the Association of American Geographers', 50, 419-38.
CARR, S. (1967) The city of the mind [reprinted in H.M. Proshansky, W. Ittelson and L.G. Rivlin (1970) 'Environmental Psychology: Man in His Physical Setting'. New York: Holt, Rinehart & Winston, 518-32.]
CARTER, H. (1972) 'The Study of Urban Geography'. London: Edward Arnold [includes The rural-urban fringe, 228-65].
CARTER, H. and ROWLEY, G. (1966) The central business district of Cardiff, 'Transactions and Papers of the Institute of British Geographers', 38, 119-34.
CASSIRER, E. (1944) 'An Essay on Man'. New Haven: Yale University Press.
CHANG, S. (1970) Some observations on the morphology of Chinese walled cities, 'Annals of the Association of American Geographers', 60, 63-91.
CHAPIN, F.S. Jnr (1964) Selected theories of urban growth and development, 'Journal of the American Institute of Planners', 30, 51-8.
CHAPIN, F.S. Jnr (1974) 'Human Activity Patterns in the City'. New York: Wiley.
CHAPIN, F.S. Jnr and WEISS, S.F. (1962) Land patterns and growth alternatives, 'Urban Growth Dynamics in a Regional Cluster of Cities', F.S. Chapin Jnr and S.F. Weiss (eds). New York: Wiley, 425-58.
CHERRY, G.E. (ed.) (1974) 'Urban Planning Problems', London: Hill.
CHILDE, V.G. (1950) The urban revolution, 'Town Planning Review', 21, 3-7.
CHISHOLM, M. and O'SULLIVAN, P. (1973) 'Freight Flows and Spatial Aspects of the British Economy'. Cambridge: University Press.
CHOMBART DE LAUWE, P.-H. (1952) 'Paris et l'agglomération

parisienne'. 2 vols, Paris: Presses Universitaires de France.
CHOMBART DE LAUWE, P.-H. (1963) 'Des hommes et des villes'.
Paris: Payot.
CHOMBART DE LAUWE, P.-H. (1965) 'Paris: essais de sociologie
1952-64'. Paris: Éditions Ouvrières
CHRISTALLER, W. (1933) 'Die zentralen Orte in Süddeutschland'.
Jena: Fischer [for translation, see C.W. Baskin].
CLARK, C. (1951) Urban population densities, 'Journal of the Royal
Statistical Society, Series A', 114, 490-6.
CLARK, W.A.V. (1972) Behaviour and the constraints of spatial
structure, 'New Zealand Geographer', 28, 171-80.
CLAVAL, P. (1973) La théorie des lieux centraux revisitée, 'Revue
géographique de l'est', 13, 225-51.
CLAVAL, P. (1974) La géographie et la perception de l'espace,
'L'Espace Géographique', 3, 179-87.
COHEN, Y.S. (1972) 'Diffusion of an Innovation in The Urban System:
The Spread of Planned Regional Shopping Centers in the United
States 1949-1968'. Chicago: University of Chicago, Department of
Geography Research Paper No. 140.
COLBY, C.C. (1933) Centrifugal and centripetal forces in urban
geography, 'Annals of the Association of American Geographers', 23,
1-20.
COLLINS, G.R. and COLLINS, C.C. (1965) 'Camillo Sitte and the Birth
of Modern City Planning'. London: Phaidon.
CROFT, M.J. (1969) 'Offices in a Regional Centre: Follow-up
Studies on Infrastructure and Linkages'. Research Paper No. 3.
London: Location of Offices Bureau.
CULLEN, G. (1961) 'Townscape'. London: Architectural Press.
CURDES, G. (1967) On a method for analyzing retail centrality and
efficiency in town and regional planning, 'Urban Core and Inner
City'. Proceedings of the International Study Week, Amsterdam,
11-17 September 1966. Leiden: Brill, 423-38.
CURRY, L. (1966) Chance and landscape, 'Northern Geographical
Essays', J.W. House (ed.). Newcastle: University Department of
Geography, 40-55.

DACEY, M.F. (1962) Analysis of central place and point patterns by a
nearest neighbour method, 'Lund Studies in Geography', Series B,
Human Geography, 24, 55-75.
DANIELS, P.W. (1974) New offices in the suburbs, 'Suburban Growth:
Geographical Processes at the Edge of the Western City', J.H.
Johnson (ed.). London: Wiley, 177-200.
DANIELS, P.W. (1975a) Strategic office centres in London, 'Town and
Country Planning', 43, 209-14.
DANIELS, P.W. (1975b) 'Office Location: an Urban and Regional
Study'. London: Bell.
DARLING, F.F. (1952) Social behaviour and survival, 'Auk', 69,
183-91.
DAVIES, D.H. (1959) Boundary study as a tool in CBD analysis: an
interpretation of certain aspects of the boundary of Cape Town's
central business district, 'Economic Geography', 35, 322-45.
DAVIES, D.H. (1960) The hard core of Cape Town's central business
district: an attempt at delimitation, 'Economic Geography', 36,
53-69.

DAVIES, R.L. (1972a) Structural models of retail distribution: analogies with settlement and land use theories, 'Transactions of the Institute of British Geographers', 58, 59-82.

DAVIES, R.L. (1972b) The retail pattern of the central area of Coventry, 'The Retail Structure of Cities'. Institute of British Geographers Occasional Paper No. 1, Urban Study Group, 1-32.

DAVIES, R.L. (1973) The location of service activities, 'Studies in Human Geography', M. Chisholm and B. Rodgers (eds). London: Heinemann, 125-71.

DAVIES, W.K.D. (1966) The ranking of service centres, 'Transactions of the Institute of British Geographers', 40, 51-63.

DAVIES, W.K.D. (1967) Centrality and the central place hierarchy, 'Urban Studies', 4, 61-79.

DAVIS, P. (1974) Data description and presentation, 'Science in Geography', 3. London: Oxford University Press.

DAWSON, A.H. (1971) Warsaw: an example of city structure in free market and planned socialist environments, 'Tijdschrift voor economische en sociale geografie', 62, 104-13.

DAWSON, J.A. (1975) Hypermarket happening, 'Geographical Magazine', 48, 118.

DE JONGE, D. (1967-8) Applied hodology, 'Landscape', 17, no. 2, 10-11.

DEWEY, R. (1948-9) Peripheral expansion in Milwaukee County, 'American Journal of Sociology', 54, 118-25.

DEWEY, R. (1960) The rural-urban continuum: real but relatively unimportant, 'American Journal of Sociology', 66, 60-6.

DIAMOND, D.R. (1962) The central business district of Glasgow, 'Proceedings of the IGU Symposium in Urban Geography', K. Norborg (ed.). Lund: Gleerup, 525-34.

DICKINSON, R.E. (1951) 'The West European City'. London: Routledge & Kegan Paul.

DICKINSON, R.E. (1962) Review of L. Mumford's 'The City in History', 'Annals of the Association of American Geographers', 52, 300-6.

DOWNS, R.M. and STEA, D. (eds) (1973) 'Image and Environment: Cognitive Mapping and Spatial Behavior'. London: Edward Arnold.

DREWETT, R., GODDARD, J. and SPENCE, N. (1976) What's happening in British cities?, 'Town and Country Planning', 44, 14-24.

DUBOSCQ, J. (1970) [Contributor to] Table ronde: Des centres - pourquoi faire?. 'Urbanisme', 120-1, 136-40, 137.

DUMONT, L. (1970) 'Homo Hierarchicus', London: Weidenfeld & Nicholson.

DUNCAN, O.D. (1957) Community size and the rural urban continuum, 'Cities and Society', P.K. Hatt and A.J. Reiss (eds). New York: Glencoe, 34-45.

DUNCAN, O.D. et al. (1960) 'Metropolis and Region'. Baltimore: Johns Hopkins University Press.

DUNN, E.S. (1970) A flow network image of urban structures, 'Urban Studies', 7, 239-58.

DURKHEIM, E. (1915) 'The Elementary Forms of the Religious Life'. London: Allen & Unwin.

DWYER, D.J. (ed.) (1971) 'The City as a Centre of Change in Asia'. Hong Kong: University Press.

DZIEWONSKI, K. (1968) Present needs and new developments in urban theory, 'Geographia Polonica', 14, 331-6.

ECCLES, J.C. (1970) 'Facing Reality'. London: Longman.

ELIADE, M. (1949) 'Le mythe de l'éternel retour: archétypes et répétition'. Paris: Gallimard.

ELIADE, M. (1957a) Centre du monde, temple, maison, le symbolisme cosmique des monuments religieux, 'Série Orientale Roma', 14, 57-82.

ELIADE, M. (1957b) 'Mythes, rêves et mystères'. Paris: Gallimard.

ELIADE, M. (1961) 'Le sacre et le profane'. Paris: Gallimard [New York: Harper Torchbook edition as 'The Sacred and the Profane'].

ELIADE, M. (1964) 'Myth and Reality'. London: Allen & Unwin.

ELIADE, M. (1969) 'The Quest'. Chicago: University Press.

EMPSON, W. (1953) 'Seven Types of Ambiguity'. London: Chatto & Windus.

ERIKSEN, E.G. (1954) 'Urban Behavior'. New York: Macmillan.

ESIN, E. (1963) 'Mecca: the Blessed'. New York: Crown.

ESSER, A.H. (1971) The importance of defining spatial behavioral parameters, 'Behavior and Environment: the Use of Space by Animals and Men'. New York: Plenum, 1-8.

EVANS, A.W. (1973) The location of headquarters of industrial companies, 'Urban Studies', 10, 387-95.

EVANS, H. (ed.) (1972) 'New Towns: the British Experience'. London: Knight.

EVENSON, N. (1966) 'Chandigarh'. Los Angeles: University of California Press.

EVENSON, N. (1973) 'Two Brazilian Capitals: Architecture and Urbanism in Rio de Janeiro and Brasilia'. New Haven: Yale University Press.

FAGIN, H. (1965) Social foresight and the use of urban space, Cities and Space', L. Wingo (ed.). Baltimore: Johns Hopkins University Press, 231-49.

FAINLICHT, M. (1970) Le citadin et la centralité, 'Urbanisme', 120-1, 21-3.

FALUDI, A. (1973) What is planning theory? 'A Reader in Planning Theory', A. Faludi (ed.). Oxford: Pergamon, 1-10.

FESTINGER, L. (1957) 'A Theory of Cognitive Dissonance'. Evanston: Row, Peterson.

FICKER, V.B. and GRAVES, H.S. (1971) 'Social Science and Urban Crisis'. New York: Macmillan.

FIREY, W.I. (1946) Ecological considerations in planning for rurban fringes, 'American Sociological Review', 11, 411-21.

FIREY, W.I. (1949) 'Land Use in Central Boston'. Cambridge, Mass.: Harvard University Press.

FISHBEIN, M. (1967) Attitude and the prediction of behavior, 'Readings in Attitude Theory and Measurement', M. Fishbein (ed.). New York: Wiley, 477-92.

FISHER, R.M. (ed.) (1955) 'The Metropolis in Modern Life'. New York: Doubleday.

FOLEY, D.L. (1952) The daily movement of population into central business districts, 'American Sociological Review', 17, 538-43.

FOLEY, D.L. (1964) An approach to metropolitan spatial structure, 'Explorations into Urban Structure'. Philadelphia: University of Pennsylvania Press, 21-78.

FORD, L.R. (1973) Individual decisions in the creation of the

American downtown, 'Geography', 58, 324-7.

FORRESTER, J.W. (1969) 'Urban Dynamics'. Cambridge, Mass.: MIT Press.

FORSTALL, R.L. and JONES, V. (1970) Selected demographic, economic, and governmental aspects of the contemporary metropolis, 'Metropolitan Problems', S.R. Miles (ed.). Toronto: Methuen, 5-69.

FRIEDMANN, J. (1966) 'Regional Development Policy: a Case Study of Venezuela'. Cambridge, Mass.: MIT Press.

FRIEDMANN, J. (1972) A general theory of polarized development, 'Growth Centers in Regional Economic Development', N.M. Hansen (ed.). New York: Free Press, 82-107.

FRIEDMANN, J. and MILLER, J. (1965) The urban field, 'Journal of the American Institute of Planners', 31, 312-20.

FRY, E. MAXWELL (1944) 'Fine Building'. London: Faber & Faber.

FUSTEL DE COULANGES, N.D. (1916) 'The Ancient City'. London: Simpkin [translation of 'Le Cité antique'. (1864) Paris: Hachette].

GARNER, B.J. (1965) 'The Internal Structure of Retail Nucleations'. Northwestern Studies in Geography no. 12. Evanston: Northwestern Department of Geography.

GARNER, B.J. (1967) Models of urban geography and settlement location, 'Models in Geography', R.J. Chorley and P. Haggett (eds). London: Methuen, 303-60.

GEDDES, P. (1915) 'Cities in Evolution' [republished in 1949, London: Williams & Norgate].

GIBSON, J.J. (1950) 'The Perception of the Visual World'. Boston: Houghton-Mifflin.

GIBSON, J.J. (1968) 'The Senses Considered as Perceptual Systems'. London: Allen & Unwin.

GILMOUR, J.M. (1974) External economies of scale, inter-industrial linkages and decision-making in manufacturing, 'Spatial Perspective on Industrial Organization and Decision-making', F.E.I. Hamilton (ed.). London: Wiley, 335-62.

GINSBURG, N.S. (1972) Planning for the Southeast Asian city, 'Focus', 22, no. 9, 1-8.

GODDARD, J. (1967) The internal structure of London's central area, 'Urban Core and Inner City'. Proceedings of the International Study Week, Amsterdam, 11-17 September 1966. Leiden: Brill, 118-40.

GODDARD, J. (1973) Office linkages and location: a study of communications and spatial patterns in central London, 'Progress in Planning', 1, part 2, 109-232.

GODDARD, J. (1975) 'Office Location in Urban and Regional Development'. London: Oxford University Press.

GOLLEDGE, R. (1960) Sydney's metropolitan fringe: a study in urban-rural relations, 'Australian Geographer', 7, 243-55.

GOMBRICH, E.H. (1961) 'Art and Illusion'. 2nd edn, New York: Bollingen.

GOODEY, B. (1971) 'Perception of the Environment: an Introduction to the Literature'. Birmingham: Centre for Urban and Regional Studies.

GOODEY, B. (1974) 'Images of Place: Essays on Environmental Perception, Communications and Education'. Birmingham: Centre for Urban and Regional Studies.

GOODWIN, W. (1965) The management center in the United States,

'Geographical Review', 55, 1-16.

GOTTMAN, J. (1974) The evolution of urban centrality: orientations
for research, 'Research Papers', no. 8. Oxford: School of
Geography.

GOULD, P.R. (1966) On mental maps [reprinted in R.M. Downs and D.
Stea (eds) (1973) 'Image and Environment: Cognitive Mapping and
Spatial Behavior'. Chicago: Aldine, 182-220].

GOULD, P.R. (1972) Pedagogic review [of A.G. Wilson, 1970], 'Annals
of the Association of American Geographers', 62, 689-700.

GOULDNER, A.W. (1960) The norm of reciprocity: a preliminary
statement, 'American Sociological Review', 25, 161-78.

GRADMANN, R. (1916) Schwäbische Städte, 'Zeitschrift der Gesellschaft für Erdkunde' [Berlin], 427. [See C.W. Baskin (1966),
translator of W. Christaller (1933), 16.]

GREGORY, R.L. (1973) The confounded eye, 'Illusion in Nature and
Art', R.L. Gregory and E.H. Gombrich (eds). London: Duckworth,
49-95.

GREGORY, T. (1973) The development of corporate planning in British
local government, 'Cities and City Regions in Europe', J. Holliday,
D. Liggins and W. Ogden (eds). Coventry: Lanchester Polytechnic,
187-94.

GRIFFIN, D.W. and PRESTON, R.E. (1966) A restatement of the 'transition zone' concept, 'Annals of the Association of American Geographers', 56, 339-50.

GROPIUS, W. (1950) Tradition and the center, 'Harvard Alumni
Bulletin', 53, 68-71.

GRUEN, V. (1965) 'The Heart of Our Cities: the Urban Crisis:
Diagnosis and Cure'. London: Thames & Hudson.

GURDJIEFF, G.I. (1950) 'All and Everything'. New York: Dutton.

GUTCH, R. (1972) The use of goals, 'Journal of the Royal Town
Planning Institute', 58, 264.

GUTTENBERG, A.Z. (1960) Urban structure and urban form, 'Journal of
the American Institute of Planners', 26, 104-10.

HAGERSTRAND, T. (1952) The propagation of innovation waves, 'Lund
Studies in Geography', Series B. Human Geography, 4, 3-19.

HALL, A.D. and FAGEN, R.E. (1956) Definition of system, 'General
Systems', 1, 18-29.

HALL, E.T. (1966) 'The Hidden Dimension'. New York: Doubleday.

HALL, P.G. (ed.) (1966) 'Von Thünen's Isolated State' [an English
edition of 'Der isolierte Stadt', first published in 1826, translated by C. Wartenberg. Oxford: Pergamon].

HALL, P.G. (1974) 'Urban and Regional Planning'. Harmondsworth:
Penguin.

HAMNETT, C. (1972) The social patterning of cities, 'Social Geography: New Trends in Geography', Units 9-12. Bletchley: Open
University Press, 29-63.

HAMNETT, C. (1973) Cosmopolitans and centralists, 'The City as a
Social System', Unit 8. Bletchley: Open University Press, 93-120.

HANDLIN, O. and BURCHARD, J. (eds) (1963) 'The Historian and the
City'. Cambridge, Mass.: Harvard University Press.

HARRIES, K.D. (1973) Spatial aspects of violence and metropolitan
population, 'The Professional Geographer', 25, 1-6.

HARRIS, B. (1966) The uses of theory in the simulation of urban

phenomena, 'Journal of the American Institute of Planners', 32,
258-72.
HARRIS, C.D. and ULLMAN, E.L. (1945) The nature of cities, 'Annals
of the American Academy of Political and Social Science', 242,
13-15.
HARRISON, D. and KAIN, J.F. (1970) 'An Historical Model or Urban
Form'. Harvard University Program on Regional and Urban Economics.
Discussion Paper no. 63.
HART, R.A. and MOORE, G.T. (1973) The development of spatial cog-
nition: a review, 'Image and Environment: Cognitive Mapping and
Spatial Behavior', R.M. Downs and D. Stea (eds). Chicago:
Aldine, 246-88.
HARTENSTEIN, W. and STAACK, G. (1967) Land use in the urban core,
'Urban Core and Inner City'. Proceedings of the International
Study Week, Amsterdam, 11-17 September 1966. Leiden: Brill,
35-52.
HARTSHORNE, R. (1960) 'Perspective on the Nature of Geography'.
London: John Murray.
HARVEY, D. (1970) Social processes and spatial form: an analysis
of the conceptual problems of urban planning [reprinted in 'Readings
in Social Geography', E. Jones (ed.). London: Oxford University
Press, 288-306].
HARVEY, D. (1972) Review [of P. Wheatley (1971)], 'Annals of the
Association of American Geographers', 62, 509-13.
HARVEY, D. (1973) 'Social Justice and the City'. London: Edward
Arnold.
HAUSER, F.L. (1951) The ecological pattern of four European cities
and two theories of urban expansion, 'Journal of the American
Institute of Planners', 17, 111-30.
HAUSER, P.M. (1965) Observations on the urban-folk and urban-rural
dichotomies as forms of western ethnocentrism, 'The Study of
Urbanization', P.M. Hauser and L.F. Schnore (eds). New York:
Wiley, 503-17.
HAWKES, J.E.Y. (1973) New towns in Britain, 'Transportation and
Environment - Policies, Plans and Practice', Symposium, Session 7.
University of Southampton.
HAWLEY, A. (1946) Discussion on W. Firey's ecological consideration
of the rurban fringe, 'American Sociological Review', 11, 421-3.
HAWLEY, A. (1950) 'Human Ecology'. New York: Ronald.
HAYEK, F.A. (1969) The primacy of the abstract, 'Beyond Reduction-
ism', A. Koestler and J.R. Smythies (eds). New York: Macmillan,
309-23.
HEATHCOTE, R.L. (1960) Geographical implications of some zoological
topics, 'Annals of the Association of American Geographers', 50,
191-2.
HEBB, D.O. (1949) 'The Organization of Behavior: a Neuropsycholo-
gical Theory'. New York: Wiley.
HEBB, D.O. (1951) The role of neurological ideas in psychology,
'Journal of Personality', 20, 39-55.
HEBB, D.O. (1958) 'A Textbook of Psychology'. Philadelphia:
Saunders.
HEINEMEYER, W.F. (1967) The urban core as a centre of attraction,
'Urban Core and Inner City'. Proceedings of the International Study
Week, Amsterdam, 11-17 September 1966. Leiden: Brill, 82-99.

HEINEMEYER, W.F. and VAN ENGELSDORP GASTELAARS, R. (1971) Urban core and inner city in Amsterdam, 'Tijdschrift voor economische en sociale geografie', 57, 207-16.

HELSON, H. (1964) 'Adaptation Level Theory'. New York: Harper & Row.

HELSON, H. and BEVAN, W. (1967) 'Contemporary Approaches to Psychology'. Princeton: Van Nostrand.

HERBERT, D.T. (1961) An approach to the study of the town as a central place, 'Sociological Review', 9, 273-92.

HILBERSEIMER, L. (1944) 'The New City'. Chicago: Theobald.

HIRSCHMAN, A.O. (1958) 'The Strategy of Economic Development'. New Haven: Yale University Press.

HODDER, B.W. (1968) 'Economic Development in the Tropics'. London: Methuen.

HOLZNER, L. (1970) The role of history and tradition in the urban geography of West Germany, 'Annals of the Association of American Geographers', 60, 315-39.

HOOVER, E.M. and VERNON, R. (1959) 'Anatomy of a Metropolis: the Changing Distribution of People and Jobs within the New York Metropolitan Region'. Cambridge, Mass.: Harvard University Press.

HOPPENFELD, M. (1962) An approach to urban design, 'Potomac Valley Architect', 6.

HORWOOD, E.M. and BOYCE, R.R. (1959) The CBD core-frame concept, 'Studies of the Central Business District and Urban Freeway Development'. Seattle: University of Washington Press, Chapter 2.

HOSELITZ, B.F. (1960) Generative and parasitic cities, 'Sociological Aspects of Economic Growth'. Chicago: Free Press, 185-216.

HOTELLING, H. (1929) Stability in competition, 'Economic Journal', 39, 41-57.

HOYLE, B.S. (1972) The port function in the urban development of tropical Africa, 'La croissance urbaine en Afrique noire et à Madagascar'. Paris: Éditions du Centre National de la Recherche Scientifique, no. 539, 705-18.

HOYT, H. (1939) 'The Structure and Growth of Residential Neighborhoods in American Cities'. Washington: US Govt Printing Office.

HOYT, H. (1964) Recent distortions of the classical models or urban structure, 'Land Economics', 40, 199-212 [reprinted in L.S. Bourne (ed.) (1971), 84-96].

HOWARD, E. (1902) 'Garden Cities of Tomorrow' [with preface by F.J. Osborn (1945) republished in 1965. London: Faber & Faber].

HUDNUT, J. (1949) 'Architecture and the Spirit of Man'. Cambridge, Mass.: Harvard University Press.

HUDSON, R. (1976) Linking studies of the individual with models of aggregate behaviour: an empirical example, 'Transactions of the Institute of British Geographers', 1, no. 2, 159-73.

HURD, R.M. (1903) 'Principles of City Land Values'. New York: Real Estate Record Association.

HUXLEY, J. (1959) Introduction [to] P. Teilhard de Chardin 'The Phenomenon of Man'. London: Collins.

INGRAM, D.R. (1974) Some comments on the use of ternary diagrams in urban classification. [Draft of a paper received 26 August].
'Irvine - the Genesis of a New Community' (1974). [Third Draft.]
Newport Beach, Calif.: Irvine Company

ISAAC, E. (1959-60) Religion, landscape and space, 'Landscape', 9, no. 2, 14-18.
ISAAC, E. (1961-2) The act and the covenant: the impact of religion on the landscape, 'Landscape', 11, no. 2, 12-17.
ISARD, W. (1956) 'Location and Space-Economy'. Cambridge, Mass.: MIT Press.
ITTELSON, W.H. (ed.) (1973) 'Environment and Cognition'. New York: Seminar.

JACOBS, J. (1961) 'The Death and Life of Great American Cities'. New York: Random House.
JANELLE, D.G. (1968) Central place development in a time-space framework, 'Professional Geographer', 20, 5-10.
JANELLE, D.G. (1969) Spatial reorganization: a model and a concept, 'Annals of the Association of American Geographers' 59, 348-64.
JEANNERET-GRIS, C.E. [Le Corbusier] (1924) 'Urbanisme' [translated by F. Etchells (1929) as 'The City of Tomorrow'. New York: Payson & Clarke].
JOHNS, E. (1969) Symmetry and asymmetry in the urban scene, 'Area', 1, 48-57.
JOHNSON, J.H. (ed.) (1974) 'Suburban Growth: Geographical Processes at the Edge of the Western City'. London: Wiley.
JOHNSTON, R.J. (1970) On spatial patterns in the residential structure of cities, 'Canadian Geographer', 14, 361-7 [see R.A. Murdie, 1970].
JOHNSTON, R.J. (1971a) Some limitations of factorial ecologies and social area analysis, 'Economic Geography', 47, 314-23.
JOHNSTON, R.J. (1971b) 'Urban Residential Patterns: an Introductory Review'. London: Bell.
JOHNSTON, R.J. and KISSLING, C.C. (1971) Establishment use patterns within central places, 'Australia Geographical Studies', 9, 116-32.
JONES, E. (1956) Cause and effect in human geography, 'Annals of the Association of American Geographers', 46, 369-77.
JONES, E. (1962) 'A Social Geography of Belfast'. London: Oxford University Press.
JONES, E. (1972) Some geographical aspects of urbanization, 'The Exploding City', W.D.C. Wright and D.H. Stewart (eds). Edinburgh: University Press, 85-93.
JONES, S.B. (1954) A unified field theory of political geography, 'Annals of the Association of American Geographers', 44, 111-23.
JUNG, C.G. (1959) 'The Archetypes and the Unconscious', Collected Works, 9, part I. London: Routledge & Kegan Paul.
JUTHEIM, F. (1963) Urban space and urban design, 'Cities and Space: the Future Use of Urban Land'. L. Wingo (ed.). Baltimore: Johns Hopkins University Press, 103-31.   .

KAMERON, J. (1973) Experimental studies of environment perception, 'Environment and Cognition', W.H. Ittelson (ed.). New York: Seminar, 157-67.
KANSKY, K.J. (1963) 'Structure of Transportation Networks'. University of Chicago: Department of Geography, Research Paper no. 84.
KAPLAN, S. (1973) Cognitive maps in perception and thought, 'Image and Environment', R.M. Downs and D. Stea (eds). London: Edward Arnold, 63-86.

KAPLAN, S. and WENDT, J.S. (1972) 'Environmental Design:
Research and Practice'. Proceedings of the Third Annual Environ-
mental Design Research Association Conference [EDRA3]. Los
Angeles: University of California. 1, 6-8-1 to 6-8-5.
KEEBLE, L. (1961) 'Town Planning at the Crossroads'. London:
Estates Gazette.
KEEBLE, L. (1964) 'Principles and Practice of Town and Country
Planning'. London: Estates Gazette.
KELLY, G.A. (1955) 'The Psychology of Personal Constructs'.
2 vols, New York: Norton.
KEPES, G. (1956) 'The New Landscape'. Chicago: Theobald.
KHOSLA, R. (1971) Chandigarh: dream and reality, 'Geographical
Magazine', 43, 679-83.
KITE, E.S. (ed.) (1929) 'L'Enfant and Washington 1791-1792'.
Baltimore: Johns Hopkins University Press.
KLEIN, H.-J. (1967) The delimitation of the town-centre in the
image of its citizens, 'Urban Core and Inner City'. Proceedings
of the International Study Week, Amsterdam, 11-17 September 1966.
Leiden: Brill, 286-306.
KNIGHT, D.B. and ITO, T. (1972) Office parks: the Oak Brook
example, 'Land Economics', 48, 65-9.
KOESTLER, A. (1964) 'The Act of Creation'. London: Hutchinson.
KOESTLER, A. and SMYTHIES, J.R. (eds) (1969) "Beyond Reductionism'.
New York: Macmillan.
KORCELLI, P. (1972) Urban spatial growth: a wave-like approach,
'Geographia Polonica', 24, 45-55.
KRISTENSSON, F. (1967) The impact of changing economic and
organizational structure on urban core development, 'Urban Core and
Inner City'. Proceedings of the International Study Week, Amster-
dam, 11-17 September 1966. Leiden: Brill, 404-12.
KRUMME, G. (1969) Toward a geography of enterprise, 'Economic
Geography', 45, 30-40.
KUHN, T.S. (1970) 'The Structure of Scientific Revolutions'. 2nd
edn, Chicago: University Press.
KURTZ, R.A. and EICHER, J.B. (1958) Fringe and suburb: a confusion
of concepts, 'Social Forces', 37, 32-7.

LABASSE, J. (1970) Signification et avenir des centres, 'Urbanisme',
120-1, 8-17.
LANGER, S.K. (1953) 'Feeling and Form'. London: Routledge & Kegan
Paul.
LE CORBUSIER, see C.E. JEANNERET-GRIS.
LEE, T.R. (1968) Urban neighbourhood as a socio-spatial schema,
'Human Relations', 21, 241-67.
LEFEBVRE, H. (1970) 'La révolution urbaine'. Paris: Gallimard.
LEFEBVRE, H. (1972) 'La pensée marxiste et la ville'. Tournai:
Casterman.
LEONTIEF, W.W. (1966) 'Input-output Economics'. New York: Oxford
University Press.
LEVER, W.F. (1972) The intra-urban movement of manufacturing: a
Markov approach, 'Transactions of the Institute of British Geo-
graphers', 56, 21-37.
LÉVI-STRAUSS, C. (1969) 'The Elementary Structures of Kinship'.
Boston: Beacon.

LEWIN, K. (1935) 'A Dynamic Theory of Personality'. New York: McGraw-Hill.

LEWIN, K. (1936) 'Principles of Topological Discovery'. New York: McGraw-Hill.

LEWIS, O. (1965) Further observations on the folk-urban continuum and urbanization with special reference to Mexico City, 'The Study of Urbanization', P.M. Hauser and L.F. Schnore (eds). New York: Wiley, 503-17 [Note 2, 514-15, refers].

LEWISON, G. et al. (1969) 'Coventry: New Architecture'. Warwick: Editors.

LLEWELLYN-DAVIES, R. (1966) Town design, 'The Town Planning Review', 37, 157-72.

LOPEZ, R.S. (1963) The crossroads within the wall, 'The Historian and the City', O. Handlin and J. Burchard (eds). Cambridge, Mass.: Harvard University Press.

LOSCH, A. (1943) 'The Economics of Location' [translation of 2nd edition by W.H. Woglom and W.F. Stolper]. New York: Wiley.

LOW, N. (1975) Centrism and the provision of services in residential areas, 'Urban Studies', 12, 177-91.

LOWENTHAL, D. (ed.) (1967) 'Environmental Perception and Behavior'. Research Paper no. 109. Chicago: University of Chicago, Department of Geography.

LOWENTHAL, D. (1975) Past time, present place, 'Geographical Review', 65, 1-36.

LOWENTHAL, D. and RIEL, M. (1972) 'Environmental Structures: Semantic and Experiential Components'. New York: American Geographical Society, Publications in Environmental Perception no. 8.

LYNCH, K. (1960) 'The Image of the City'. Cambridge, Mass.: Harvard University Press.

LYCNH, K. and RODWIN, L. (1958) A theory of urban form, 'Journal of the American Institute of Planners', 24, 201-14.

LYNDON, D. et al. (1962) Toward making places: inside and outside, 'Landscape', 12, no. 1, 31-41.

MCGEE, T.G. (1971) 'The Urbanization Process in the Third World'. London: Bell.

MCKENZIE, R.D. (1933) 'The Metropolitan Community'. New York: Russell & Russell.

MCTAGGART, W.D. (1965) The reality of urbanism, 'Pacific Viewpoint', 6, 220-4.

MAGEE, B. (1973) 'Popper'. London: Fontana-Collins.

MAJEWSKI, J. (1971) The development of the street patterns in four town cores of medieval origin, 'Svensk Geografisk Arbosk', 47, 163-83 [Summary in English].

MALIN, J.C. (1950) Ecology and history, 'The Scientific Monthly', 70, 295-8.

MANN, P. (1965) 'An Approach to Urban Sociology'. London: Routledge & Kegan Paul.

MANNERS, G. (1974) The office in metropolis: an opportunity for shaping metropolitan America, 'Economic Geography', 50, 93-110.

MARCUSE, H. (1964) 'One Dimensional Man: Studies in the Ideology of Advanced Industrial Society'. London: Routledge & Kegan Paul.

MARUYAMA, M. (1963) The second cybernetics: deviation amplifying mutual causal processes, 'American Scientist', 51, 164-79.

MASSEY, D. (1975) Behavioural research, 'Area', 7, 201-3.
MATHUR, O.P. (1973) 'Growth Poles and Growth Centres in Regional
Development: a Bibliography'. Monticello, Illinois: Council of
Planning Librarians, Exchange Bibliography no. 387.
MAUSS, M. (1954) 'The Gift'. London: Cohen & West [English
translation of 'Essai sur le don', by I. Cunnison].
MAYER, H.M. and KOHN, C.F. (1959) 'Readings in Urban Geography'.
Chicago: University Press.
MEDAWAR, P.B. (1961) 'The Future of Man'. London: Methuen.
MEDAWAR, P.B. (1967) 'The Art of the Soluble'. London: Methuen.
MEDAWAR, P.B. (1969) 'Induction and Intuition in Scientific Thought'.
Philadelphia: American Philosophical Society [and London:
Methuen].
MEDDIN, J. (1975) Attitudes, values and related concepts: a system
of classification, 'Social Science Quarterly', 55, 889-900.
MEIER, R.L. (1962) 'A Communications Theory of Urban Growth'.
Cambridge, Mass.: MIT Press.
MERCER, D. (1971) Discretionary travel behaviour and the urban
mental map, 'Australian Geographical Studies', 9, 133-43.
MERLIN, P. (1971) 'New Towns'. London: Methuen.
METTON, A. (1969) Le quartier: étude géographique et psycho-
sociologique, 'Canadian Geographer', 13, 299-316.
METTON, A. and BERTRAND, M.-J. (1974) Les espaces vécus dans une
grande agglomération, L'Espace Géographique', 3, 137-46.
METZNER, R. (1971) 'Maps of Consciousness'. New York: Macmillan.
MEYERSON, M. et al. (1963) 'The Face of the Metropolis'. New York:
Random House.
MICHELSON, W. (1970) 'Man and His Urban Environment: a Sociological
Approach'. Reading, Mass.: Addison-Wesley.
MILLER, I.R.W. (1972) A synopsis of corridor development, 'Royal
Australian Planning Institute Journal', 10, no. 3, 100-4.
MILLS, C.W. (1959) 'The Sociological Imagination'. London: Oxford
University Press.
MINER, H. (1952) The folk-urban continuum, 'American Sociological
Review', 17, 529-37.
MOLES, A.A. (1957) 'La création scientifique'. Geneva: Kister.
MOLES, A.A. and ROHMER, E. (1972) 'Psychologie de l'espace'.
Tournai: Casterman.
MONOD, J. (1972) 'Chance and Necessity'. London: Collins.
MONTGOMERY, R. (1968) Urban design - illusive reality, 'Planning
1968', American Society of Planning Officials, 189-205.
MORI, A. (1964) Il valore della finalità in geografia umana,
'Bollettino della Societa Geografica Italiana', 84, 3-13.
MOSELEY, M.J. (1972) The impact of growth centres in rural regions -
I and II, 'Regional Studies', 7, 57-94.
MOSELEY, M.J. (1973) Growth centres: a shibboleth?, 'Area', 5,
143-50.
MOSELEY, M.J. (1974) 'Growth Centres in Spatial Planning'. Oxford:
Pergamon.
MUMFORD, L. (1961) 'The City in History'. London: Secker & Warburg.
MUMFORD, L. (1962) On the origin of cities, 'Landscape', 12, no. 3,
14-16.
MURDIE, R.A. (1969) The social geography of the city: theoretical
and empirical background [reprinted in L.S. Bourne (ed.) (1971)

'Internal Structure of the City'. New York: Oxford University Press, 279-90].

MURDIE, R.A. (1970) A reply to 'On spatial patterns in the residential structure of cities' [see R.J. Johnston, 1970]. 'Canadian Geographer', 14, 367-9.

MURPHEY, R. (1964) The city in the swamp: aspects of the site and early growth of Calcutta, 'Geographical Journal', 130, 241-56.

MURPHY, R.E. (1972) 'The Central Business District'. Chicago: Aldine.

MURPHY, R.E. and VANCE, J.E. (1954) Delimiting the CBD, 'Economic Geography', 30, 189-222.

MURPHY, R.E. and VANCE, J.E. (1954) A comparative study of nine central business districts, 'Economic Geography', 30, 301-36.

MURPHY, R.E., VANCE, J.E. and EPSTEIN, B.J. (1955) Internal structure of the CBD, 'Economic Geography', 31, 21-46.

MUSIL, J. (1968) The development of Prague's ecological structure, 'Readings in Urban Sociology', R.E. Pahl (ed.). London: Pergamon, 232-59.

'Nation's Capital [The] - a Policies Plan for the Year 2000' (1961). Washington: National Capital Planning Commission and Regional Planning Council.

NEALE, W.C. (1967) The market in theory and history, 'Trade and Market in the Early Empires', K. Polanyi, C.M. Arensberg and H.W. Pearson (eds). New York: Free Press, 357-71.

NEEDHAM, B. (1971) Concrete problems, not abstract goals, 'Journal of the Royal Town Planning Institute', 57, 317-19.

NELSON, R.L. (1958) 'The Selection of Retail Locations'. New York: Dodge.

NEUTRA, R.J. (1955) The adaptation of design to the metropolis, 'The Metropolis in Modern Life', R.M. Fisher (ed.). New York: Doubleday, 261-7.

NEWLING, B.E. (1969) The spatial variation of urban population densities [reprinted in L.S. Bourne (ed.) (1971) 'Internal Structure of the City'. New York: Oxford University Press, 329-37].

NEYRET, R. (1970) Les quartiers historiques: musees ou elements du centre, 'Urbanisme', 120-1, 36-43.

NORDBECK, S. (1971) Urban allometric growth, 'Geografiska Annaler', 53B, 54-67.

NORTH, D.C. (1955) Location theory and regional economic growth [reprinted in J. Friedmann and W. Alonso (1964) 'Regional Development and Planning'. Cambridge, Mass.: MIT Press, 240-55].

NUTTALL, G. (1972) The £1 million gamble on the rebirth of Regent St., 'Sunday Times', 12 March, 63.

OGDEN, C.K. (1932) 'Opposition: a Linguistic and Psychological Analysis' [republished 1967, Bloomington: Indiana University Press].

OLMSTED, F.L. and VAUX, C. (1858) 'Description of a Plan for the Improvement of Central Park'. New York: Aldine [reprinted in D.R. Weimer (1962) 'City and Country in America'. New York: Meredith, 173-80].

OSBORN, F.J. and WHITTICK, A. (1963) 'The New Towns: the Answer to Megalopolis'. New York: McGraw-Hill.

PAHL, R.E. (1965) 'Urbs in Rure: the Metropolitan Fringe in Hertfordshire'. London: London School of Economics and Political Science Geographical Papers, no. 2.

PAHL, R.E. (ed.) (1968) 'Readings in Urban Sociology'. London: Pergamon [includes his The rural-urban continuum, 263-97].

PAPAGEORGIOU, A. (1971) 'Continuity and Change'. London: Pall Mall.

PARETO, V. (1935) 'The Mind and Society: a Treatise on General Sociology', A. Livingston (ed.), A. Bongiorno, A. Livingston and J.H. Rogers (translators). 4 vols, New York: Dover [reprinted 1963].

PARKER, A.J. (1975) Hypermarkets: the changing pattern of retailing, 'Geography', 60, 120-4.

PARR, A.E. (1964-5) Environmental design and psychology, 'Landscape', 14, no. 2, 15-18.

PARR, A.E. (1965) In search of theory [reprinted in H.M. Proshansky, W.H. Ittelson and L.G. Rivlin (eds) (1970) 'Environmental Psychology: Man and his Physical Setting'. New York: Holt, Rinehart & Winston, 11-16].

PEARSON, H.W. (1957) The economy has no surplus: critique of a theory of development, Trade and Market in the Early Empires, K. Polanyi, C.M. Arensberg and H.W. Pearson (eds). Chicago: Free Press, 320-41.

PEARSON, K. (1930) 'The Life, Letters and Labours of Francis Galton'. 3 vols, Cambridge: University Press.

PECKHAM, M. (1965) 'Man's Rage for Chaos'. Philadelphia: Chilton.

PERROUX, F. (1950) Economic space: theory and applications, 'Quarterly Journal of Economics', 64, 89-104.

PERROUX, F. (1955) Note sur la notion de 'pôle de croissance' [translated and reprinted in D.L. McKee, R.D. Dean and W.H. Leahy (eds) (1970) 'Regional Economics: Theory and Practice'. New York: Free Press, 93-103].

PIGGOTT, S. (1972) Conclusion, 'Man, Settlement and Urbanism', P.J. Ucko, R. Tringham and G.W. Dimbleby (eds). London: Duckworth, 947-53.

PILLSBURY, R. (1970) The urban street pattern as a culture indicator: Pennsylvania, 1682-1815, 'Annals of the Association of American Geographers', 60, 428-46.

PINDER, D.A. and WITHERICK, M.E. (1972) The principles, practice and pitfalls of nearest-neighbour analysis, 'Geography', 57, 277-88.

PIRENNE, H. (1925) 'Medieval Cities: their Origins and the Revival of Trade'. New Haven: Princeton University Press.

Planning of a New Town [The]: 'Data and Design based on a Study for a New Town at Hook, Hampshire' (1965). London: Greater London Council.

POPPER, K.R. (1961) 'The Poverty of Historicism'. London: Routledge & Kegan Paul [originally published 1957].

POPPER, K.R. (1968) 'The Logic of Scientific Discovery'. London: Hutchinson [first published in 1934].

POPPER, K.R. (1972a) 'Conjectures and Refutations: the Growth of Scientific Knowledge'. London: Routledge & Kegan Paul [originally published 1963].

POPPER, K.R. (1972b) 'Objective knowledge: An Evolutionary Approach'. London: Oxford University Press.

POTTIER, P. (1963) Axes de communications et développement économique, 'Revue Économique', no. 1, 58-132.

POUNDS, N.J.G. (1947) Port and outport in North-west Europe, 'Geographical Journal', 109, 216-28.

POWERS, W.T. (1973) 'Behavior: the Control of Perception'. Chicago: Aldine.

PRED, A. (1962) 'The External Relations of Cities during "Industrial Revolution", with a Case Study of Göteborg, Sweden, 1868-1890'. Chicago: University Department of Geography Research Papers, no. 76.

PRED, A. (1965) Industrialization, initial advantage, and American economic growth, 'Geographical Review', 55, 158-85.

PRED, A. (1973) The growth and development of systems of cities in advanced economies, 'Systems of Cities and Information Flows'. Lund: Gleerup, 9-82.

PRESTON, R.E. (1966) The zone in transition: a study of urban land use patterns, 'Economic Geography', 42, 236-60.

PRESTON, R.E. (1971a) The structure of central place systems, 'Economic Geography', 47, 136-55.

PRESTON, R.E. (1971b) Toward verification of a 'classical' centrality model, 'Tijdschrift voor economische en sociale geografie', 67, 301-7.

PRICE, E.T. (1968) The central courthouse square in the American county seat, 'Geographical Review', 58, 29-60.

PRICE, H.H. (1969) 'Thinking and Experience'. London: Hutchinson.

PROKOP, D. (1967) Image and functions of the city, 'Urban Core and Inner City'. Proceedings of the International Study Week, Amsterdam, 11-17 September 1966. Leiden: Brill, 22-34.

PROSHANKSY, H.M., ITTELSON, W.H. and RIVLIN, L.G. (eds) (1970) 'Environmental Psychology'. New York: Holt, Rinehart & Winston.

PRYOR, R.J. (1968) Defining the rural-urban fringe, 'Social Forces', 47, 202-15 [reprinted in L.S. Bourne (ed.) (1971) 'Internal Structure of the City'. New York: Oxford University Press, 59-68].

QUEEN, S.A. and CARPENTER, D.B. (1953) 'The American City'. New York: McGraw-Hill.

QUINN, J.A. (1940) The Burgess zonal hypothesis and its critics, 'American Sociological Review', 5, 210-18.

RACINE, J.-B. (1973) La centralité commerciale relative des municipalités du système métropolitaine montréalais: un exemple d'utilisation des méthodes d'analyse statistique en géographie, 'L'Espace Géographique', 4, 275-89.

RAND, G. (1969) Pre-Copernican views of the city, 'Architectural Forum', 131, no. 2, 77-81.

RANNELS, J. (1956) 'The Core of the City'. New York: University of Columbia Press.

RAPOPORT, A. and HAWKES, R. (1970) The perception of urban complexity, 'Journal of the American Institute of Planners', 36, 106-11.

RAPOPORT, A. and KANTOR, R.E. (1967) Complexity and ambiguity in environmental design, 'Journal of the American Institute of Planners', 33, 210-21.

RAY, A.S. (1973) Shopping policy in Leeds, 'Town and Country Planning', 41, 559-62.

RAY, D.M. and BREWIS, T.N. (1976) The geography of income and its correlates, 'Canadian Geographer', 20, 41-71.

READE, E. (1968) 'Community' and the 'rural-urban continuum' - are the concepts outdated?, 'Journal of the Town Planning Institute', 54, 426-9.

REDFIELD, R. and SINGER, M.B. (1954) The cultural role of cities, 'Economic Development and Cultural Change', 3, 53-73.

REES, J. (1972) The industrial corporation and location decision analysis, 'Area', 4, 199-205.

REES, J. (1974) Decision-making, the growth of the firm and the business environment, 'Spatial Perspectives on Industrial Organization and Decision-making', F.E.I. Hamilton (ed.). London: Wiley, 189-211.

REISSMAN, L. (1964) 'The Urban Process: Cities in Industrial Societies'. New York: Free Press.

RENDU, P. (1970) Rôle fonctionelle du centre, 'Urbanisme', 20-1, 18-20.

RENFREW, C. (1972) 'The Emergence of Civilisation'. London: Methuen.

RENFREW, C. (1975) Trade as action at a distance: questions of integration and communication, 'Ancient Civilisation and Trade', J.A. Sabloff and C.C. Lamberg-Karlovsky (eds). Albuquerque: University of New Mexico Press, 3-59.

REPS, J.W. (1965) 'Town Planning in Frontier America'. Princeton: University Press.

RICHARDS, P. (1974) Kant's geography and mental maps, 'Transactions of the Institute of British Geographers', 61,1-16.

RIMMER, P.J. (1967) The search for spatial regularities in the development of Australian seaports 1861-1961/2, 'Geografiska Annaler', 49B, 42-54.

ROBBINS, S.M. and TERLECKYJ, N.E. (1960) Money Metropolis: a Locational Study of Financial Activities in the New York Region'. Cambridge, Mass.: Harvard University Press.

ROBINSON, G.W.S. (1967) [Secretary's report on] Section VIII: Regional Geography, 'Twentieth International Geographical Congress Proceedings', J.W. Watson (ed.). London: Nelson, 177-80.

ROBSINON, R. and SHAW, J. (1973) Density gradients and urban shape in the Illawara Corridor, 1954-66, 'Australian Geographical Studies', 11, 211-27.

ROBSON, B.T. (1973) A view on the urban scene, 'Studies in Human Geography', M. Chisholm and B. Rodgers (eds). London: Heinemann, 203-41.

ROBSON, B.T. (1975) 'Urban Social Areas'. London: Oxford University Press.

RODWIN, L. (1956) 'The British New Towns Policy: Problems and Implications'. Cambridge, Mass.: Harvard University Press.

RODWIN, L. (1970) 'Nations and Cities: a Comparison of Strategies for Urban Growth'. Boston: Houghton-Mifflin.

ROGERS, A. (1967) Theories of intra-urban spatial structure [reprinted in L.S. Bourne (ed.) (1971) 'Internal Structure of the City'. New York: Oxford University Press, 210-15].

ROSE, A.J. (1966) Metropolitan primacy as the normal state, 'Pacific Viewpoint', 7, 1-27.

ROSE, A.M. (1962) A systematic summary of symbolic interaction

theory, 'Human Behavior and Social Processes', A.M. Rose (ed.).
London: Routledge & Kegan Paul, 3-19.
ROSENAU, H. (1974) 'The Ideal City: its Architectural Evolution'.
London: Studio Vista.
ROWLEY, G. (1965) A note on central business research in Britain,
'Professional Geographer', 17, 15-16.
ROWLEY, G. (1974) Notions and realities within central place
studies: an assessment, 'Die Erde', 105, 265-74.
RUSSELL, J.C. (1972) 'Medieval Regions and their Cities'.   Newton
Abbot: David & Charles.
RUSSWURM, L. (1970) 'Development of an Urban Corridor System:
Toronto to Stratford Area 1941-66'.   Research Paper no. 3.
Toronto: Regional Development Branch, Ontario Department of
Treasury and Economics.

SAARINEN, E. (1943) 'The City'.   Cambridge, Mass.:   MIT Press.
SADLER, B. (1970-1) Perception of environment: some theoretical
aspects, 'The Albertan Geographer', 7, 52-7.
SARGENT, C.S. (1972) Toward a dynamic model of urban morphology,
'Economic Geography', 48, 357-74.
SARRE, P. (1972) Perception, 'Channels of Synthesis', Unit 16.
Bletchley: Open University Press, 15-43.
SARRE, P. et al. (1973) 'The Future City', Units 30-3.   Bletchley:
Open University Press.
SCHAFFER, F. (1970) 'The New Town Story'.   London: MacGibbon &
Kee.
SCHEIN, I. (1970) La notion d'espace global polyvalent, 'Urbanisme',
120-1, 28-30, 137-9.
SCHNORE, L.F. (1965) 'The Urban Scene: Human Ecology and Demo-
graphy'.   New York: Free Press.
SCHNORE, L.F. (1966) The rural-urban variable: an urbanite's
perspective, 'Rural Sociology', 31, 131-43.
SCHÖLLER, P. (1966) Centre-shifting and centre mobility in Japanese
cities, 'Proceedings of the IGU Symposium in Urban Geography',
K. Norborg (ed.).   Lund: Gleerup, 577-93.
SCHORSKE, C.E. (1963) The idea of the city in European thought:
Voltaire to Spengler, 'The Historian and the City', O. Handlin and
J. Burchard (eds).   Cambridge, Mass.:   Harvard University Press,
95-114.
SCHULTZ, T.W. (1953) 'The Economic Organization of Agriculture'.
New York: McGraw-Hill.
SEAMON, D. (1972) Environmental imagery: an overview and tentative
ordering, 'Environmental Design: Research and Practice'.   Proceed-
ings of the Third Annual Environmental Design Research Association
Conference [EDRA3].   Los Angeles: University of California, 1, 23,
7-1-1 to 7-1-7.
SELF, P. (1972) Show me a structure plan, daddy!, 'Town and Country
Planning', 40, 558-60.
SENNETT, R. (1970) 'The Uses of Disorder'.   Harmondsworth: Penguin.
SHEVKY, E. and BELL, W. (1955) 'Social Area Analysis: Theory,
Illustrative Application and Computational Procedures'.   Stanford:
University Press.
'Shopping for Pleasure: a Survey of Shopping Centres in North
America' (1969).   London: Capital and Counties.

SIDDALL, W.R. (1961) Wholesale-retail trade ratios as indices of urban centrality, 'Economic Geography', 37, 124-52.

SIMMONS, J.W. (1965) Descriptive models or urban land use, 'Canadian Geographer', 9, 170-4.

SINCLAIR, R. (1967) Von Thünen and urban sprawl, 'Annals of the Association of American Geographers', 57, 72-87.

SITTE, C. (1889) 'Der Städtebau' [translated by C.T. Stewart (1945) as 'The Art of Building Cities'. New York: Reinhold].

SJOBERG, G. (1960) 'The Preindustrial City'. Chicago: Free Press.

SMAILES, A.E. (1971) Urban systems, 'Transactions and Papers of the Institute of British Geographers', 53, 1-14.

SMITH, B.A. (1972) Shopping in the seventies - Velizy 2, 'Town and Country Planning', 41, 122-6.

SMITH, P.F. (1974) 'The Dynamics of Urbanism'. London: Hutchinson.

SMITH, P.F. (1975) Symbolic meaning in contemporary cities, 'Ekistics', 39, 159-64.

SMITH, P.J. Calgary: a study in urban pattern, 'Economic Geography', 38, 315-29.

SMITH, T.L. (1937) 'The Population of Louisiana: its Composition and Changes', Louisiana Agricultural Experiment Station Bulletin, 293, 24-6.

SMITH, T.L. (1947) 'The Sociology of Rural Life'. New York: Harper.

SMOLENSKY, E. and RATAJCZAK, D. (1965) The conception of cities, 'Explorations in Entrepreneurial History', 2, 2nd series, 90-131.

SMOLSKI, C.E. (1972) European new towns: focus on London, 'Focus', 22, no. 6.

SMYTHIES, J.R. (1969) Aspects of consciousness, 'Beyond Reductionism', A. Koestler and J.R. Smythies (eds). New York: Macmillan, 233-45.

SOJA, E.W. (1971) 'The Political Organization of Space'. Washington: Association of American Geographers Resource Papers no. 8.

SOLESBURY, W. (1975) Ideas about structure plans; past, present and future, 'Town Planning Review', 46, 245-54.

SONNENFELD, J. (1966) Variable values in space and landscape: an enquiry into the nature of environmental necessity, 'Journal of Social Issues', 22, no. 4, 71-82.

SOROKIN, P. and ZIMMERMAN, C.C. (1929) 'Principles of Rural-Urban Sociology'. New York: Holt.

'South Hampshire Structure Plan: Draft Document for Participation and Consultation' (1972). Hampshire County Council, Portsmouth and Southampton City Councils.

STAFFORD, H.A. (1962) The dispersed city, 'Professional Geographer', 14, 8-10.

STANILAWSKI, D. (1946) The origin and spread of the grid-pattern town, 'Geographical Review', 36, 105-20.

STANLEY, W.R. (1970) Transport expansion in Liberia, 'Geographical Review', 60, 529-47.

STEA, D. (1967) Reasons for our moving, 'Landscape', 17, no. 1, 27-8.

STEIN, C.S. (1966) 'Toward New Towns for America'. Cambridge, MASS.: MIT Press.

STEINITZ, C. (1968) Meaning and the congruence of urban form and activity, 'Journal of the Institute of American Planners', 34, 233-48.

STEISS, A.W. (1974) 'Urban Systems Dynamics'. Lexington: Heath.

STEWARD, J.H. (1955) 'Theory of Culture Change'. Urbana: University of Illinois Press.

STEWART, C.T. (1958) The urban-rural dichotomy: concepts and uses, 'American Journal of Sociology', 64, 152-8.

STEWART, T.C. (1970) 'The City as an Image of Man: a Study of the City Form in Mythology and Psychology'. London: Latimer.

STOW, J. (1603) 'A Survey of London' [C.L. Kingston (ed.) (1908), 2 vols. Oxford: Clarendon].

STRAUSS, A.L. (1961) 'Images of the American City'. New York: Free Press.

STUDER, R.G. (1971) Discussant [on communal behavior and environment], 'Behavior and Environment: the Uses of Space by Animals and Men'. New York: Plenum, 325-8.

SULLIVAN, H.S. (1953) 'The Interpersonal Theory of Psychiatry'. New York: Norton.

SVART, L. (1974) On the priority of behaviour in behavioural research: a dissenting view, 'Area', 6, 301-5.

TAAFE, E.J., MORRILL, R.L. and GOULD, P.R. (1963) Transport expansion in underdeveloped countries: a comparative analysis, 'Geographical Review', 53, 503-29.

TAYLOR, E.G.R. (1938) [opening contributor to] Discussion on the geographical distribution of industry, 'Geographical Journal', 92, 22-7.

TAYLOR, G.R. (1915) The outer ring of industry, 'Satellite Cities', 1-20 [reprinted in C.N. Glaab (1963) 'The American City: a Documentary History'. Homewood: Dorsey, 438-49].

TAYLOR, J. (1971) The shadow of the mind, 'New Scientist and Science Journal', 735-7.

TEILHARD DE CHARDIN, P. (1959) 'The Phenomenon of Man'. London: Collins,

TER HART, H.W. (1967) List of terms used in the study of urban core and inner city problems, 'Urban Core and Inner City'. Proceedings of the International Study Week, Amsterdam, 11-17 September 1966. Leiden: Brill, 550-72.

THIEL, P. (1970) Notes on the description, scaling notation, and scoring of some perceptual and cognitive attributes of the physical environment, 'Environmental Psychology', H.M. Proshansky, W.H. Ittelson and L.G. Rivlin (eds). New York: Holt, Rinehart & Winston, 593-619.

THOMAS, D. (1970) 'London's Green Belt'. London: Faber & Faber.

THOMAS, D. (1972) Problems in planning the rural-urban fringe with special reference to London, 'Geographia Polonica', 24, 81-94.

THOMAS, R. and CRESSWELL, P. (1972) 'The New Town Idea'. Milton Keynes: Open University Press.

THOMAS, R.W. (1972) The retail structure of the central area, 'The Retail Structure of Cities', Institute of British Geographers, Occasional Paper no. 1, Urban Study Group, 69-93.

THORNBURY, W.D. (1954) 'Principles of Geomorphology'. New York: Wiley.

THORNGREN, B. (1967) External economies of the urban core, 'Urban Core and Inner City'. Proceedings of International Study Week, Amsterdam, 11-17 September 1966. Leiden: Brill, 413-20.

THORNGREN, B. (1970) How do contact systems affect regional

development?, 'Environment and Planning', 2, 409-27.
THORPE, D. and RHODES, T.C. (1966) The shopping centers of the Tyneside urban region and large scale grocery retailing, 'Economic Geography', 42, 52-73.
THORPE, H. (1949) The green villages of County Durham, 'Transactions and Papers of the Institute of British Geographers', 15, 155-80.
THRUPP, S.L. (1963) The city as an idea of social order, 'The Historian and the City', O. Handlin and J. Burchard (eds). Cambridge, Mass.: Harvard University Press, 121-32.
TIEBOUT, C.M. (1957) Location theory, empirical evidence, and economic evolution, 'Papers and Proceedings of the Regional Science Association', 3, 74-86.
TIMMS, D. (1971) 'The Urban Mosaic'. Cambridge: University Press.
TOLMAN, E.C. (1948) Cognitive maps in rats and men, 'Psychological Review', 55, 189-208.
TÖNNIES, F. (1887) 'Gemeinschaft und Gesellschaft' [translated by C.P. Loomis (1955) as 'Community and Association'. London: Routledge & Kegan Paul].
'Trans-Canada Field Excursion Guide Book' (1972), A.L. Farley (ed.). Montreal: International Geographical Congress, August.
TSURU, S. (1963) The economic significance of cities, 'The Historian and the City', O. Handlin and J. Burchard (eds). Cambridge, Mass.: Harvard University Press, 44-55.
TUAN, Y.-F. (1971) 'Man and Nature'. Washington: Association of American Geographers Resource Paper no. 10.
TUAN, Y.-F. (1973) Ambiguity in attitudes toward environment, 'Annals of the Association of American Geographers', 63, 411-23.
TUAN, Y.-F. (1975) Images and mental maps, 'Annals of the Association of American Geographers', 65, 205-13.
TUNNARD, C. and PUSHKAREV, B. (1963) 'Man-made America: Chaos or Control'. New Haven: Yale University Press.
TUZET, H. (1965) 'Le cosmos et l'imagination'. Paris: Corti.

UCKO, P.J., TRINGHAM, R. and DIMBLEBY, G.W. (eds) (1972) 'Man, Settlement, and Urbanism'. London: Duckworth.
ULLMAN, E.L. (1958) Regional development and the geography of concentration [reprinted in J. Friedmann and W. Alonso (1964) 'Regional Development and Planning'. Cambridge, Mass.: MIT Press, 153-72].
ULLMAN, E.L. (1962) Discussant on the city centre in K. Norborg (ed.) (1962) 'Proceedings of the IGU Symposium in Urban Geography', 596-600.
ULLMAN, E.L. (1974) Space and/or time: opportunity for substitution and prediction, 'Transactions of the Institute of British Geographers', 63, 125-39.
'Urban Core and Inner City' (1967). Proceedings of the International Study Week, Amsterdam, 11-17 September 1966. Leiden: Brill.
'Urbanisme', vol.120-1 (1970). [Issue devoted to] Centralité: éclatement et mobilité, action sur les structures et les formes, approches et solutions, bibliographie, 1-144 [with abstracts in English, 1-6].
'Urban Models in Shopping Studies' (1970). London: National Economic Development Office.

VANCE, J.E. (1960) Labor-shed, employment field, and dynamic analysis in urban geography, 'Economic Geography', 36, 189-220.
VANCE, J.E. (1964) 'Geography and Urban Evolution in the San Francisco Bay Area'. Berkeley: University of California Institute of Government Studies.
VANCE, J.E. (1966) Focus on downtown [reprinted in L.S. Bourne (ed.) (1971) 'Internal Structure of the City'. New York: Oxford University Press, 112-20].
VANCE, J.E. (1970) 'The Merchant's World: the Geography of Wholesaling'. Englewood Cliffs, N.J.: Prentice-Hall.
VENEKAMP, P.E. and KRUIJT, B. (1967) Structure, spread and development of the retail trade in the inner city of Amsterdam, 'Urban Core and Inner City'. Proceedings of the International Study Week, Amsterdam, 11-17 September 1966. Leiden: Brill, 226-36.
VENTURI, R., SCOTT BROWN, D. and IZENOUR, S. (1973) Learning from Las Vegas, 'Environment and Cognition', W.H. Ittelson (ed.). New York: Seminar, 99-112.
VERNON, P.E. (ed.) (1970) 'Creativity'. Harmondsworth: Penguin.
VERNON, R. (1957) Production and distribution in the large metropolis [reprinted in C.E. Elias, J. Gillies and S. Riemer (eds) (1964) 'Metropolis: Values in Conflict'. Belmont, Calif.: Wadsworth, 85-8].
VINCENT, L.G. (1960) The town centre, Stevenage, 'Town Planning Review', 33, 103-6.
VON BERTALANFFY, L. (1968) 'General Systems Theory'. New York: Braziller.

WADE, R.C. (1959) 'The Urban Frontier: the Rise of Western Cities 1790-1830'. Cambridge, Mass.: Harvard University Press.
WALLACE, D.A. (ed.) (1957) Planning the city's center, 'Journal of the American Institute of Planners', 23 [no. 1 Special Issue], 1-73, 82-91.
WALMSLEY, D.J. and DAY, R.S. (1972) 'Perception and Man-Environment Interaction: a Bibliography and Guide to the Literature'. Armidale, N.S.W.: Geographical Society of New South Wales, New England Branch.
WATANABE, Y. (1975) Some notes on the research methodology in a field of Japanese geography - on the empirical study of the formation of Japanese cities based on central place concept, 'Geographical Reports of Tokyo Metropolitan University', 10, 1-24.
WATERHOUSE, A. (1971) Dominant values and urban planning policy, 'Journal of the Town Planning Institute', 57, 9-14.
WATSON, J.W. (1975) Perception and place, 'Geographical Journal', 141, 271-4.
WEAVER, D.C. (1969) Changes in the morphology of three American central business districts, 'Professional Geographer', 21, 406-10.
WEAVER, W. (1967) Science and complexity, 'Science and Imagination'. New York: Basic Books, 25-33.
WEBBER, M.J. (1971) Empirical verifiability of central place theory, 'Geographical Analysis', 3, 15-28.
WEBBER, M.J. (1972) 'Impact of Uncertainty on Location'. Canberra: Australian National University Press.
WEBBER, M.M. (1963) Order in diversity: community without propinquity, 'Cities and Space: the Future Use of Urban Land',

L. Wingo (ed.). Baltimore: Johns Hopkins University Press.
WEBBER, M.M. (1964) The urban place and nonplace urban realm,
'Explorations into Urban Structure'. Philadelphia: University of
Pennsylvania Press, 79-153.
WEBBER, M.M. (1968) The post-city age [reprinted in L.S. Bourne
(ed.) (1971) 'Internal Structure of the City'. New York: Oxford
University Press, 496-501].
WEBER, A. (1909) 'Über den Standort der Industrien' [translated as
Alfred Weber's Theory of Location (1929) by C.J. Friedrich.
Chicago: University Press].
WEBER, A.F. (1899) 'The Growth of Cities in the Nineteenth Century'.
New York: Macmillan [republished in 1963 by Cornell University
Press].
WEBER, M. (1960) 'The City'. London: Heinemann [first published
in German in 1921].
WEHRWEIN, G.S. (1942) The rural-urban fringe, 'Economic Geography',
18, 217-28.
WEISS, S.F. (1964) The downtown mall experiment, 'Journal of the
American Institute of Planners', 30, 60-73.
WELLS, H.G. (1902) The probable diffusion of great cities, 'Anti-
cipations'. London: Chapman & Hall, 33-65.
WERTHEIM, W.F. (1974) 'Evolution and Revolution'. Harmondsworth:
Penguin.
WHEATLEY, P. (1969) 'City as Symbol'. An Inaugural Lecture, 1967.
London: University College.
WHEATLEY, P. (1971) 'The Pivot of the Four Quarters: a Preliminary
Enquiry into the Origins and Character of the Ancient Chinese City'.
Edinburgh: University Press.
WHEBELL, C.F.J. (1969) Corridors: a theory of urban systems,
'Annals of the Association of American Geographers', 59, 1-26.
WHITE, O. (1969) 'Societal Determinants of Urban Form - Some
Thoughts on the City in the Year 2000'. London: Centre for
Environmental Studies, WP45.
WHITEHAND, J.W.R. (1972) Building cycles and the spatial pattern of
urban growth, 'Transactions of the Institute of British Geogra-
phers', 56, 39-55.
WHITNEY, V.H. (1948) Rural-urban people, 'American Journal of
Sociology', 54, 48-54.
WILLEY, G.R. (1962) Mesoamerica, 'Courses toward Urban Life', R.J.
Braidwood and G.R. Willey (eds). Chicago: Aldine, 84-105.
WILSON, A.G. (1970) 'Entropy in Urban and Regional Modelling'.
London: Pion.
WINGO, L. (ed.) (1963) 'Cities and Space: the Future Use of Urban
Land'. Baltimore: Johns Hopkins University Press.
WIRTH, L. (1938) Urbanism as a way of life, 'Americal Journal of
Sociology', 44, 1-24.
WISSINK, G.A. (1962) 'American Cities in Perspective'. Assen:
Vangorcum.
WITTFOGEL, K.A. (1956) The hydraulic civilizations, 'Man's Role in
Changing the Face of the Earth', W.L. Thomas (ed.). Chicago:
University Press, 152-64.
WITTFOGEL, K.A. (1957) 'Oriental Despotism: a Comparative Study of
Total Power'. New Haven: Yale University Press.
WOHLWILL, J.F. (1966) The physical environment: a problem for a

psychology of stimulation, 'Journal of Social Issues', 22, 29-38.

WOOD, P.A. (1970) Industrial location and linkage, 'Area', 1, 32-9.

WOODBURY, C. (ed.) (1953) 'The Future of Cities and Urban Redevelopment'. Chicago: University Press.

WRIGHT, F. LLOYD (1936) Broadacre City: a new community plan, 'Architectural Record', 77, 243-54.

WURSTER, C.B. (1963) The form and structure of the future urban complex, 'Cities and Space', L. Wingo (ed.). Baltimore: Johns Hopkins University Press, 73-101.

YAZAKI, T. (1963) 'The Japanese City'. Tokyo: Japan Publications Trading Company.

YEATES, M.H. (1965) Some factors affecting the spatial distribution of land values, 1910-1960, 'Economic Geography', 41, 57-70.

YOUNG, O.R. (1964) A survey of general systems theory, 'General Systems', 9, 61-80.

ZELINSKY, W. (1967) Classical town names in the United States: the historical geography of an American idea. 'Geographical Review', 57, 463-95.

ZUCKER, P. (1959) 'Town and Square'. New York: Columbia University Press.

AUTHOR INDEX

Underlined figures indicate main references, often a summary of an argument, concept, or idea.

SUBJECT INDEX

Underlined figures indicate main references. Entries preceded by an asterisk particularly refer to concepts, ideas, etc.